Transfer Pricing and Corporate Taxation

Elizabeth King

Transfer Pricing and Corporate Taxation

Problems, Practical Implications and Proposed Solutions

 Springer

Elizabeth King
Beecher Consulting, LLC
9 Beecher Road
Brookline, MA 02445
USA
www.beecherconsultinggroup.com

ISBN: 978-0-387-78182-2   e-ISBN: 978-0-387-78183-9
DOI: 10.1007/978-0-387-78183-9

Library of Congress Control Number: 2008937177

Printed on acid-free paper

springer.com

For Ella, an extraordinary person and a wonderful daughter

Acknowledgements

I have worked with many people—clients, attorneys and international examiners, fellow transfer pricing economists and others—over the years, all of whom have contributed greatly to my understanding of the issues addressed in this book. I thank all of these individuals for their professionalism, their willingness to share their knowledge, and their friendship. I would also like to thank several people for their extremely helpful and insightful comments on this manuscript. Confidentiality constraints prevent me from mentioning anyone by name. Finally, my profound thanks to Marianne Burge, in memoriam, for her mentoring and personal friendship.

USA   Elizabeth King

Contents

Part II   Alternative and Supplementary Approaches to Transfer Pricing

Part III   Case Studies

Chapter 1
Introduction

National tax authorities individually determine multinational firms' country-specific tax liabilities by applying one or more sanctioned transfer pricing methodologies. These methodologies are founded on basic assumptions about market structure and firm behavior that are rarely empirically valid. Moreover, for the most part, the transfer pricing methodologies now in vogue were developed before the Internet became a dominant factor in the world economy, and hedge and private equity funds transformed financial and commodities markets. For these reasons, multinational firms are unable to accurately anticipate their tax liabilities in individual countries, and remain at risk of double taxation.

Uncertainties in corporate tax liability are extremely costly, both for individual corporations and from an economy-wide perspective. Firms pay exorbitant fees to have tax attorneys, accountants and economists prepare the documentation required by tax authorities to substantiate their intercompany pricing practices and defend their tax positions on audit. Corporate tax liabilities are also potentially much higher than they would be under a more transparent and predictable transfer pricing regime (due to the potential for double taxation and penalties), and investors' returns are reduced accordingly. The FASB's Interpretation No. 48, *Accounting for Uncertainty in Income Taxes* (released on July 13, 2006), has motivated multinational firms to increase their reserves substantially (in many cases at the insistence of their auditors), reducing the total funds available for productive investment.

The current transfer pricing regimes are embodied in the OECD Guidelines,[1] individual OECD member countries' interpretations thereof, the U.S. regulations promulgated in 1994 (governing intercompany tangible and intangible property transfers) in combination with the Temporary Regulations governing services issued in 2006, and other, country-specific laws and regulations. These transfer pricing regimes' failure to provide the requisite level of certainty regarding corporate tax liabilities can often be traced directly back to the flawed economic underpinnings

---

[1] The *Transfer Pricing Guidelines for Multinational Enterprises and Tax Administrations* was issued by the OECD in segments on July 1995, April 1996 and October 1997. Section 482 of the U.S. Internal Revenue Code of 1986, as amended, and the Treasury Regulations promulgated thereunder, contain the U.S. transfer pricing provisions.

E. King, *Transfer Pricing and Corporate Taxation,*
DOI 10.1007/978-0-387-78183-9_1, © Springer Science+Business Media, LLC 2009

of specific transfer pricing methods. As applied to profits-based transfer pricing methods in particular, they are caused, or compounded, by the substitution of accounting rates of return (and other accounting measures of profitability) for economic rates of return. While accounting measures of profitability serve numerous useful purposes in other contexts, they are not compatible with the transfer pricing regulations' economic foundations. The use of accounting rates of return in lieu of economic rates of return to allocate multinational firms' income among the tax jurisdictions in which they operate yields arbitrary and unpredictable results.

Leaving aside the logical flaws in the current transfer pricing regimes, the range of methods that individual countries sanction, each of which presupposes a certain division of labor or type of transaction among members of a multinational group, is no longer consonant with the much wider range of fact patterns that one observes "on the ground," due in significant part to the emergence of new, Internet-based activities and the growing influence of hedge and private equity funds. The Internet has caused the rapid depreciation of certain traditional intangible assets, given rise to new types of intangible assets (e.g., online user communities), transformed marketing and distribution activities and altered (or eliminated) the division of labor among affiliated companies. The development of global private equity funds, with portfolio companies headquartered in numerous countries, has resulted in the segmentation of capital-raising, due diligence and investment management functions. The same segmentation between distribution and investment advisory functions is evident in the hedge fund industry as well.

It is relatively uncommon for individual members of a multinational group that has evolved organically to maintain separate research facilities, or otherwise independently develop intangible assets other than trademarks. Some notable exceptions to this general observation, ironically, are e-commerce companies. Despite the fact that such firms often have a limited physical presence, and national boundaries do not exist in cyberspace, there are numerous impediments to the formation of genuinely border-free e-commerce websites. Such obstacles include (a) language; (b) local customs, tastes and preferences, not only for particular types of goods and services but also for the "look and feel" of sites and user interface features; (c) legal protections vis-a-vis the transfer of personal information on the Internet, and consumers' comfort level in doing so; (d) legal restrictions on the types of products that can be sold on the Internet; (e) the extent to which users benefit from free speech protections; (f) currency; (g) payment mechanisms; (h) customs duties; and (i) shipping.

As a result of these impediments to the development of border-free Internet sites, certain affiliated companies with Internet-based operations have separately developed their own, distinct user communities. Conversely, certain other types of Internet-based businesses, where user communities as such are not overly important, have originated in one country, and expanded by replicating the same business model in other countries (with relatively minor or cosmetic adaptations to accommodate country-specific preferences, laws and regulations). This pattern of international expansion generally entails the transfer of a bundle of intangible assets, including the business model, proprietary IT and marketing tools and strategies.

Certain of these assets are not ordinarily bought and sold individually at arm's length. At the other extreme, the Internet has spawned entire industries, such as Content Delivery Network (CDN) services providers, that entail the provision of services on a worldwide basis and require the location of network infrastructure assets in all major geographic markets. The absence of any meaningful division of labor itself creates a transfer pricing conundrum, as those familiar with the global trading of commodities and financial instruments will immediately recognize.

This book is organized into three main parts and a concluding section. Part I contains a detailed review of the economic premises that underpin individual transfer pricing methods. More particularly, Chapter 2 contains a brief overview of the key differences between economic and accounting measures of profit rates and the "big picture" practical implications of substituting accounting measures for economic measures in the transfer pricing regulations. Chapter 3 contains an overview of individual transfer pricing methodologies currently in use, the implicit economic rationale for each, and the reasons that such economic justifications do not hold when accounting rates of return (and other accounting measures of profitability) are substituted for economic profit rates, or when certain implicit assumptions about market structure are not warranted.

Part II contains a discussion of certain proposed alternative transfer pricing methods. The first such method is simply an extension or reinterpretation of the inexact comparable uncontrolled price method. The second, third and fourth methods presuppose that the legal entities comprising a multinational corporation perform distinct functions. The last two proposed methods presuppose that all legal entities constituting a multinational corporation perform the same range of functions and employ similar types of assets. These proposed methods have a more solid economic footing than existing methods and can be applied to certain transfer pricing issues that the extant transfer pricing regimes do not effectively address.

Part III, consisting of Chapters 5 through 12, contains a series of highly detailed case studies. Where feasible, individual case studies contain an analysis of the subject intercompany transactions under both the existing regimes and the proposed alternative regime, and a review of their relative merits. Where the fact pattern typified by a particular case study is not adequately addressed under the existing transfer pricing regimes, the analysis is limited to proposed methods. The case studies encompass a broad range of industries, both traditional and new, and are based on actual cases. *All* specific numerical results cited in these case studies have been altered, relative to the actual cases on which they are based, to preserve confidentiality. Moreover, certain key aspects of the underlying fact patterns have been changed. In some instances, features of more than one industry have been blended to maintain confidentiality. As such, background information on the cited industry should not be taken at face value.

Tax policy-makers, business school students and tax practitioners are the target audience for this book. Policy-makers should find the critique of existing transfer pricing regimes of particular interest, insofar as it elucidates how and why these regimes contribute to (a) extremely high compliance costs; (b) frequent disputes over transfer pricing issues; and (c) the limited efficacy of existing dispute resolution venues. The proposed alternative methods may also be helpful to policy-makers in identifying useful modifications to the existing transfer pricing regulations, whether on a small or large scale. Business school students will obtain a clear understanding of (a) the key role that transfer pricing plays in determining multinational firms' effective tax rates and, thereby, their investment decisions across geographic markets, and (b) how transfer pricing issues are currently addressed in practice. Tax practitioners can utilize the critique of existing transfer pricing methodologies, in combination with the case studies, as a guide in developing and defending their own transfer pricing policies and practices. The proposed alternative methods may also provide some useful insights into how certain transfer pricing issues that are not adequately addressed under the current transfer pricing regime can be analyzed.

Part I
Economic and Accounting Rates and Concepts Should Not be Conflated

Chapter 2
Economic vs. Accounting Profit Rates

This chapter contains a brief overview of the key differences between economic and accounting measures of profit rates, and the "big picture" practical implications of substituting accounting measures for economic measures in the transfer pricing regulations.

The transfer pricing methodologies written into the U.S. and OECD regulations and guidelines are loosely founded on economic concepts of equilibrium under specific competitive conditions. These concepts are taken to justify comparisons of rates of return (and other "profit level indicators") across firms. Such comparisons are the cornerstone of our current transfer pricing regimes. More particularly, individual members of a multinational firm are generally likened to a set of quasi-comparable standalone companies, and their gross or operating profits are determined, for tax purposes, by imputing the independent sample companies' rates of return, gross margins, operating margins or other measures of profits thereto.

In theory, economic rates of return in product markets *are* equalized (albeit only in the infamous "long run" under competitive conditions). However, as noted, the U.S. and OECD transfer pricing regulations and guidelines substitute accounting measures of profit, rates of return and asset values for economic profits, rates of return and asset values. As described below, accounting measures do not play the same signaling and resource allocation roles that economic rates of return play in an economy. Therefore, they would not be equalized even in competitive markets poised in long–run equilibrium, much less in the imperfectly competitive markets in various states of disequilibrium that are the norm. Stated differently, there is no reasonable basis for assuming that one firm will earn the same accounting rate of return as a similarly situated competitor. This observation applies equally to other accounting measures of profit.

The fields of economics and accounting serve very different purposes. Microeconomic and financial theories seek to explain the allocation of resources in an economy through firm, consumer and investor behavior and market mechanisms. Economic profits drive firm behavior and lead to the maximization of shareholders' wealth (and, thereby, their lifetime consumption). The calculation of such profits reflects the actual timing of investments (rather than smoothing out periodic capital expenditures via depreciation) and incorporates *all* costs, including the cost of

E. King, *Transfer Pricing and Corporate Taxation*,
DOI 10.1007/978-0-387-78183-9_2, © Springer Science+Business Media, LLC 2009

equity capital (and, potentially, other opportunity costs). The economic profit *rate* is defined as that rate which equates (a) the discounted present value of forecasted after-tax free cash flows generated by a given investment project with (b) the initial outlays required.[1] It is extremely difficult, if not impossible, to quantify a firm-wide economic profit rate as a practical matter.

Under conditions of free entry and exit, and absent financing constraints, firms will continue to enter a given market until the net present value of market participation (that is, the present value of projected after-tax free cash flows, discounted at the opportunity cost of capital and reduced by the initial investment required) is driven to zero. Until this point is reached, incumbent firms will earn positive economic profits (i.e., profits in excess of a "normal" return), and shareholders' wealth will be increased thereby. Through the process of market entry, additional resources are dedicated to the manufacture of those products that consumers value more highly than the resources necessary to produce them.

Accounting analyses present a snapshot of firm performance at a point in time, or generally over a relatively short period of time, to facilitate "mid-course corrections" and incremental decision-making on the part of management and shareholders. Accounting rates of return are computed as the ratio of operating profits to total assets, fixed assets or some other measure of the book value of resources committed by the firm. Costs are measured by explicit expenditures only, and one attempts to match revenues and the expenditures necessary to generate them on a year-by-year basis. As such, assets are depreciated over their useful lives, in lieu of deducting investment outlays in full when they are made. Firms generally do not maximize their accounting rates of return (or their ratios of operating profits to revenues or costs, or gross profits to cost of goods or operating expenses), because such courses of action will not result in the highest possible shareholder value. Therefore, as noted, there are no market mechanisms at work to equalize these profit level indicators across firms, and, by implication, no particular reason to expect similarly situated firms to earn the same accounting rates of return, operating margins or operating markups, as noted.

The use of accounting measures of profit to determine multinational firms' country-specific income tax liabilities under profits-based methods has several important practical implications, enumerated below.

(1) *Tax authorities in different jurisdictions are likely to allocate individual multinational firms' consolidated income across countries in different ways.* This statement would be true even if tax authorities utilized the *same* transfer pricing methodology, given the sensitivity of one's results to the particular "comparable companies" included in one's sample (and, in the case of the CPM, the particular profit level indicator used). However, as a practical matter, tax authorities are likely to use different transfer pricing methodologies in analyzing a given case.

---

[1] In this context, free cash flow, constituting income that actually accrues to investors, is defined as the after-tax cash flows earned by the legal entity under consideration, assuming that it had no debt.

Most countries endorse the arm's length standard in principle, and the U.S. and OECD provisions contain the same specific set of transfer pricing methodologies (discussed at length in Chapter 3). However, the IRS has a clear predilection to use one particular profits-based method (the CPM), while OECD countries prefer transactions-based methods. Different approved methodologies will generally produce different allocations of income, because the assumed unifying foundation across methods—primarily the basic concept of market equilibrium—does not in fact apply. The large number of cases handled by the competent authorities of different countries attests to this conundrum, which in turn creates the potential for double taxation on a significant scale.

(2) *Individual multinational corporations cannot accurately anticipate their country-specific tax liability in the absence of an Advance Pricing Agreement.*[2] Corporate taxpayers and tax authorities, respectively, also frequently utilize different firm samples and/or transfer pricing methodologies to determine their tax liability (taxpayers before an audit and tax authorities during an audit). Because the use of different samples and/or methods will often produce inconsistent results, firms acting in good faith may report substantially less income in a given jurisdiction than the tax authority in that jurisdiction believes is warranted.

(3) *The current transfer pricing regime produces inequitable results.* Because the existing transfer pricing laws and regulations are not based on defensible economic principles, or on transparent rules that all countries apply uniformly, they produce arbitrary results. Arbitrary apportionments of multinational firms' income across the countries in which they operate are inherently inequitable.

(4) *Multinational and domestic firms are not treated uniformly for tax purposes.* In the abstract, the arm's length principle appears to ensure that domestic and multinational firms will be treated uniformly for tax purposes, essentially by definition. However, individual standalone competitors in a given market often report markedly different operating results in the same reporting period. By requiring individual members of a multinational group to report gross margins, markups or accounting rates of return that are contained in the interquartile range of third parties' results (a U.S. regulatory provision that the OECD Guidelines do not endorse), multinational firms are treated more favorably for tax purposes than a subset of their domestic counterparts, and less favorably than others.

Inequity is inherently problematic, and uncertainty is costly, both for tax authorities and individual corporations and from an economy-wide perspective. Explicit costs, from tax authorities' perspectives, include costs incurred in conducting audits and analyzing transfer pricing issues, and in resolving conflicts over income allocations with their opposite numbers in other tax jurisdictions. Moreover, to reduce the

---

[2] An Advance Pricing Agreement, as the term suggests, is a vehicle for tax authorities and firms to agree well in advance of an audit on a particular transfer pricing methodology and the way that it will be applied, thereby minimizing disputes at a later date.

likelihood of penalties, firms generally commission costly transfer pricing studies, and, as part of this process, make their personnel available to respond to analysts' questions and requests for documentation and information. Inasmuch as uncertainties regarding tax liability require firms to set aside funds that would otherwise be invested productively, they also entail substantial opportunity costs. Lastly, firms maximize their *after-tax* free cash flows. Their inability to accurately anticipate their effective tax rates in individual countries, whether due to double taxation or simply to inconsistent allocations of income across jurisdictions (that are subsequently adjusted without penalties), may distort investment decisions.

Chapter 3
Overview and Critique of Existing Transfer Pricing Methods

In this Chapter, we provide an overview of the current transfer pricing regulations pertaining to intra-group transfers of tangible and intangible property, the performance of services, cost-sharing and global dealing. Our discussion consists of (a) a description of individual methodologies and the circumstances in which they are applied; (b) a review of the economic rationale for each methodology; (c) a critique of such rationale; and (d) an assessment of practical implications.

3.1 Comparable Profits Method and TNMM

The U.S. and OECD transfer pricing regulations and guidelines sanction five transfer pricing methodologies:

1. The comparable profits method or "CPM" (referred to in the OECD Guidelines as the transactional net margin method or "TNMM");
2. The resale price method or "RPM";
3. The cost plus method;
4. The comparable uncontrolled price (or "CUP") method; and
5. The profit split method.

Taxpayers are also permitted to establish fees for intercompany services rendered to affiliates based on costs alone (without a profit element) under certain circumstances. Affilated lenders may charge a published safe harbor floating loan rate (the "Applicable Federal Rate"), or, alternatively, they may determine the prevailing market loan rate given the credit rating of the borrower and the loan terms.

The U.S. transfer pricing regime also encompasses intra-firm "cost-sharing" and "global dealing" as special cases, addressed in separate provisions. Cost-sharing regulations govern circumstances in which related companies jointly contribute to research and development activities, and are assigned specific, non-overlapping ownership rights in the research results. The term "global dealing operation" refers to multinational financial intermediaries that buy and sell financial products, manage

E. King, *Transfer Pricing and Corporate Taxation*,
DOI 10.1007/978-0-387-78183-9_3, © Springer Science+Business Media, LLC 2009

risk and execute transactions on behalf of customers.[1] The proposed global dealing regulations do not formally encompass the global trading of physical commodities (as distinct from financial products), although "the IRS solicit[ed] comments on whether these regulations should be extended to cover dealers in commodities ..."[2]

In this section, we consider the merits and shortcomings of the CPM, frequently the IRS' and U.S. practitioners' method of choice. For those readers who are not familiar with the U.S. and OECD transfer pricing regulations, certain key terms are defined below:

- A "controlled group of companies" is a multinational firm.
- A "tested party" is an individual member of a controlled group that one selects to be the subject of analysis under certain transfer pricing methods. It is generally the entity that owns little or no intangible assets and performs comparatively simple functions.
- A "profit level indicator" refers to one of several financial ratios that constitute accounting measures of operating results.
- The "arm's length standard" is the guiding principle underlying all transfer pricing methods. It requires individual members of a controlled group of companies engaging in intra-group transactions to charge the same prices, fees, and royalty or loan rates in such transactions that they would charge unafffiliated companies.

3.1.1 Description of CPM and TNMM

The CPM is used to establish arm's length prices or royalty rates for (a) tangible property sold to, (b) intangible property licensed or otherwise transferred to, or (c) services performed on behalf of, affiliated companies. Application of the CPM entails assembling a sample of standalone companies that are similar to the tested party principally in terms of resources employed and risks assumed. Functional and product comparability between the tested party and the unaffiliated companies with which it is compared is considered significantly less important under the CPM than under other transfer pricing methods.[3] Unaffiliated firms need only perform broadly similar functions and operate in broadly similar product markets as the tested party.

---

[1] More specifically, as defined in the relevant proposed regulations, a global dealing operation "consists of the execution of customer transactions, including marketing, sales, pricing and risk management activities, in a particular financial product or line of financial products, in multiple tax jurisdictions and/or through multiple participants ... The taking of proprietary positions is not included within the definition of a global dealing operation unless the proprietary positions are entered into by a regular dealer in securities in its capacity as such a dealer ...". See Prop. Treas. Reg. 1.482-8(a)(2).

[2] Ibid.

[3] See Treas. Reg. Section 1.482-5(c)(2)(ii) and (iii).

In a second series of steps, one (a) computes accounting rates of return (or one of several other profit level indicators) for each sample company[4]; (b) applies the resulting arm's length profit level indicators to the tested party's corresponding denominator (operating assets, sales, total cost, etc.); (c) establishes a range of the tested party's potential arm's length results thereby (the "arm's length range"); (d) determines the interquartile range of such results; and (e) generally selects a profit level contained in the interquartile range. This level of profitability directly determines the tested party's tax liability; its affiliated counterparty's operating income and tax liability are determined as a residual.[5]

Application of the CPM to establish arm's length services fees entails essentially the same steps, except that the sample selection criteria (or "comparability requirements") differ, and the U.S. Temporary Regulations favor a different profit level indicator. The Temporary Regulations emphasize accounting consistency for sample selection purposes under the CPM as applied to services, rather than resources employed and risks assumed.[6] The use of similar intangible assets in performing the subject services, if any, is also an important sample selection criterion. Whereas an accounting rate of return is the profit level indicator of choice under the CPM vis-a-vis intra-group tangible or intangible property transfers, operating profits over total cost is the preferred profit level indicator vis-a-vis services. This preference presumably reflects the fact that services providers often employ limited assets, and do not consistently report cost of services separately from total cost.

The OECD Guidelines' TNMM closely resembles the CPM, although the Guidelines do *not* favor the use of statistical tools, such as the interquartile range, to select a particular value within the arm's length range. Rather, the Guidelines focus on comprehensive comparability analyses (a point forcefully reiterated in the series of Draft Issue Notes released by the OECD's Center for Tax Policy and Administration on May 10, 2006).[7] More generally, the OECD Guidelines take a less formulaic approach to comparability standards and differentiate between methods in establishing comparability criteria to a lesser extent. In all cases, the character of the property or service, the functions performed by the parties, contractual terms,

---

[4] Under the U.S. regulations, an accounting rate of return is the preferred profit level indicator for purposes of applying the CPM to transfers of tangible or intangible property. Other profit level indicators include operating profits to sales or total cost, gross profits to operating expenses, etc.

[5] Application of the CPM to establish arm's length royalty rates reflects the proposition, incorporated into the U.S. transfer pricing regulations, that an unaffiliated licensee would not retain any income attributable to the licensed intangible asset. Rather, all such income would be transferred to the licensor by means of royalty payments. See Treas. Reg. Section 1.482-(4)(f)(2).

[6] However, the examples given in Treas. Reg. Section 1.482-9T(f)(3) to illustrate how the comparability requirements should be applied indicate that the CPM is the preferred method when one *cannot* ascertain whether unaffiliated companies follow the same accounting conventions as the tested party.

[7] See *Comparability: Public Invitation to Comment on a Series of Draft Issue Notes*, Center for Tax Policy and Administration, Organization for Economic Cooperation and Development, May 10, 2006.

economic circumstances and business strategies should be considered in selecting sample companies.

3.1.2 Circumstances when CPM and TNMM Are Applied

As originally conceived, the CPM and TNMM were to be used only when the comparability standards applied under other methods could not be satisfied or accounting ambiguities precluded their use. OECD member countries often take a dim view of the CPM/TNMM. However, it is *very* widely applied in the United States, accounting for the substantial majority of transfer pricing cases analyzed by IRS agents in the field, and almost all of the *Advance Pricing Agreements* negotiated among companies, the National Office of the IRS and tax authorities in other jurisdictions. (For the sake of decorum, the methodology may be referred to differently in the accompanying documentation, such as a resale price method with adjustments for higher-than-normal operating expenses.)

There are at least two reasons for the CPM's widespread use in the United States. First, as a practical matter, IRS agents in the field and National Office personnel have tended to apply higher comparability standards under the resale price and cost plus methods than a strict reading of the regulations would appear to require, significantly limiting their applicability. Moreover, the CPM is amenable to "cookie-cutter" analyses that apply across a range of transactions and industries. As such, it is cost-effective for corporations and the IRS alike. (Hence, if history is a reliable guide, U.S. practitioners will also frequently resort to the CPM to establish arm's length services fees when the services cost method, which provides for a cost-based fee, cannot be used.)

3.1.3 Underlying Economic Rationale

The CPM and TNMM depend on the following key assumptions for their economic legitimacy:

1. Product markets are generally competitive and in equilibrium;
2. For this reason, accounting rates of return (defined in the U.S. regulations as operating profits divided by operating assets) are equalized across manufacturing or distribution firms in broadly similar product markets;
3. Service markets are generally competitive and in equilibrum; and
4. Under these circumstances, operating markups over total cost are equalized across service providers rendering broadly similar services.

Such reasoning has also been generalized, to some degree, to the other profit level indicators used in applying the CPM to transactions in tangible and intangible property. However, in principle, greater functional comparability is required when using a financial ratio other than accounting rates of return under the U.S. regulations.

One might argue that the CPM and TNMM are not based on economic notions of equilibrium and specific market structure assumptions. Admittedly, the drafters are not explicit on this point, beyond asserting (inaccurately) that "[a]n operating profit represents a return for the investment of resources and assumption of risks" (thereby equating accounting profits per annum with the discounted present value of free cash flows),[8] and sanctioning comparisons of accounting rates of return across firms. However, if one determines the tax liabilities of individual *affiliated* companies by imputing to them accounting rates of return realized by similarly situated *unaffiliated* companies, there must be some expectation that accounting rates of return (and other profit level indicators) will be uniform across firms. Other than an unvarnished assumption to this effect (which is belied by the wide arm's length ranges that one routinely observes in practice), or the belief that affiliated companies can legitimately be likened to a "median" unaffiliated firm for purposes of determining their tax liabilities, an economic rationale is all that remains.

3.1.4 Critique of Economic Reasoning

As previously noted, in theory, *economic* rates of return, as distinct from *accounting* rates of return, are equalized, albeit only in competitive markets and in equilibrium.[9] There are no market mechanisms at work to equalize accounting-based profit level indicators across firms, and, by implication, no reason to expect similarly situated firms to earn the same accounting rates of return, operating margins or operating markups, even in competitive markets.

The corollary assumptions that product markets are generally competitive and normally in long-run equilibrium are equally invalid. "Perfect" competition is characterized by (a) a large number of incumbent firms, each of which sells an undifferentiated product, makes up a very small share of the total market and can therefore take selling prices as fixed (that is, independent of its own output decisions); (b) potential entrants do not face barriers to entry (or existing firms, impediments to expansion); (c) buyers are numerous, knowledgeable and can obtain the undifferentiated product from a number of different suppliers without bearing additional costs; and (d) buyers themselves are indistinguishable from the perspective of producers. As a consequence of these characteristics, product prices will be equalized and, over time, firms will be forced to utilize the (same) most efficient technology available.

More loosely speaking, product markets can generally be considered competitive if products are homogenous, incumbent firms can readily expand or new firms can enter (even if only with the investment of potentially significant resources and over a potentially long period of time), buyers are well informed as to their alternative sources of supply, and switching suppliers is not excessively costly.

---

[8] See Treas. Reg. Section 1.482-5(c)(2)(ii).

[9] However, as noted, the economic rate of return is a much more difficult magnitude to measure than an accounting rate of return, particularly on a firm-wide basis.

Very few product markets were competitive in the strict sense when the basic tenets of microeconomic theory were first put forward by Alfred Marshall circa 1891. However, the discrepancy between archetype and economic reality was not as marked then as it is now. Firms have become progressively larger, vertically integrated and both horizontally and geographically diversified. Products other than commodities are routinely differentiated along numerous dimensions (trademarks, functionality, levels of customer service and technical support, product quality, etc.). As such, the pure competitive market model has become largely a figment of the imagination (with the exception of securities markets and commodity markets in some instances). In fact, relatively few product markets are competitive in the broader sense described above. While this statement is probably more obviously apparent vis-a-vis consumer product markets, it is often true of producer product markets as well. Switching costs are relatively common among producer products, as is product differentiation in certain forms.

Moreover, the traditional concept of long-run equilibrium is a theoretical construct, rather than a description of real product markets at any point in time. It implies a stasis in the number of firms operating in a given market, the types of products they produce, the technologies they utilize, the terms of competition, etc. In most markets, new product introductions are the norm, firms continuously strive to improve their production technologies and techniques, barriers to foreign competition (e.g., quotas and tariffs) are revisited, competitors merge, and regulatory requirements change. Hence, even supposing that product markets were generally competitive, economic rates of return would only be equalized in the long run, not on a year-by-year basis. Product markets are almost invariably in a state of disequilibrium.

Two other shortcoming with the use of accounting rates of return in a transfer pricing context also bear noting, the second of which is widely recognized:

1. Affiliated manufacturers' accounts receivables and affiliated distributors' accounts payables reflect intercompany pricing. As such, their asset bases, inclusive of working capital, will potentially be distorted by intercompany pricing and cannot reliably be used for purposes of evaluating such pricing.
2. The book value of assets, as shown on financial statements, reflects particular accounting conventions, over which firms have a certain amount of discretion. If unaffiliated firms utilize different conventions (e.g., different depreciation methods), all other things equal, their accounting rates of return will differ for this reason alone. Moreover, accounting rates of return will be strongly influenced by the age of operating assets through two mechanisms: (a) the price paid for individual assets at the outset (in that prices vary over time) and (b) the extent to which the assets have been written off. Lastly, individual firms rely on intangible assets to widely differing degrees.[10]

---

[10] Certain of the limitations noted above regarding accounting rate of return measures are acknowledged in the U.S. Regulations, and one is cautioned to consider them in evaluating comparability. However, as a practical matter, the potential for distortions is so great as to preclude the use of

Clearly, differences in accounting rates of return across firms could not be ascribed solely to transfer pricing, even if such comparisons were otherwise meaningful.

3.1.5 Summary and Practical Implications

In short, the imputation of accounting rates of return, operating markups or operating margins derived from unaffiliated companies to individual members of controlled groups, to determine the latter firms' tax liabilities, cannot be justified by economic principles. Moreover, the implicit assumption that such financial ratios will be equalized across small samples of firms on a year-by-year basis is indefensible on empirical grounds alone, in view of the wide range of results reported by sample companies in most instances. Consequently, a tested party's tax liability under the CPM/TNMM is entirely dependent on the particular profit level indicator chosen and the specific unaffiliated companies included in one's firm sample. Different profit level indicators and/or different sample companies can produce markedly different allocations of income across countries. Moreover, because the comparability criteria applied under the CPM and TNMM are not restrictive, the universe of potential sample companies is quite large.

Therefore, even if companies correctly anticipate that the IRS will utilize the CPM in assessing their tax liability after the fact, they will not be able to determine with a reasonable degree of certainty, before the fact, how much taxable income they should report in the United States. As previously noted, this state of affairs imposes both explicit and opportunity costs, the former in the form of professional and legal fees (and, potentially, double taxation and penalties), and the latter resulting from monies held in reserve, in conformity with the FASB's standards of practice vis-a-vis uncertain tax liabilities. Moreover, if firms maximize their after-tax free cash flows, and gauge their country-specific tax liabilities incorrectly, this will result in a sub-optimal allocation of resources.

3.2 Resale Price and Cost Plus Methods

Consider next the resale price and cost plus methods. Both are transactions-based methods that the OECD favors over the CPM/TNMM.

---

accounting rates of return in most cases involving manufacturing firms. Because distributors' assets are composed principally of inventories and accounts receivables, for which book value approximates market value, the potential for distortion is not as problematic, except as regards intercompany pricing.

3.2.1 Circumstances when Resale Price and Cost Plus Methods Apply

The resale price and cost plus methods (and, under the U.S. Temporary Regulations, the gross services margin method and the cost of services plus method) can be applied under the following fact patterns:

1. A single manufacturer sells similar products to both affiliated and unaffiliated distributors;
2. A single distributor sources similar products from both affiliated and unaffiliated suppliers;
3. A single services provider renders similar liaison or agency services (in the case of the gross services margin method) to both affiliated and unaffiliated companies, and, if relevant, utilizes the same intangible assets in doing so;
4. A single services provider renders similar services (other than liaison services in the case of the cost of services plus method) under the same contractual terms to both affiliated and unaffiliated companies and utilizes the same intangible assets, if any, in doing so;
5. Two or more manufacturers sell similar products, in one instance to affiliated distributors, and in the other instances, to unaffiliated distributors;
6. Two or more distributors source similar products, in one instance from affiliated suppliers and in the other instances, from unaffiliated suppliers; and
7. A group member performs routine manufacturing or distribution functions and licenses intellectual property from another group member.

Given one of the above fact patterns, one's choice between the resale price and cost plus methods depends principally on whether (a) one of the group members engages in internal arm's length transactions, and (b) the affiliated manufacturer or the affiliated distributor is the least complex entity (and therefore, the designated tested party). For example, under the first fact pattern, one would ordinarily apply the cost plus method, and under the second, the resale price method. As indicated above, the gross services margin method generally applies when the services at issue are intermediary in nature, and the cost of services plus method applies when the tested party renders the same services to both affiliated and independent companies. Under the fifth and sixth fact patterns, one's choice between the resale price and cost plus methods would be dictated by each group member's ownership of intellectual property and the relative values thereof. Under the last fact pattern, the choice of methods depends on whether the licensee is a manufacturer or a distributor.

The U.S. regulations impose higher standards of comparability under the resale price and cost plus methods, as compared to the CPM: Products must be "of the same general type (e.g., consumer electronics),"[11] and the parties being compared should perform similar functions, bear similar risks and operate under similar contractual terms. As previously noted, the OECD Guidelines do not differentiate

---

[11] See Treas. Reg. Section 1.482-3(c)(3)(ii)(B).

between transfer pricing methods in establishing comparability criteria to the same degree as the U.S. regulations. Such criteria include the character of the property or service, the functions performed by the parties, contractual terms, economic circumstances and business strategies.

3.2.2 Description of Resale Price and Cost Plus Methods

Briefly stated, under the resale price method, one compares the captive distributor's gross margin on product sourced from affiliated companies with its gross margin on product sourced from unaffiliated companies. If the captive distributor does not source similar products from both affiliated and unaffiliated companies, one can compare its resale margin on products sourced from affiliated suppliers with the resale margins reported by unaffiliated distributors that source similar products from independent suppliers. An analogous comparison is made under the cost plus method and the cost of services plus method, except that the profit level indicator differs. More particularly, under the cost plus and cost of services plus methods, the profit level indicator is equal to gross profits divided by cost of goods (or services) sold.

3.2.3 Underlying Economic Rationale

Under one interpretation, the resale price method, applied to *internal* transactions, presupposes that individual distributors would pay similar purchase prices to their multiple suppliers on an arm's length basis and charge their unrelated customers similar selling prices. This set of assumptions, in turn, implies that (a) suppliers operate in the same competitive market or have no binding capacity constraints and value the subject distributor's business relatively highly, and (b) the distributor cannot (and is not forced to) differentiate among its customers in establishing its selling prices. If the resale price method depends on these assumptions for its validity, gross margin comparisons would only be valid if the products generating such margins are *quite* similar, not simply of the "same general type". Similarly, the cost plus method, applied to internal transactions, may presuppose that individual manufacturers are unable to differentiate among customers in establishing their selling prices, and employ the same or similar technologies in producing product for different customers. Again, under this rationale, the products on which markups are being compared must be closely similar.

Alternatively, the economic rationale for *internal* comparisons of resale margins or cost plus markups may simply be that individual distributors and manufacturers would necessarily earn a reasonably uniform gross margin or markup across transactions, consistent with the return that investors would require. As applied to *external* transactions, the only economic rationale for the resale price and cost plus methods would seem to be that market forces will equalize resale margins and gross markups across firms.

3.2.4 Critique of Economic Reasoning

As previously discussed, there is no reason to expect gross margins or gross markups to be equalized across firms, and, therefore, no good reason to compare an affiliated distributor's (or manufacturer's) resale margin (or gross markup) with the corresponding results reported by its unaffiliated counterparts. Therefore, as with the CPM, the resale price and cost plus methods, as applied to *external* transactions, are not founded on valid economic principles.

Absent suppliers' manufacturing capacity constraints and the potential for price discrimination, comparisons of an individual distributor's resale margins on product sourced from related and independent suppliers, respectively, makes a certain amount of sense. On an arm's length basis, the distributor would source exclusively from the lowest cost supplier if its suppliers' selling prices differed, thus forcing them to charge the same price (or similar prices, in the case of similar products). Therefore, if the distributor cannot freely choose to price discriminate, and its customers do not insist on different prices (where "price" encompasses co-op advertising arrangements, volume discounts, etc.), it should earn similar resale margins across suppliers on an arm's length basis. Similarly, an individual manufacturer producing similar products for related and independent customers will generally use the same facilities (and, therefore, the same or similar manufacturing technologies and processes), absent dedicated production lines. If the manufacturer cannot freely choose to price discriminate, and its customers would not insist on different prices at arm's length, it should earn similar gross markups across customers on an arm's length basis. Such internal comparisons do not depend on theoretical concepts of market equilibrium (although certain market structure assumptions are implicit), but rather, the profit-maximizing behavior of a single firm.

However, as a practical matter, the circumstances that permit such internal comparisons are relatively unlikely to arise. If we do not require internal arm's length transactions to take place in the same geographic market as the parallel intercompany transactions, price discrimination will often be feasible. Most geographic markets are segmented to one degree or another, and both demand and supply conditions in individual markets will likely differ. For obvious reasons, this possibility undermines the reliability of comparisons across geographic markets. Conversely, if we require the transactions being compared to take place in the same geographic market, the fact patterns permitting internal comparisons will rarely arise. Manufacturers are unlikely to sell to both affiliated and unaffiliated distributors in the same geographic market, because doing so would undermine the affiliated distributor. The same reasoning applies to distributors sourcing from affiliated and independent suppliers (unless affiliated suppliers are capacity-constrained, usually a temporary state of affairs). Moreover, price discrimination within geographic markets may take place: Large merchandisers possess considerable market power in certain markets (notably, the United States) and routinely negotiate exceptionally favorable pricing arrangements with their suppliers. Stated differently, large retailers often have the power to impose certain advantageous forms of price discrimination on their suppliers.

There are certain instances in which internal comparisons may be feasible. For example, an affiliated distributor may be appointed in place of a predecessor unaffiliated distributor in a particular geographic market, seek to round out its product offerings by sourcing from related and unrelated suppliers, or make a strategic decision to dual-source. An affiliated manufacturer may seek to reach different types of customers in the same geographic market, or the same types of customers in different locales, and employ both affiliated and independent distributors to these ends. However, in many of these instances, comparisons of resale margins or gross markups will still not be valid. If an affiliated distributor is stepping into the shoes of an unaffiliated predecessor, it may incur start-up costs. If an affiliated distributor dual-sources as a matter of course, it may be doing so in part to limit its exposure to country-specific risks (e.g., strikes, natural disasters, political instability, etc.). Therefore, its affiliated and independent suppliers will probably not operate in the same geographic market. If a manufacturer sells to both affiliated and unaffiliated distributors in the same geographic market, they in turn will likely sell to distinct customer bases (e.g., large discount chains and small independent companies), and obtain different volume discounts or otherwise insist on different purchase prices, consistent with their disparate selling costs.

3.2.5 Summary and Practical Implications

In sum, comparisons of an individual distributor's resale margins or an individual manufacturer's gross markups on internal transactions with related and unrelated parties, respectively, are valid in certain hypothetical circumstances, but are rarely feasible in practice. Comparisons of resale margins or gross markups across firms have the same shortcomings as comparisons of accounting rates of return, operating markups, and other accounting measures of performance.

As previously noted, both IRS agents in the field and IRS personnel in the National Office hold prospective comparable companies to a higher standard of comparability than the U.S. regulations themselves would seem to require under both the resale price and the cost plus methods. As a result, U.S. firms and the IRS use these methods very sparingly. On the other hand, the OECD Guidelines look substantially more favorably on these transactions-based methods than the CPM and TNMM, and favor internal comparable uncontrolled transactions over external comparable uncontrolled transactions. The aforementioned series of Draft Issue Notes released by the OECD's Center for Tax Policy and Administration reiterate the OECD's negative view of the CPM and TNMM, insofar as they entail "mechanical comparisons of financial indicia."

Just as there is no reason to expect close correlations in accounting rates of return, gross margins and gross markups across firms, there is no compelling reason to believe that two unafffiliated companies with similar accounting rates of return will also have similar gross margins or gross markups. Hence, if OECD member countries apply the resale price and/or cost plus methods to the same intercompany transactions that the IRS analyzes under the CPM, the two (or more) tax authorities are likely to arrive at different conclusions regarding the arm's length allocation of income thereon, even if the sample companies are identical. This preference for different methods defeats one of the key purposes of the existing transfer pricing regime: To minimize the incidence of double-taxation.

3.3 Comparable Uncontrolled Price Method

In this segment, we review the comparable uncontrolled price method.

3.3.1 Description of Comparable Uncontrolled Price Method

The CUP method (aka the "comparable uncontrolled transactions method" as applied to intangible property and the "comparable uncontrolled services price method" as applied to services) entails comparing the prices, royalty rates or services fees that one member of a controlled group charges other members and unaffiliated companies, respectively. As with the resale price and cost plus methods, one can also apply the CUP method when two companies, one of which is a member of a controlled group and one of which is a standalone entity, sell virtually identical products, license the same intangible assets or perform the same services, in the former instance to (or for) affiliated buyers, and in the latter instance, to (or for) independent companies.

The standard of comparability applied under the CUP method is very high. Under the U.S. regulations, and in relation to *tangible* property, the transactions must be closely similar in terms of product type, functionality and quality, contractual terms, level of market, geographic market, timing, associated intangible property, foreign currency risks, and alternatives realistically available to buyers and sellers. If the products or transactions are dissimilar along any of these dimensions (that is, if the CUPs are "inexact"), price comparisons are valid only insofar as one can make reliable adjustments to the arm's length price to reflect such differences. The OECD Guidelines, similarly, emphasize product comparability, coupled with adjustments for differences. However, they also note that "[t]he difficulties that arise in attempting to make reasonably accurate adjustments should not routinely preclude the possible application of the CUP method. Practical considerations dictate a more flexible approach to enable the CUP method to be used ..."[12]

In relation to *intangible* property, the assets licensed to affiliated and unrelated companies, respectively, must either be identical or "comparable" under the U.S. regulations. One intangible asset will be considered comparable to another only

---

[12] See para. 2.9, Chapter II, *Transfer Pricing Guidelines for Multinational Enterprises and Tax Administrations*, Organization for Economic Cooperation and Development, July 1995.

if they are used in connection with similar products or processes within the same general industry or market and have similar profit potential. In comparing controlled and arm's length transfers of intangible assets, one should also consider the terms and circumstances of the transfers, the assets' respective stages of development, the licensees' rights to receive updates, the duration of the license, liability risks and collateral transactions. As applied to services transactions, one should consider the similarity of services, the intangible assets used in providing them (if any), contractual terms, and the economic conditions in which the transactions take place.[13]

3.3.2 Underlying Economic Rationale

With regard to tangible property and services, the (exact) CUP method presupposes that competitive pressures will cause prices and services fees to be equalized. With regard to intangible property, the comparable uncontrolled transactions method presupposes that an individual licensor will generally charge independent licensees the same royalty rate for the same rights to identical property, as will two licensors of comparable intangible property. This reasoning, in turn, implies one of several economic backdrops:

1. Different licensees value the intellectual property available from a single licensor equally, and have similar bargaining power in relation to the licensor (that is, they have similar alternatives available to them);
2. An individual licensor cannot effectively price discriminate in establishing its license terms and royalty fees, whether due to the costs of ascertaining the value of the intellectual property to different prospective licensees or because it is precluded from price discriminating as a practical or legal matter; or,
3. Two unaffiliated licensors of comparable intellectual property, dealing with separate licensees, will either independently negotiate precisely the same contractual terms and royalty rates or be forced to charge a uniform royalty rate and offer standardized terms by some unarticulated competitive dynamic.

3.3.3 Critique of Economic Reasoning

With regard to tangible property and services, prices and fees may or may not be equalized, depending on the degree to which the market at issue is competitive. In this context, the OECD Guidelines' and Draft Issue Notes' emphasis on comparability analyses, beginning with a broad-based analysis encompassing the industry, value-drivers, the nature of competition, and economic and regulatory factors, is well placed.

---

[13] See Treas. Reg. Section 1.482-9T(c)(2).

As previously noted, markets can generally be considered competitive for practical purposes if products or services are homogenous, incumbent firms can readily expand or new firms can enter, buyers or services recipients are well informed as to their alternative sources of supply or services, and switching suppliers or services providers is not excessively costly. Conversely, if products or services are differentiated in any material way, there are barriers to entry and expansion, buyers are not especially knowledgeable about the alternatives available to them, or firms would bear significant switching costs if they opted to segue to another supplier, prices or services fees may persistently differ across suppliers. Whether a given market can be characterized as competitive in a *de facto* sense is very much a matter of facts and circumstances. Moreover, although prices will generally be equalized more rapidly than economic rates of return in competitive product markets, there may be some "stickiness" in the adjustment process, which one should consider in determining whether price comparisons are valid in a given instance.

Items of intellectual property are inherently distinctive to greater or lesser degrees, and closely similar alternatives available from different entities are unlikely to exist (with the important exceptions of franchise arrangements and trademarks). By definition, truly unique intangible assets are not available from more than one source. Moreover, licensees generally cannot obtain rights to highly valuable "comparable" intellectual property from separate licensors. Therefore, absent internal arm's length licensing arrangements, the comparable uncontrolled transactions method will rarely apply to these types of intellectual property transactions, as practitioners have generally found.

However, even if, by some quirk of fate, external arm's length licensing transactions involving the same rights to comparable intangible property as those transferred intra-group could be found, the royalty rates charged in the external transactions may not be a satisfactory measure of an arm's length royalty rate in the controlled licensing arrangement at issue. Royalty rates are negotiated bilaterally between individual pairs of firms, and the parties to these private transactions do not generally make information on the terms and conditions agreed on publicly available.[14] Relatedly, buyers may incur significant costs simply to ascertain whether substitutable alternatives exist; such costs may deter them from doing so. Therefore, market pressures that might serve to equalize royalty rates across licensors rarely come into play. Moreover, the comparability criteria set forth under the comparable uncontrolled transactions method in the U.S. regulations would not suffice to ensure that two separate licensors would independently negotiate the same royalty rate and terms for the same set of rights to comparable intellectual property.

Different prospective licensees of the same intangible asset available from a single licensor may also ascribe substantially different values to it, depending on how

---

[14] U.S. firms can, and frequently do, request confidential treatment of information relating to the license or sale of intangible assets. If granted such treatment, they generally redact royalty rates from their public filings with the Securities and Exchange Commission.

the asset will contribute to the incremental generation of their free cash flows.[15] Further, a licensor can generally ascertain whether prospective licensees attach different values to its intellectual property without incurring significant costs, in part because there is a finite—and often quite limited—number of potential licensees, and considerable information is exchanged in the course of negotiating license agreements. Even if two licensees attach the same value to the same intellectual property, they may not be in the same bargaining position vis-a-vis the licensor (i.e., they may not have the same alternatives available to them). These factors may also influence the outcome of bilateral negotiations. Lastly, licensors are afforded legal protections that enable them to price discriminate and prevent licensees from engaging in arbitrage (i.e., by negotiating sublicensing arrangements).

In short, one cannot automatically assume that a single licensor will charge two unaffiliated licensees the same royalty rate for the same rights to identical intellectual property. Similarly, two licensors are unlikely to charge their respective licensees the same fees for the same rights to comparable intellectual property. (In any event, as a practical matter, one is unlikely to find satisfactory external comparables.) Therefore, there is limited support for the comparable uncontrolled transactions method, except as applied to franchises and trademarks.

It should also be noted that the *Commensurate with Income* requirement implies that a single licensor, or two licensors, will charge the same royalty rates per annum for identical or comparable intangible property *only* if their licensees will earn the same amount of intangible income, per dollar of sales, in *each* year over the terms of the licensing arrangements being compared.[16] Therefore, internal consistency would dictate that this extremely high standard of comparability be applied to both internal and external arm's length licensing transactions.

Trademarks are comparatively common intangible assets, they are frequently licensed, and, from many licensees' perspectives, they are substitutable to a significant degree (within categories). There is also a reasonable amount of publicly available information on license terms and royalty rates. As such, licensees often have viable alternatives and are cognizant of this fact, and they are therefore in a similar bargaining position vis-a-vis licensors. Lastly, licensees are generally motivated by one of a limited number of considerations to enter into trademark licensing arrangements:

1. An existing supplier of brand name products may want to diversify its portfolio of brands;
2. An established private label supplier may want to add brand name products to its offerings; or,

---

[15] To some extent, the U.S. regulations anticipate and allow for this possibility, as illustrated by the examples given in Treas. Reg. Section 1.482-4(c)(4).

[16] The *Commensurate with Income* or *Periodic Adjustment* requirement in the U.S. regulations provides that, "[i]f an intangible is transferred under an arrangement that covers more than one year, the consideration charged in each taxable year may be adjusted to ensure that it is commensurate with the income attributable to the intangible." See Treas. Reg. Section 1.482-4(f)(2).

3. An established or new company may be entering a new market and seek to simplify and streamline the market penetration process by utilizing a well-known brand.

Individual franchisors generally offer standardized contracts to all comers, and their terms are publicly available. As with trademarks, one franchise is generally substitutable for another within categories. Franchisees have minimal bargaining power, because of the enormous discrepancy in size between national franchisors and individual franchisees. Lastly, prospective franchisees generally research various franchising opportunities extensively before entering into a franchise agreement. As such, they are knowledgeable about the alternatives available to them.

3.3.4 Summary and Practical Implications

In sum, when an affiliated company operates in a truly competitive market, the exact CUP method, applied to tangible property or services, is based on well-accepted economic principles. By the same token, when the controlled group at issue operates in markets with differentiated products or services, or the markets are otherwise imperfectly competitive, the exact CUP method does not have the same economic validity (and generally would not be applied in any event).

The rarity of competitive product markets limits the usefulness of the CUP method, as it is framed in the U.S. regulations and construed in the field. However, product pricing in imperfectly competitive markets (or "inexact CUPs") can often yield quite useful information, even when the effects of differences in product attributes cannot be precisely quantified. Unfortunately, the U.S. regulations do not provide for the use of such information to any significant degree.

Conversely, in circumstances where the provision of services is predicated on ownership of unique intangible assets, comparisons of services fees across firms are unlikely to be reliable or helpful. Moreover, the comparable uncontrolled transactions method often does *not* have a solid economic foundation, even where the transactions being compared involve the same licensor, the same rights and identical intangible property. (For the reasons enumerated above, the license of trademarks and franchise arrangements are often exceptions to this general rule.)

3.4 Services Cost Method

For U.S. tax purposes, an arm's length services fee must be levied when one member of a group of controlled entities performs marketing, managerial, administrative, technical or other services that (a) jointly benefit the group members as a whole, or (b) benefit one or more individual group members. Charges for services that benefit more than one member should reflect "the relative benefits intended from the services, based on the facts known at the time the services were rendered," and must be levied whether or not the potential benefits are realized.[17] The OECD Guidelines provide that cross-charges for services rendered to affiliates are justified when the recipient derives economic or commercial value from such services. Duplicative or stewardship services rarely confer economic or commercial benefits on the recipient(s), and hence, do not generally warrant intra-group services fees.[18]

The U.S. Treasury Department issued Temporary Regulations governing intra-group services on July 31, 2006. These transfer pricing regulations provide that arm's length services fees should be determined (under specified circumstances) by application of one of the following methods: The services cost method; the comparable uncontrolled services price method; the gross services margin method; the cost of services plus method; the comparable profits method; the profit split method; and, unspecified methods. All these methods, with the exception of the services cost method, apply to transactions in tangible and/or intangible property as well, are applied in an analogous manner and are addressed elsewhere in this Chapter. (The OECD Guidelines on services are far less detailed, and generally favor the CUP and cost plus methods.[19]) In this segment, we review the services cost method.

3.4.1 Description of Services Cost Method

The services cost method, or SCM, sanctions a cost-based charge for certain types of services ("covered services") rendered to affiliated companies.[20] Covered services may either be generic support services that are common across many industries,[21] or other types of "low margin services" (defined as services for which the median comparable arm's length markup on total services costs is less than or equal to 7.0%). Where these covered services do not contribute significantly to key competitive advantages, core capabilities or the fundamental chances of success or failure in

---

[17] See Treas. Reg. 1.482-2(b)(2)(i).

[18] "Pure" shareholder activities performed by a parent or regional holding company benefit these entities in their capacity as owners, and do not justify charges to recipient group members.

[19] The CUP method can be used "where there is a comparable service provided between independent enterprises in the recipient's market, or by the associated enterprise providing the service to an independent enterprise in comparable circumstances." (See Chapter 7, "Special Considerations For Intra-Group Services," para. 7.31.) Where the CUP method cannot be applied, the cost plus method "would likely be appropriate," assuming the requisite standard of comparability is satisfied.

[20] The Temporary Regulations were originally intended to apply to taxable years beginning after December 31, 2006. However, *Notice 2007-5*, released on December 21, 2006, postponed the effective date of the SCM for 1 year (with the exception of the Business Judgment Rule under Temp. Treas. Reg. 1-482-9T(b)(2)).

[21] These services were provisionally identified by the Commissioner in a concurrently issued proposed revenue procedure, and subsequently expanded in *Rev. Proc. 2007-13*, released on December 21, 2006.

one or more businesses of the controlled group, in the opinion of the taxpayer (the "Business Judgment Rule"), a cost-based charge will suffice.[22,23]

Certain types of services cannot be charged out at cost. This list of services (the "black list") includes the following:

1. Manufacturing;
2. Production;
3. Extraction, exploration or processing of natural resources;
4. Construction;
5. Reselling, distribution, acting as a sales or purchasing agent or acting under a commission or other similar arrangement;
6. Research, development or experimentation;
7. Engineering or scientific;
8. Financial transactions, including guarantees; and
9. Insurance or reinsurance.

Although a standalone services provider would generally establish its fees with a view to recovering its costs and earning an element of profit, the OECD Guidelines also contemplate circumstances in which a profit should not be included in charges to affiliated services recipients. For example, if intra-group services fees, inclusive of a profit factor, are more costly than the economic alternatives available to the recipient, it would presumably be unwilling to pay more, on an arm's length basis, than these alternatives would entail. This constraint may reduce or eliminate the profit element that the affiliated services provider would otherwise have charged. There are also circumstances in which an independent services provider would render services at cost (e.g., to complement its other activities).

3.4.2 Rationale for Services Cost Method

Most multinational companies centralize certain routine support services. It would be extremely burdensome to require that companies conduct exhaustive transfer pricing studies to support cross-charges for each such service. The services cost method is an effort to lighten the administrative load on taxpayers; it does not have an economic justification per se.

The OECD Guidelines covering services reflect the basic tenet that rational economic actors will consider the alternatives available to them and select the most advantageous option. In some instances, this consideration will dictate a cost-based

---

[22] A literal reading of the Temporary Regulations indicates that a cost-based charge will be considered the best method when the requirements described above are met. However, in various public forums, the IRS has described the SCM as a safe harbor.

[23] The Business Judgment Rule was originally framed in terms of the key competitive advantages, core capabilities or the fundamental chances of success or failure of the renderer or the recipient. *Notice 2007-5* modified this definition by substituting "controlled group" for "renderer or recipient".

intercompany services fee. As a practical matter, many European taxing authorities are more concerned with the services cost base than the particular markup applied thereto, because it is generally more consequential from a tax revenue perspective.

3.5 Profit Split Methods

The profit split methods address circumstances in which two (or more) members of a controlled group own valuable intangible property. In these instances, neither the traditional transactions methods nor the CPM/TNMM apply. The U.S. regulations contain two profit split methods: The residual profit split method and the comparable profit split method. The OECD Guidelines take a more flexible approach and allow for a range of profit split methods, including the residual and comparable profit splits (and, seemingly, game-theoretic analyses.[24])

3.5.1 Residual Profit Split Method

Consider first the residual profit split method.

3.5.1.1 Description of Residual Profit Split Method

The residual profit split method (RPSM) is applied in several discrete steps. In the first step, each member of a controlled group engaged in a joint endeavor is allocated a portion of combined before-tax operating income. Such allocations are generally quantified by application of the CPM: Individual group members earn a certain markup over associated costs or tangible assets for their "routine contributions," such as sales functions, manufacturing functions, etc. These markups are determined by reference to samples of functionally comparable standalone companies.

In the second step of the RPSM, "residual" income is quantified by reducing adjusted operating profits by each entity's returns to routine functions, as determined in Step 1. Adjusted operating profits, in turn, are computed by eliminating deductions for investments in intangible assets from combined reported operating profits, and imputing deductions for the amortization of such assets (thereby conforming the accounting treatment of intangible assets to that of tangible assets).

Lastly, residual income is allocated among group members based on the relative value of intangible property that they each contribute to the joint endeavor. U.S. practitioners generally determine the relative value of intangible assets by capitalizing and amortizing intangibles-creating expenditures. This procedure necessitates (a) identifying all expenditures that give rise to intellectual property; (b) estimating the gestation lag between these outlays and the realization of benefits (improved

---

[24] See Organization for Cooperation and Development, para. 3.21, Chapter III. *Transfer Pricing Guidelines for Multinational Corporations and Tax Administrations,* July 1995.

process technologies and/or product features and functionality) from the resulting intellectual property; and (c) estimating the economically useful lives of individual intangible assets.

3.5.1.2 Underlying Economic Rationale

The basic premise underlying the RPSM is that before-tax operating profits are generated jointly by tangible and intangible assets.

3.5.1.3 Critique of Economic Reasoning

Inasmuch as the economic reasoning underlying the CPM applies equally to Step 1 of the RPSM, so too do the CPM's shortcomings. Additionally, assuming for the moment that the CPM *could* accurately measure the value of each controlled company's routine contributions, the difference between combined before-tax operating profits and combined returns to routine contributions would *not* yield income attributable to intangible assets. Combined after-tax free cash flows, rather than combined before-tax operating profits, should be the starting point of these computations. After-tax free cash flows and before-tax operating profits are generally very different magnitudes. Further, the practice of amortizing intangible assets for purposes of applying the residual profit split method exacerbates this problem: The discrepancy between before-tax operating profits (which reflect the depreciation of assets) and after-tax free cash flows (which reflect the deduction of investment outlays in full when they are made) is thereby magnified.

In short, the pool of allocable income is incorrectly measured both in total and as a residual under the residual profit split method: After-tax free cash flows should be used in lieu of before-tax operating profits, and the portion of free cash flows that is attributable to tangible assets should be netted out of this total, rather than arbitrary markups over cost, as determined by application of the CPM. In fact, there is no need to distinguish between income attributable to tangible and intangible assets, respectively. Rather, the relative values of *all* assets combined, both tangible and intangible, can be used to allocate free cash flows.

Relatedly, as noted, U.S. transfer pricing practitioners frequently value intangible assets by capitalizing and amortizing certain marketing, advertising and R&D expenditures, a methodology that the transfer pricing regulations endorse.[25] This valuation methodology presupposes a close correlation between the development costs and the fair market value of intangible assets that simply does not exist. R&D activities are fundamentally risky in nature, and in many cases, will not yield assets of material value. Conversely, a relatively modest R&D outlay can give rise to highly valuable intangible assets. Moreover, assumptions about gestation lags and useful lives are highly subjective. Finally, this method of valuation is contrary to well-established and widely accepted valuation principles and methodologies: Both

---

[25] See Treas. Reg. Section 1.482-6(c)(3)(i)(B).

the discounted cash flow (DCF) method and the market comparison method have considerably more merit from an economic standpoint.

In sum, the magnitudes that are allocated under the residual profit split method, and the approximations of relative asset values used for purposes of allocating residual income, are incorrectly defined and inaccurately measured.

3.5.2 Comparable Profit Split Method

Consider next the comparable profit split method.

3.5.2.1 Description of Comparable Profit Split Method

In principle, the U.S. regulations favor the comparable profit split method over the residual profit split method because it relies more heavily on external market benchmarks.[26] The comparable profit split method entails constructing a "hypothetical" multinational firm from two unrelated firms considered comparable to two individual members of a controlled group. Comparability, in this context, requires that each of the two unrelated companies artificially joined together engages in similar activities, employs similar resources (as measured by the book value of tangible assets), and incurs similar risks as the affiliated company with which it is paired. The combined operating profits of the two unaffiliated companies should not "vary significantly" from the combined operating profits of the affiliated companies with which they are being compared. Under these circumstances, one can quantify the proportional division of combined before-tax operating income between the unaffiliated companies, and apply the same proportion to the before-tax operating income earned jointly by the affiliated companies to determine their individual taxable income. Practitioners rarely use the comparable profit split method, because pairs of sufficiently comparable companies can rarely be found.

3.5.2.2 Underlying Economic Rationale

The comparable profit split method rests more on analogy than economic reasoning. It presupposes that the division of labor and risks between two unaffiliated companies, coupled with the book value of their respective assets, enables one to infer the relative fair market value of assets (both tangible and intangible) that each employs. Stated differently, the comparable profit split method presupposes that, if two pairs of unaffiliated companies divide functions and risks between themselves, and individually have approximately the same book value of assets, as their respective affiliated opposite number, the relative fair market value of assets across pairs will likewise be the same.

---

[26] See Treas. Reg. Section 1.482-6(c)(2)(ii)(D)) and Treas. Reg. Section 1.482-6(c)(3)(ii)(B).

3.5.2.3 Critique of Economic Reasoning

The division of labor and risks between two unaffiliated companies bears no necessary relationship to the value of their tangible assets, much less to their intangible assets. Functionally similar companies often differ in the degree to which their manufacturing processes are automated, the technologies they utilize, and the significance of intangible assets to their operations. Moreover, any extrapolation from the book value of assets to their fair market value is unlikely to be accurate. The assumed link between before-tax operating profits and assets is simply incorrect: As previously noted, after-tax free cash flows are an entirely separate and distinct measure of profits than before-tax operating income, and the two measures often differ significantly. Assets generate, and derive their value from, free cash flows. As such, relative asset values should determine the proportional division of after-tax free cash flows (which can be converted into before-tax operating profits as a separate step).

3.5.3 Summary and Practical Implications

In sum, the residual profit split method, as typically applied, incorrectly measures both combined income attributable to intangible assets and the relative fair market values of these assets, used to allocate "residual income" among controlled parties. The comparable profit split method, similarly, incorrectly measures income attributable to combined tangible and intangible assets. While assets are not explicitly valued under this variant of the profit split method, an entirely unfounded connection is forged between functions, risks and the book value of assets employed, on the one hand, and the relative fair market values of total assets employed, on the other. As such, application of these methods results in arbitrary allocations of income, with the attendent potential for double-taxation, inequity and unpredictability.

3.6 Proposed Cost-Sharing Regulations and Coordinated Issue Paper

The cost-sharing provisions in the U.S. transfer pricing regulations permit multinational firms to establish intra-group "cost-sharing agreements" (research joint ventures). Typically, one group member contributes pre-existing intangible assets to the cost-sharing arrangement for research purposes, for which the remaining participants must compensate it at arm's length. Additionally, from the start of the cost-sharing arrangement forward, all participants pay a share of ongoing research and development expenditures, based on their relative anticipated benefits therefrom. Research is frequently carried out by the group member that contributes pre-existing intellectual property at the outset. In a Coordinated Issue Paper (CIP) on the subject released in 2007, the IRS defines cost-sharing arrangements as follows:

A CSA is an arrangement by which the participants agree to share the costs of developing one or more intangibles (cost shared intangibles) that will be separately exploited by each of the participants. By participating in a CSA, each participant obtains a separate interest in such cost shared intangible.[27]

Many firms have opted to establish cost-sharing arrangements in lieu of licensing arrangements, as an alternative means of providing affiliated companies access to technology. However, the U.S. Treasury Department and the IRS presently view cost-sharing as a large loophole that companies have extensively exploited to reduce their U.S. tax liabilities. Such purported income-shifting is accomplished principally by under-compensating the entity contributing pre-existing intangible assets to the cost-sharing arrangement. As in other areas of transfer pricing requiring the valuation of intangible assets, practitioners have generally valued pre-existing intangible assets contributed to a cost-sharing arrangement by means of the residual profit split method. This methodology results in a declining buy-in payment for pre-existing intangibles, structured as a running royalty, because analysts typically assume a finite useful life for contributed assets.

Proposed cost-sharing regulations were issued on August 22, 2005. They were roundly criticized at the time by practitioners, professional associations and academic economists.[28] At the time of this writing, final cost-sharing regulations have not yet been issued, although they are expected to be released in the comparatively near future. The IRS has indicated in numerous forums, as well as in its CIP cited above, that the final regulations will look very much like the 2005 proposed regulations. As such, the latter (and the 2007 CIP on cost-sharing) are the focus of this discussion.

The proposed cost-sharing regulations and the CIP are based on the "Investor Model," as the U.S. Department of Treasury and the IRS have christened it, and are premised on the following key assumptions:

1. Research joint ventures between third parties are fundamentally different from intercompany cost-sharing arrangements. Such purported differences, cited in the CIP, include the following:

   (a) *All* participants in third party research joint ventures (or "co-development arrangements") typically contribute valuable intangible property to the venture;
   (b) Co-development agreements are more limited in scope;
   (c) Co-development agreements may contemplate *joint* exploitation of intangible assets; and,

---

[27] See Internal Revenue Service, *Coordinated Issue Paper: Section 482 CSA Buy-In Adjustments*, LMSB-04-0907-62, September 27, 2007, "Executive Summary".

[28] See, for example, a submission by Dr. William Baumol to the Internal Revenue Service, entitled "The IRS Cost Sharing Proposals: Implications for Innovative Activity, Outsourcing and the Public Interest," dated November 28, 2005.

    (d) Co-development agreements may tie the division of actual results to each
party's contributions.

2. Pre-existing intangible assets contributed to an intercompany cost-sharing
   arrangement (referred to as external contributions and Preliminary or Contemporaneous Transactions (PCTs) in the proposed regulations) have a useful life
   equal to or greater than the anticipated period of intangibles development *and*
   subsequent exploitation of newly developed intangibles. (Therefore, a declining
   royalty payment, such as that obtained by application of the residual profit split
   method, would not constitute sufficient consideration for pre-existing intellectual
   property.)
3. Third parties would base payments for external contributions purely on *ex ante*
   expectations, and would not renegotiate these terms if actual results differed
   significantly from expectations. As such, affiliated companies participating in
   a cost-sharing arrangement cannot modify either the amount or the form of payment for external contributions over time. (However, the IRS can revisit payments for external contributions due to a divergence between *ex ante* projections and *ex poste* results annually, through the Periodic Adjustment provision.[29]
   Moreover, absent contemporaneous projections, the IRS may rely on actual
   results in lieu of such projections, per the CIP.)
4. Third parties would regularly revisit cost-sharing contributions to fund ongoing
   research, however, if anticipated relative benefits diverge from actual relative
   benefits. As such, affiliated cost-sharing participants are required to do the same.
5. The group member (or members) that possessed pre-existing intellectual property would consider the alternatives realistically available to it (or them)—most
   notably, self-development and licensing—in deciding whether to enter into a
   cost-sharing agreement in the first instance. It (or they) would only opt to participate if this course of action yielded an equal or higher expected return than
   the next best alternative (measured in terms of the net present value of before-tax
   operating profits).
6. The participants that contribute funding alone are performing a routine financing
   function and should receive a rate of return equal to their cost of capital (i.e.,
   zero economic profits).

    The proposed regulations differ from the current cost-sharing regulations pri-
marily in their treatment of buy-in payments. Under both existing and proposed
regulations, each cost-sharing participant's share of pooled costs must reflect their
anticipated relative benefits from exploitation of the developed intangible assets,
as measured indirectly by units used, produced or sold, sales, operating profit or
other reasonable proxies. Adjustments to cost shares must be made "to account
for changes in economic conditions, the business operations and practices of the

---

[29] See Treas. Reg. Section 1.482-4(f)(2).

participants, and the ongoing development of intangibles under the CSA."[30] Stock-based compensation must be included in the base of costs to be shared.[31]

The proposed regulations provide much more detailed guidance than the current cost-sharing regulations as to how one should determine the amount of a buy-in payment. More particularly, the proposed regulations contain the following specified "valuation" methods:

- The comparable uncontrolled transaction method;
- The income method;
- The acquisition price method;
- The market capitalization method; and,
- The residual profit split method.

The above methods are referred to as unspecified methods in the CIP, because the cost-sharing regulations remain in proposed form at this point. However, the CIP emphasizes that unspecified methods may produce more reliable results than specified methods, thus elevating the former's status for audit purposes. The comparable uncontrolled transaction and residual profit split methods have been discussed elsewhere in this Chapter. Hence, in this discussion, we concentrate on the income method, the acquisition price method and the market capitalization method.

3.6.1 Income Method

Under the 2005 proposed cost-sharing regulations, the income method applies only when a single group member contributes pre-existing intangible property to the cost-sharing arrangement. However, the more recent CIP relaxes this restriction. The income method is based on the aforementioned assumption that the group member contributing pre-existing intangible assets would only enter into a cost-sharing arrangement if such participation is at least as advantageous as the best feasible alternative. The income method can be applied in conjunction with the comparable uncontrolled transaction (CUT) method or the comparable profits method.

As indicated above, the entity contributing pre-existing intangible assets could opt instead to incur all intangibles development costs itself, and license the resulting intellectual property to affiliated companies. Under the CUT variant of the income method, one establishes an arm's length royalty rate for rights to pre-existing intellectual property by reference to a sample of third party license agreements. This royalty rate is then reduced by the ratio of (a) the discounted present value of

---

[30] See Treas. Reg. Section 1.482-7(e)(1).

[31] This issue is currently being litigated. Xilinx Inc. challenged an upward adjustment in its U.S. taxable income, predicated on the inclusion of the value of certain employee stock options in the pool of costs to be shared under a CSA, in Tax Court. The Tax Court recently ruled in favor of Xilinx. (See Xilinx v. Comm'r., 125 TC No. 4, 4142-01, 702-03, Filed August 30, 2005.) However, the IRS is appealing the Tax Court's decision.

projected cost-sharing payments, to (b) the discounted present value of the payee's projected sales of product incorporating the developed intangible property. (The proposed regulations refer to this step as the "cost contribution adjustment.") Stated differently, all cost-sharing participants other than the contributor of pre-existing intangible assets would pay a buy-in fee, structured as a running royalty, that is roughly equal, at the outset, to the prevailing arm's length royalty rate for rights to exploit the pre-existing intangible assets, reduced by the payee's approximate cost-sharing contributions per dollar of sales. This is, in essence, a means of reimbursing the cost-sharing participants for their projected contributions and converting the cost-sharing arrangement into a licensing arrangement.

Consider next the income method applied in conjunction with the comparable profits method. As with applications of the comparable profits method in other contexts, one first establishes returns to the routine functions that participants *not* making external contributions to the cost-sharing arrangement perform. The present value of total projected operating profits in these companies' markets, reduced by the present value of their projected routine returns and divided by the present value of their projected sales, constitutes the "alternative rate." This alternative rate, reduced by the "cost contribution adjustment" (as defined above) and applied to realized sales, is the amount paid to the contributor of pre-existing intellectual property. Equivalently, all other participants are reimbursed for their projected cost contributions, and pay over to the contributor all projected operating profits in excess of their routine returns.

3.6.2 Acquisition Price Method

The acquisition price method is a special case of the CUT method. It applies only when an unaffiliated company is acquired at the outset or during the term of a cost-sharing agreement, and substantially all the target company's non-routine assets constitute external contributions thereto.[32] It entails adjusting the acquisition price upward for liabilities assumed and downward for tangible (and routine intangible) assets purchased. Additionally, the total adjusted value (that is, the buy-in charge in total) must be allocated among cost-sharing participants based on their relative anticipated benefits.

3.6.3 Market Capitalization Method

The market capitalization method is similar to the acquisition price method in concept, although it is applied to the controlled group establishing a cost-sharing

---

[32] As is evident in the CIP, the IRS anticipates that the acquisition price method will be used primarily, if not exclusively, to establish buy-in fees for assets contributed to an ongoing cost-sharing agreement.

arrangement, and the fair market value of assets in total is derived from the group's publicly traded shares (increased by the value of its liabilities), rather than an acquisition price. To obtain the fair market value of intangible assets constituting an external contribution, the fair market value of tangible assets owned by the group is netted out of its total market capitalization.

If more than one entity owns intangible property, the market capitalization method necessitates that one compute market capitalization on an entity-specific basis. This is clearly not feasible (although one can value individual group members by other means). Therefore, while not explicitly stated in the proposed cost-sharing regulations or the CIP, the market capitalization method can only be applied when ownership of intellectual property is centralized in a single group member. The market capitalization method also presupposes that all of this entity's intangible assets constitute external contributions.

3.6.4 Critique

The 2005 proposed cost-sharing regulations are based on a set of assumptions that the IRS simply asserts are valid, despite an abundance of theory and evidence to the contrary. Arm's length research joint ventures cannot be distinguished from intercompany cost-sharing arrangements by a bright line and may shed considerable light on how the latter should be structured and evaluated, consistent with the arm's length standard in general. While pre-existing intangible assets that are further developed often retain some of their separate identity and original value, this value does not persist indefinitely, and does not account for *all* of the next-generation intangible assets' value. Further, third parties can and do regularly revisit commercial contracts when the benefits to each party differ significantly from those expected at the outset, and often incorporate provisions in long-term contracts that permit adjustments in terms.[33]

The comparable uncontrolled transaction, acquisition price and market capitalization methods are very limited in their applicability and have certain innate drawbacks. Those associated with the comparable uncontrolled transaction method are discussed elsewhere in this Chapter. The acquisition price method only applies when a target company has been purchased for the express purpose of obtaining access to specific identifiable assets, all of which will be contributed to an ongoing cost-sharing arrangement (while all remaining acquired assets will be abandoned). Under most other circumstances, the acquisition price method will result in an overvaluation of external contributions, because goodwill and going concern value will be included in this valuation.

---

[33] See, for example, King, Elizabeth, "Is the Section 482 Periodic Adjustment Requirement Really Arm's Length? Evidence from Arm's Length Long Term Contracts." *Tax Notes International*, April 11, 1994.

The market capitalization method is limited to situations in which only one group member owns intellectual property, and *all* such property is contributed to the cost-sharing arrangement at the outset. The market capitalization method will also generally result in an over-valuation of intangible assets constituting external contributions by including goodwill and going concern value. (Because the value of these intangible assets is almost always determined as a residual, one cannot carve them out of the combined value of all intangible assets.) Moreover, even the *comparatively* straightforward valuation of tangible assets can prove difficult. Accounting measures of tangible asset values often bear little relationship to their fair market value.

The residual profit split method, also discussed elsewhere in this Chapter, has virtually no economic foundation. Moreover, the IRS does not hold it in very high regard. Hence, as a practical matter, it will probably cease to be widely used in a cost-sharing context.

Given the extremely limited applicability of all methods other than the residual profit split and income methods, and the IRS' discomfort with the former, it follows that intercompany cost-sharing arrangements will frequently be evaluated under the income method. Consistent with this view, the CIP states that "the income or foregone profits method will generally constitute the most reliable method for measuring an initial buy-in . . ."[34] This is quite unfortunate, because the income method is flatly inconsistent with the arm's length standard, as explained in detail below. Moreover, the income method permits the IRS to recharacterize intercompany transactions in a manner that other portions of the U.S. transfer pricing regulations expressly prohibit:

> The contractual terms, including the consequent allocation of risks, that are agreed to in writing before the transactions are entered into will be respected if such terms are consistent with the economic substance of the underlying transactions. In evaluating economic substance, greatest weight will be given to the actual conduct of the parties, and the respective legal rights of the parties.[35]

Independent companies contemplating an investment opportunity will only commit capital (and will only maximize shareholder value thereby) if the undertaking yields a *positive* expected net present value, accurately measured:

> The objective of the firm is assumed to be the maximization of shareholders' wealth. Towards this end, managers should [under]take projects with positive NPVs [net present values] down to the point where the NPV of the last acceptable project is zero. When cash flows are properly defined for capital budgeting purposes and are discounted at the weighted average cost of capital, the NPV of a project is exactly the same as the increase in shareholders' wealth.[36]

---

[34] Internal Revenue Service, *Coordinated Issue Paper: Section 482 CSA Buy-In Adjustments*, LMSB-04-0907-62, September 27, 2007. See IV, "Initial Buy-In: Best Method Analysis – Income Method is Generally the Best Method."

[35] Treas. Reg. Section 1.482-1(d)(3)(ii)(B).

[36] Thomas E. Copeland and J. Fred Weston, *Financial Theory and Corporate Policy*, Addison-Wesley Publishing Company: New York, 1988.

Cash flows for capital budgeting purposes are defined as "free operating cash flows minus taxes on free operating cash flows. .... This definition is very different from the accounting definition of net [or operating] income. Cash flows for capital budgeting purposes can be thought of as the after-tax cash flows that the firm would have if it had no debt."[37]

Interestingly, the drafters of the CIP use precisely this argument in justifying the allocation of *all* income attributable to jointly developed intangible assets to the contributor of pre-existing intangible assets:

> [T]he notion that USP [U.S. parent] would accept a buy-in with an expected net present value significantly less than the expected NPV of the project as a whole in the CFC's [Controlled Foreign Corporation's] territory would violate an established principle of corporate finance. USP would in that case be investing an asset (the buy-in intangible as it pertains to the CFC's territory) for an anticipated return with a smaller expected NPV than the value of the asset invested. USP's investment thus would have a negative anticipated NPV. In general, however, *a corporation will undertake a project only if its NPV is greater than zero* [my emph.] ...[38]

In other words, *all* income generated through the exploitation of newly developed intangible assets can ultimately be traced back, and is attributable in full, to pre-existing intangible assets; hence their fair market value. As such, the buy-in payment should be equal to (or greater than) the discounted present value of all such income. By implication, intangible assets created as a result of joint efforts have no value in and of themselves, but only as an extension of the original intellectual property on which they build.

It is indisputably true that, for the contemplated research undertaking to make economic sense, whether funded solely by the owner of the pre-existing assets or jointly funded through a CSA, the discounted present value of projected after-tax free cash flows (rather than before-tax operating profits) must exceed the value of the buy-in assets. That is, the net present value of the project must be positive. However, this does *not* mean that, having opted to establish a cost-sharing arrangement, all income attributable to pre-existing and yet-to-be-developed intangible assets should flow to USP. Rather, USP should systematically compare the discounted present value of after-tax free cash flows associated with the following two options:

1. Fund the further development of intangibles independently and exploit the resulting assets directly or through licensing (or a combination thereof) on a worldwide basis; or
2. Contribute the pre-existing intellectual property to a cost-sharing arrangement, receive a buy-in payment, share the costs of further development and exploit the resulting assets in a more limited territory.

---

[37] Ibid, pp. 39–40.

[38] See Internal Revenue Service, *Coordinated Issue Paper: Section 482 CSA Buy-In Adjustments*, LMSB-04-0907-62, September 27, 2007, "Taxpayer Methods and Positions".

Taking as given a particular buy-in payment, one can determine which of these two options yields a higher NPV. Alternatively, one can treat the buy-in payment as a variable and derive a minimum payment by (a) equating the NPVs associated with each option (taking into account USP's projected development expenses under each scenario, licensing fees, etc.), and (b) solving for the unknown (the minimum buy-in payment). Moreover, it is not sufficient that USP have an incentive to enter into a cost-sharing arrangement; the net present value of joining for *each* prospective participant must be positive. One can derive a maximum buy-in payment for each participant that does not make external contributions using the same analytics.

However, the proposed regulations do not take this more nuanced approach. Instead, they convert the cost-sharing arrangement into a *de facto* licensing arrangement by brute force under the income method, applied in conjunction with the comparable uncontrolled transaction method. Participants' incentives to enter into a cost-sharing arrangement, and the cost-sharing option in substance, are taken off the table entirely.

The mechanics are slightly different when one applies the income method in conjunction with the comparable profits method. However, such applications produce at least as draconian an allocation of intangible income. Moreover, the comparable profits variant of the income method eliminates non-U.S. participants' incentives to invest not only in cost-shared intangibles, but *all independently developed, territory-specific intangible assets* as well. With a return capped at some arbitrarily determined "routine" level, non-U.S. cost-sharing participants would earn a negative NPV if they invested in the development of any intangible assets, cost-shared or otherwise, inasmuch as the cash flows generated thereby would flow directly to USP.[39]

Clearly, regulations that require affiliated companies to agree to and abide by terms that third parties would never negotiate cannot be considered arm's length. Correspondingly, regulations that do not permit commonly controlled companies to enter into collaborative research joint ventures, while third parties routinely do so, cannot be considered arm's length. As such, the 2005 proposed cost-sharing regulations' income method is markedly inconsistent with the arm's length standard.

In short, the income method incorporated into the 2005 proposed cost-sharing regulations, and embroidered on in the CIP, flagrantly violates the foundational arm's length principle, as well as the U.S. transfer pricing regulations' stricture against recharacterizing the form of an intercompany transaction if the parties

---

[39] There are more narrowly defined problems with the mechanics of the income method as well. As described in Example 1.482-7(g)(4)(iii)(C) of the proposed regulations, the ratio of cost-sharing payments to sales is calculated by separately discounting projected cost-sharing payments and projected sales. Therefore, contrary to what one would logically expect, the more risky the research project jointly undertaken, the *smaller* the discount from an arm's length royalty charge for rights to pre-existing intellectual property. Moreover, because cost-sharing payments are made over a shorter period of time than royalty payments, the should be calculated on a lump-sum basis (that is, using the discounted present value of projected royalty payments as well), rather than on a contingency basis, as the proposed regulations contemplate.

thereto have acted in conformity with it. Despite these enormous drawbacks, the CIP indicates that the income method will generally be the best method for purposes of analyzing intra-group cost-sharing arrangements. The comparable uncontrolled transaction method is flawed for the reasons discussed elsewhere in this chapter and can rarely be applied in practice. The acquisition price method is extremely limited in its applicability as well. The market capitalization method will systematically result in an over-valuation of external contributions on those comparatively rare occasions that it applies.

3.7 Global Dealing Regulations and Notice 94–40

The proposed global dealing regulations are intended to provide guidance vis-a-vis transfer pricing to multinational financial intermediaries that deal in various financial products and services. These proposed regulations expressly exclude global trading firms that deal in non-financial products (e.g., physical commodities). In lieu of specific regulations (proposed or otherwise), Notice 94–40 is used by the latter in formulating their transfer pricing policies under certain circumstances.

3.7.1 Circumstances in Which the Proposed Global Dealing Regulations and Notice 94–40 Apply

Many tax practitioners, both in and outside the government, believe that the global trading of commodities and financial instruments presents unique difficulties vis-a-vis the application of transfer pricing regulations. A number of features set trading activities apart from many other types of economic activity: (a) there is often limited division of labor among legal entities constituting a controlled trading group; (b) traders in different jurisdictions may work collectively on a single "book of business" or otherwise collaborate quite closely; (c) debt and equity capital used to finance trades may be fungible across legal entities; (d) traders are not physically tied to a particular geographic location by necessity (that is, they could make the same contributions to the generation of trading profits independent of their geographic base of operations); and (e) by its nature, trading is a multi-jurisdictional activity.

Given the limited division of labor among controlled trading group members, transfer pricing methods that presuppose a particular division of labor (the resale price and cost plus methods) are generally not applicable. Because individual members of a trading group can contribute to the generation of joint trading profits in a variety of ways, and, depending on booking conventions, may not purchase (or sell) commodities or financial products from (or to) one another, the comparable uncontrolled price method, likewise, is often not a viable approach. By virtue of the fungibility of financial capital, traders' flexibility regarding their physical location, and the fact that commodities and financial products trading requires a broad geographic reach, the nexus between geographic location and particular profit-generating activities is, in the view of many practitioners, not clearly drawn, and standalone firms operating in a single geographic market are not comparable essentially by definition. This perceived lack of fixed correspondence between contribution and location, and the dearth of genuinely comparable standalone firms, effectively precludes other traditional transfer pricing methods as well. In lieu of the "separate entity" approach that underlies all the conventional U.S. and OECD transfer pricing methods,[40] the IRS has more or less endorsed a formulary apportionment methodology for certain types of global trading firms.[41]

In *Notice 94–40*, issued in 1994, the IRS described certain key characteristics of Advance Pricing Agreements (APAs) that it has negotiated with taxpayers engaged in the global trading of derivative financial instruments or commodities on a "functionally fully integrated" basis. According to the *Notice*, fully integrated trading operations manage their business "as one global position for purposes of risk management rather than several discrete businesses." The trading book is not independently maintained for each trading location, but instead, one book (the "global book") is passed from one trading location to another in the adjacent time zone at the close of each trading day. To facilitate the effective management of risk, a central credit department monitors the group's credit-related exposure and establishes credit guidelines and customer credit limits to be applied by traders in all locations. In addition, in a functionally fully integrated global trading operation, the book for each product (or group of products) typically has one head trader who allocates trading limits for each trading location and determines guidelines for the book. The head trader is also responsible for the economic performance of that book, and, as such, he or she is in frequent communication with, and oversees, other traders employed by the company.

Notice 94–40 is "not intended to prescribe a method or factors that will necessarily apply in all APAs with functionally fully integrated global trading operations, limit the use of other methods or factors"[42] or be used to allocate the trading profits of firms that are not functionally fully integrated.

The U.S. Treasury Department issued proposed transfer pricing regulations addressing transactions among participants in a global dealing operation in 1998.[43] For purposes of these proposed regulations, a global dealing operation "consists of the execution of customer transactions, including marketing, sales, pricing and risk

---

[40] The "separate entity" approach is part and parcel of the arm's length standard, in that the objective is to determine the amount of taxable income that each member of a controlled group would earn on a separate, standalone basis.

[41] See Notice 94–40, *Global Trading Advance Pricing Agreements*, 1994-1 C.B. 351; 1994 IRB LEXIS 213; 1994-17 I.R.B. 22, April 25, 2004.

[42] Ibid.

[43] *IRS Proposed Rules on Allocation and Sourcing of Income and Deductions Among Taxpayers Engaged in Global Dealing Operations*, REG-208299-90, 63 Fed. Reg. 11177, 3/6/98.

management activities, in a particular financial product or line of financial products, in multiple tax jurisdictions and/or through multiple participants . . . The taking of proprietary positions is not included within the definition of a global dealing operation unless the proprietary positions are entered into by a regular dealer in securities in its capacity as such a dealer . . ."[44] The proposed global dealing regulations do *not* encompass commodities, although "the IRS solicit[ed] comments on whether these regulations should be extended to cover dealers in commodities . . ."[45] To date, these regulations have not been finalized. Moreover, financial transactions in which members of a global dealing operation engage are expressly exempted from the Temporary Regulations issued under Treas. Reg. Section 1.482-9T in 2006, which might otherwise have provided useful (and much-needed) guidance:

> Pending finalization of the global dealing regulations, taxpayers may rely on the proposed global dealing regulations, not the temporary services regulations, to govern financial transactions entered into in connection with a global dealing operation as defined in proposed Section 1.482-8. Therefore, proposed regulations under IRC Section 1.482-9(m)(5) issued elsewhere in the Federal Register clarify that a controlled services transaction does not include a financial transaction entered into in connection with a global dealing operation.[46]

Hence, global commodities and financial products trading firms have been in a regulatory limbo of sorts with regard to transfer pricing matters. *Notice 94–40* is not expressly relevant outside the context of an APA, and the proposed global dealing regulations exempt global traders of non-financial products, as noted, as well as firms that engage exclusively in proprietary trading activities. Further, the weight that one should attach to proposed regulations, as distinct from temporary regulations, is somewhat unclear. As such, global trading firms have been faced with even greater uncertainty in the transfer pricing arena than firms engaged in other types of economic activity (and they were among the first to avail themselves of the APA option when it was introduced).

3.7.2 Description of Notice 94–40 and Proposed Global Dealing Regulations

Notice 94–40 states that, in the APAs that the IRS has concluded with functionally fully integrated global traders, all parties (the IRS, the taxpayer and the relevant treaty partner) agreed that worldwide income for each global book covered by the APA should be allocated among the taxpayer's trading locations pursuant to a profit split method that is keyed to three critical factors:

---

[44] See Prop. Treas. Reg. Section 1.482-8(a)(2).

[45] Ibid.

[46] See *IRS Final, Temporary Rules on Services Treatment Under Section 482, Allocation of Income and Deductions From Intangibles, Stewardship Expenses*, 26 CFR Parts 1 and 31, RIN 45-BB31, 1545-AY38, 1545-BC52, "Explanation of Provisions," Item 12, Coordination with Other Transfer Pricing Rules – Temp. Treas. Reg. Section 1.482-9T(m).

- The relative value of the trading location (the "value factor");
- The risk associated with the trading location (the "risk factor"); and
- The extent of activity at each trading location (the "activity factor").

The "value factor" is intended to measure each trading location's contribution to the worldwide profits of the group and is often equated with the compensation paid to all traders at individual trading locations. The "risk factor" measures the risk to which a particular trading location exposes the worldwide capital of the organization. Risk has been measured in a variety of ways (e.g., the maturity-weighted volume of swap transactions or open commodity positions at year-end by trading location). Finally, the "activity factor" is a measure of each trading location's contributions to key support functions. It is frequently quantified by the compensation paid to such personnel at each trading location. Value, risk and activity factors must also be weighted in accordance with their relative importance.

Under the proposed global dealing regulations, the allocation of combined income across tax jurisdictions must be determined by application of one of the following methods:

- The comparable uncontrolled financial transaction (CUFT) method;
- The gross margin method;
- The gross markup method; and
- The profit split method (consisting of either a total or residual profit split).

Under the CUFT method, one looks to the pricing of uncontrolled financial transactions to establish or evaluate intercompany prices among members of a group engaged in global dealing. Pricing data from public exchanges or quotation media are acceptable under some circumstances, as are applications of internal proprietary pricing models used to establish pricing on arm's length financial dealings. Judging from the examples given in the proposed global dealing regulations, the CUFT method would generally apply when (a) a controlled group trades standardized financial instruments, (b) each group member operates as a dealer in its own right vis-a-vis its separate customer base, and (c) intercompany financial transactions take place contemporaneously with third party transactions. While the CUFT approach is reasonable on its face, its applicability is somewhat limited, inasmuch as many trading firms deal in non-standard financial products and commodities and enter into relatively few (albeit large) trades per day. Moreover, individual trading offices may conclude contracts in a broad range of geographic markets and are motivated to do so in part by arbitrage opportunities (i.e., because prices differ across markets). As such, pricing comparisons across geographic markets are frequently unreliable.

As with the CUFT method, the gross margin and gross markup methods presuppose that each member of a global dealing operation has a substantial book of business that it carries out independently. The gross margin and gross markup methods can be applied when individual group members act as market-makers vis-a-vis third parties, and a market-determined bid/ask spread can therefore readily be established in the relevant time frame (that is, when an intercompany transaction takes place).

The proposed global dealing regulations' profit split methods are intended to address more complex situations in which individual group members' activities are more closely integrated. Consistent with *Notice 94–40*, the proposed regulations advocate apportioning a group's combined operating profits (or losses) by reference to each legal entity's contributions thereto. However, the proposed regulations are more open-ended as to the particular factors that should be incorporated into the allocation formula. Depending on the facts and circumstances that characterize individual cases, a multi-factor formula may be indicated, and, in this event, each factor will need to be weighted.

3.7.3 *Underlying Economic Rationale*

The proposed global dealing regulations and *Notice 94–40* are, in essence, an attempt to devise a transfer pricing methodology in the absence of an economic rationale. They are based on the uncontroversial, albeit generic, proposition that each entity's share of trading profits should reflect its relative contributions to the generation thereof. However, the proposed regulations and *Notice 94–40* do not embody the foundational premise that profits (specifically, after-tax free cash flows) are generated through the employment of assets rather than "allocation keys," variously defined in individual cases.

3.7.4 *Critique of Formulary Method*

The formulary apportionment methodologies described in *Notice 94–40* and the proposed global dealing regulations produce highly arbitrary results, for the following reasons:

- Most fundamentally, formulary methods do not preserve the nexus between assets and after-tax free cash flows, as noted above.
- Trading companies engage in a wide variety of transactions, each of which poses different types of risks. The diversity of risks cannot be distilled down to a single reliable measure;
- The weights assigned to each allocation factor in individual cases are entirely subjective; and
- Trading is intrinsically fluid and dynamic. As such, it is uniquely ill-suited to tax treatment that, for analytical purposes, holds constant both the activities that contribute to the generation of trading profits and their relative importance over time (the term of an APA or the number of years that individual taxpayers rely on a fixed formula, absent an APA).

Moreover, conventional wisdom substantially understates the degree to which particular trading activities and assets can be identified with specific geographic locales. A "separate entity" framework is often viable and may produce more reasonable results than the formulary apportionment method (albeit less reasonable results than a straightforward profit split based on assets employed).

3.7.4.1 "Factors" Should Be Replaced with Assets

Assets alone generate free cash flows. Factors other than assets, such as "trader expertise" and "activity levels," should not be used to *allocate* free cash flows, because they do not *generate* free cash flows in the first instance. Rather, traders, marketers and key support personnel are paid the fair market value of their services,[47] and, for accounting purposes, compensation is included in cost of goods sold and/or below-the-line expenses. Stated differently, operating profits and free cash flows do not embody the fair market value of services rendered by traders, marketers and key support personnel. In allocating after-tax free cash flows (i.e., the return to providers of debt and equity capital), one should look *only* to the fair market values of income-generating assets leased or purchased with such capital.

3.7.4.2 Risk is Multi-faceted

The formulary apportionment method outlined in *Notice 94–40* incorporates a single "risk factor," variously measured as the maturity-weighted volume of swap transactions, open commodity positions at year-end, etc. Leaving aside the reasonableness of including this type of factor in the allocation formula, risk, in a trading context, cannot be reduced to single measure. Nor is the nature of risk constant over time.

As discussed in Chapter 11 at much greater length, the current commodities trading environment, characterized by extremely volatile prices, has greatly exacerbated trading firms' price and credit risk, and effectively precluded open positions of any duration. Non-performance risk is probably the single most important risk at present, and it is not reflected at all in the measures of risk briefly described in *Notice 94–40*. There is also much greater risk that delayed payment (and the attendent interest costs) will eliminate the narrow margins that firms currently earn in traditional merchant trading activities. Additionally, commodities trading firms' investments in upstream hard assets (e.g., stakes in bauxite, alumina and copper mining companies) have given rise to other risks not contemplated in *Notice 94–40*.

3.7.4.3 Weights are Subjective and Factors Change in Relative Importance

Again, leaving aside the appropriateness of including non-asset "factors" in the apportionment formula, the weights assigned to individual factors under the formulary apportionment method are purely subjective, and are held fixed for the multi-year term of an APA agreement. Given the highly fluid nature of global trading, such constancy is not a viable working assumption.

---

[47] If such individuals were compensated at less than their fair market value, they would presumably seek employment elsewhere.

The subjective nature of weighting is self-evident. However, even if one could objectively establish the relative importance of core trading assets and activities at a given point, these "objective" weights would not remain the same for long. Access to financial capital and effective risk management have increased in importance over the past several years. At the same time, the relative importance of trading expertise and established supplier relationships has diminished with the narrowing of potential trading strategies, and China's substantially increased mining and refining capacity.

3.7.4.4 The Formulary Apportionment Methodology Is Unnecessary

As discussed in Chapter 11, the core elements of a global commodities trading operation include (1) access to financing, (2) access to product, (3) a reputation for reliability, (4) a set of administrative controls that prevents enormously costly errors and facilitates the effective management of risk, (5) a sophisticated IT system that enables traders and risk managers to track activity in real time, and (6) expertise in market fundamentals, infrastructural and logistical features, trading strategies and risk management.

With the exception of expertise possessed by traders, risk managers and logistical specialists (i.e., "human capital"), these core elements can be linked to specific tangible and intangible assets, most of which can in turn be identified with individual trading offices:

- The "worldwide capital" available to a trading group is fungible only if lenders agree to these terms. It is by no means always the case that a single group member has large credit lines and allocates borrowed funds freely among group members, as dictated by trading opportunities. Rather, in many instances, credit is extended directly from third party lenders to individual group members, and the latter have limited flexibility with regard to the reallocation of borrowed funds. Moreover, even where loans *are* made to a single entity that performs a centralized treasury function, the relevant metric for profit split purposes (that is, the associated intangible asset) is access to capital in the first instance, not the extent to which individual trading locations put the "worldwide capital" of the group at risk. Such access is often measurable on an entity-by-entity basis.
- Where access to product is formalized in a written contract, generally only one member of a controlled trading group is the counterparty. While other entities may have assisted in the negotiation of the contract or provided pre-financing, and should be compensated accordingly, the counterparty is the legal "owner" of the established relationship. Where a relationship with a customer or supplier is well-established but not formalized, an individual originator or trader will generally have developed the relationship in the first instance. The entity that employs this individual should be deemed to "own" the customer or supplier relationship.
- Administrative controls, risk management systems and proprietary IT systems are often developed in one trading location and used by other locations. The

developer (or, if different, the legal owner) of these controls and systems should be treated as the owner for transfer pricing purposes.

- A reputation for reliability may have originated with a single trading location, or it may be a natural outgrowth of the integrated operation. In the first case, the single trading location should be deemed to own the goodwill intangible. In the second case, goodwill should not be used to allocate income across trading locations, inasmuch as it is jointly developed and owned.

3.7.5 Summary and Practical Implications

In summary, the proposed global dealing regulations and *Notice 94–40*, taken together, constitute an attempt to address situations in which individual group members coordinate very closely and perform the same or closely similar functions. Under these circumstances, many practitioners and tax policy-makers believe that a separate entity approach is infeasible. While the general principle that each group member's share of profits should reflect its relative contributions to the generation of such profit is sound, the measures of both profit and contributions vary from one case to the next, and have no real economic basis. As such, the results produced by formulary apportionment methods are arbitrary. The use of (a) after-tax free cash flows in lieu of accounting measures of profit, (b) assets in lieu of factors, and (c) fair market values in lieu of weights, would significantly improve on the formulary apportionment approach, and may also be preferable to a separate entity approach.

Part II
Alternative and Supplementary Approaches to Transfer Pricing

Chapter 4
Some Alternative Approaches to Transfer Pricing

This segment of the book contains descriptions of a number of alternative approaches to transfer pricing. Several proposed methods are relatively minor modifications of existing methodologies, although their application requires more flexibility and a greater appreciation of the market dynamics at work in individual cases. Other proposed methods constitute more radical departures from current practice.

The first proposed method is simply an extension or reinterpretation of the inexact comparable uncontrolled price method. The second and third methods, and one variant of the fourth method, presuppose that the legal entities comprising a multinational corporation contribute in differing ways to the generation of profits. The other variant of the fourth method can be applied whether individual group members perform the same or differing functions. The last proposed method presupposes that all legal entities constituting a multinational corporation perform the same range of functions and employ similar types of assets. These proposed methods, summarized briefly below and addressed in greater detail subsequently, have a more solid economic footing than existing methods (with the exception of the "numerical standards" approach), and address certain fact patterns to which the extant transfer pricing regimes give short shrift.

- **Modified Comparable Uncontrolled Price Method.** As previously discussed, under certain circumstances, the comparable uncontrolled price method is a sound means of establishing arm's length prices. Yet, in the United States, applications of the CUP method are frequently rejected out-of-hand due to the difficulty in finding "exact CUPs." However, arm's length prices often contain useful information even when they are inexact, and this information should be utilized to the extent possible. (Chapter 5 contains a case study illustrating the proposed modified inexact comparable uncontrolled price method, along with the resale price method and the comparable profits method.)
- **Numerical Standards.** For comparatively simple cases, taxing authorities in different jurisdictions could establish numerical results that they would apply uniformly. For example, tax authorities could agree that an affiliated distributor of personal care products should report a resale margin of 35%–40% (or an operating margin of 3%–5%) in consideration for its commitment of capital to

E. King, *Transfer Pricing and Corporate Taxation*,
DOI 10.1007/978-0-387-78183-9_4, © Springer Science+Business Media, LLC 2009

distribution activities and its assumption of related inventory and other risks, absent exceptional circumstances. "First tier" trademarks owned by a distributor (i.e., marks that are household names) might, for example, entitle it to an additional 8% of net sales, second tier marks, 5%, and third tier marks, 2%. These incremental revenues would be offset by the associated intangibles development expenses borne by the distributor.

The safe harbor services provisions in the U.S. Temporary Regulations could be expanded along the same lines. For example, services requiring relatively unskilled labor and limited tangible assets that cannot be analyzed under the services cost method could be charged out at a standardized cost plus 5%, services requiring higher-level skills, 10%, and services requiring very specialized skills (e.g., those requiring a Ph.D. or a particular talent to perform), 15%. (This proposed safe habor provision should not apply where the services at issue can only be rendered in conjunction with intangible property. In this case, the provider should be compensated for both the services it renders and its contribution of intellectual property.)

The numerical standards approach has the obvious virtue of greatly reducing compliance, audit and dispute resolution costs and the likelihood of double-taxation. It is also equitable. (The second and third case studies, in Chapters 6 and 7, respectively, illustrate the numerical standards approach, as well as the resale price, comparable uncontrolled price, comparable uncontrolled transaction and comparable profits methods.)

- **Required Return Method.** For more complex cases, including those involving genuinely unique intangible property, one can, in principle, determine individual group members' tax liabilities by assuming that they will earn their estimated required return on debt and equity capital per annum. A required return analysis necessitates that one quantify (a) the fair market value of individual group members' equity capital, (b) their required return thereon, and (c) their arm's length cost of debt. As such, this methodology would be extremely laborious unless taxing authorities agree on certain valuation conventions. The required return methodology may also produce a fairly wide range of results, and the scope for such variability in results should be bounded by agreed-on conventions as well. Lastly, certain standard valuation methodologies, such as the discounted cash flow method, *cannot* be used to determine the fair market value of individual group members' assets (and, thereby, their equity capital), because such cash flows incorporate potentially non-arm's length transfer pricing.

  However, in circumstances where a group member has a reliable measure of its fair market value and cost of capital, or if taxing authorities can agree on (a) the use of valuation methods that do not reflect transfer pricing, and (b) certain conventions that reduce the scope for subjective judgement, the required return method may be a viable approach. Moreover, a required return analysis has a far more solid theoretical foundation than the current transfer pricing methodologies. Finally, as noted, the required return methodology can be used in situations where one or both parties utilize unique or highly valuable intangible assets, inasmuch as the value of these assets will be reflected in the value of the group members' equity capital. (The cases analyzed in Chapters 9 and 10 illustrate the required return methodology, as well as the resale price and simplified profit split methods.)

- **Simplified Profit Split and Joint Venture Models.** For cases in which ownership of highly valuable intellectual property is not centralized in one entity, the apportionment of a controlled group's combined after-tax free cash flows can also be based on (a) the relative values of tangible and intangible assets employed by individual group members, where such values can be determined with reasonable accuracy, or (b) the ownership shares of unrelated joint venture partners, where individual joint venture partners' asset contributions correspond approximately to those that individual members of the controlled group make. (Alternatively, joint venture agreements may provide for various formulaic divisions of income.) Both of these approaches preserve the nexus between after-tax free cash flows and asset values. The second approach also eliminates the need to value assets explicitly and to draw unfounded inferences regarding the relative fair market values of assets from observable, but largely irrelevant, factors. Ownership shares in joint ventures are an accurate gauge of the relative value of contributions that each partner makes (or will make), as determined by the parties at the outset. (The case studies in Chapters 10 and 11 illustrate the proposed simplified profit split method, along with the required return method and the formulary approach. Chapter 12 illustrates the joint venture method and the 2005 proposed cost-sharing regulations, along with the residual profit split method.)
- **Franchise Model.** Where there is no real division of labor among the individual legal entities that comprise a multinational corporation, but (a) one entity developed a core business model and other intangible assets on which the remaining legal entities subsequently based their operations, and (b) each entity operates largely independently in a distinct geographic territory, one can utilize arm's length franchise arrangements to determine the arm's length division of income among group members in different taxing jurisdictions. (This approach does not presuppose that individual licensor of unique intellectual property would separately negotiate the same royalty rate and other license terms for "comparable" intellectual property, or that a single licensor of unique intellectual property would invariably offer the same terms to each of its licensees. Rather, it is empirically true that individual franchisors offer standardized terms to their franchisees). The case study in Chapter 8 illustrates the proposed franchise model approach.

Each of these supplementary or alternative approaches to transfer pricing are discussed at greater length below.

4.1 Modified Comparable Uncontrolled Price Method

The proposed modified comparable uncontrolled price method would simply provide for more flexible applications than the current version of this method. Prices generally contain useful information that can be exploited in one form or another, not solely by using them essentially "as is" to directly establish transfer prices between affiliated companies. The particular ways in which one can use arm's length pricing data is very much fact-driven and difficult to characterize in the abstract. As noted, the first case study (in Chapter 5) illustrates one such application, but it is by no means exhausive.

4.2 Numerical Standards

As previously noted, the current transfer pricing regime imposes significant compliance costs on multinational corporations. To demonstrate that they have made a good faith effort to comply with the arm's length standard, and thereby minimize the likelihood of double-taxation and penalties, multinational firms routinely commission extensive transfer pricing studies every several years, and frequently have updates done in the interval. In addition to the explicit costs of such studies, which can be quite high, they entail significant opportunity costs in the form of senior executives' time and attention. Tax authorities also incur enormous costs in auditing individual multinational firms' treatment of their transfer pricing issues after the fact, and resolving conflicts with tax authorities in other jurisdictions. Lastly, the endemic uncertainty engendered by the existing transfer pricing regime requires firms to hold additional financial resources in reserve and may bias investment decisions, inasmuch as effective tax rates across jurisdictions may not be accurately anticipated.

Through their transfer pricing studies, corporations with very similar fact patterns individually recreate the wheel over and over again. However, confidentiality and antitrust concerns generally preclude coordination among firms. Taxing authorities are not constrained by such concerns, though, and could readily pool their knowledge and experience to the end of establishing numerical norms regarding the margins, markups or royalty rates that certain routine activities (e.g., distribution and specific types of services) and relatively common intangible assets (e.g., trademarks) should command.[1] The use of such norms would greatly reduce compliance, audit, dispute resolution and other costs. Moreover, numerical norms would be equitable if such norms were uniformly applied by different tax authorities. Numerical standards do *not* address the theoretical shortcomings associated with the resale price, cost plus and comparable profits methods. Rather, this approach is put forth in recognition of the fact that genuinely arm's length results are time-consuming and difficult to develop, and perhaps such efforts should be reserved for the more complex transfer pricing issues.

This proposed numerical approach, if adopted at some point in the future, should be somewhat more nuanced than the term suggests. More particularly, taxing authorities could conduct annual benchmarking studies, by industry and geographic

---

[1] Tax authorities currently utilize similar rules of thumb during the audit process as a means of determining whether a transfer pricing issue exists, and, if so, whether it is worth pursuing.

market, to determine suitable numerical norms each year. As applied to distributors, tax authorities might agree on safe harbor ranges of (a) resale margins,
(b) advertising-to-sales ratios, (c) inventory-to-sales ratios, and (d) SG&A to sales
ratios. Where individual multinational firms' results deviate from these norms, further analysis would be warranted.

Clearly, a substantial percentage of transfer pricing cases are not amenable to this
type of simplified treatment. The proposals outlined below are intended to address
more complex fact patterns.

4.3 Required Return on Debt and Equity Capital

Financial economists have long held that individual firms have reasonably quantifiable risk-adjusted required rates of return on equity capital, as determined chiefly
by shareholders' opportunity costs. Similarly, a firm's arm's length cost of debt at a
point in time is equal to the yield to maturity on its outstanding debt (as determined
jointly by its credit rating, the specific characteristics and seniority of the indebtedness and prevailing conditions in the markets for various types of debt), reduced
by the debt tax shield. On average, an individual firm's after-tax free cash flows
must be at least equal to the returns that all contributors of capital must receive,
commensurate with the risks they bear, in order to retain the use of their funds.

In the context of transfer pricing, one can utilize individual group members'
estimated required return on equity capital and their market-determined cost of
debt to derive their taxable income. More particularly, this procedure would entail
(a) applying an appropriate risk-adjusted required rate of return on equity to the
estimated fair market value of an individual group member's equity capital, and
(b) adding to this magnitude the group member's arm's length, market-determined
cost of outstanding debt, net of the tax shield thereon. Before-tax net income, *prior
to incorporating firm-specific credits, deductions, loss carryforwards, etc.*, can be
computed, using the results obtained in the preceding step as a starting point, by
adding back the tax shield on debt, deducting interest expenses, adding investment
in tangible and intangible assets and changes in working capital, deducting depreciation, and dividing the resulting magnitude by $(1-t)$ (where t denotes the applicable
country-specific, statutory corporate tax rate).

However, large multinational corporations typically have numerous tax credits
and deductions that cause their effective tax rates to differ from statutory rates
(among them the deductibility of interest expense). Because our preliminary estimate of arm's length before-tax net profits is based on statutory rates, the tax benefits
enjoyed by individual members of a controlled group should be factored into the
analysis as a separate step.

If one applies the proposed required return methodology to one member of a
controlled group, and consistently determines its affiliated counterparty's taxable
income as a residual, the latter group member's reported taxable income may be
greater or lesser than the level of income necessary to just compensate its investors

and debt-holders in any given year. However, on average, the allocation should be approximately consistent with each entity's required return, provided that the tested party's beta and the fair market value of its equity capital can be reliably estimated.[2]

The individual steps required under this proposed method are described below. Many of the steps entail subjective judgement and would generally be quite labor-intensive. As such, if the method is to be viable, certain measures to simplify and standardize the analytical steps are necessary. While the rationale for these measures will be readily apparent in the step-by-step discussion following, for convenience, we summarize them below:

- Comprehensive valuations of equity capital should only be required every several years, absent significant changes in the business. In the interim, firms should be able to adjust the valuations incrementally (as a percentage of the total value), based on prevailing market conditions. Percentage changes in the values of publicly traded companies operating in the same line(s) of business (and the same geographic market) should be used as the "baseline" adjustment. Firm-specific considerations can be incorporated as refinements to this baseline.
- Tax authorities should sanction the use of, and publish monthly, industry betas, safe harbor loan rates, the risk-free rate and the price of risk.

The discussion below does not presuppose that the recommendations summarized above would be implemented, but underscores their importance.

4.3.1 Required Return on Equity

Under the Capital Asset Pricing Model (CAPM), estimated required rates of return on equity are a function of (a) the degree of systematic risk that firms bear, (b) the "price" of risk, and (c) the risk-free rate of return.[3] Systematic risks are those risks that shareholders cannot eliminate through portfolio diversification, because they are economy-wide. (Shareholders do not need to be compensated for non-systematic risks, because they can be eliminated through diversification.)

The systematic risk associated with a given asset (e.g., a firm's stock) is equal to (i) the covariance between the return on the asset and the return on the market portfolio (consisting of all stocks or assets, held according to their market value weights),

---

[2] Equilibrium in financial markets, a much shorter-term proposition than equilibrium in product markets, would ensure that firms would earn their required return on a standalone basis, on average, or be forced to exit the industry. If we equate one affiliated company's results in a given reporting period with its estimated required return, the same must be true of the other entity as well, on average, because the multinational group as a whole must earn its required return as well.

[3] More specifically, under the Capital Asset Pricing Model, the required return on equity is equal to (i) the risk-free rate, plus (ii) the price of risk multiplied by a given firm's systematic risk. See, for example, Copeland, Thomas E. and J. Fred Weston, *Financial Theory and Corporate Policy*, Addison-Wesley Publishing Co.: Mass., 1988.

divided by (ii) the variance of the market portfolio.[4] The measure of systematic risk for an individual firm is referred to as its "beta." A number of academics and private sector firms regularly quantify and publicly report individual corporations' betas and industry-wide betas.

The least labor-intensive approach to determining betas for transfer pricing purposes is to utilize published industry betas. In general, different betas would apply to individual group members, because they operate both in different geographic markets and, often, at different market levels. Unlevered published betas should be used, rather than levered betas, because the former measure business risk alone. As a separate step, published unlevered betas should be "relevered" to reflect individual affiliated companies' actual leverage.

In principle, one could also estimate betas for individual tested parties. However, inasmuch as individual members of controlled groups are not publicly traded, some modifications to the standard analysis are necessary in a transfer pricing context.

4.3.1.1 Measurements of Firm-Specific Betas

An individual member of a publicly held multinational group will not have a directly measurable beta. Rather, betas can only be quantified by means of the standard regression analysis for the group as a whole, because its stock price reflects its operations as a whole. Therefore, in applying the proposed required return methodology to establish transfer prices, and assuming that industry betas are not satisfactory approximations, one must develop estimates of the relevant entity-specific betas. In a valuation context, the following approaches have been proposed:[5]

1. **Management comparisons:** Discuss with senior management the types of risks borne by the relevant legal entity in relation to a range of firms for which betas are published, and select a beta on this basis.
2. **Comparability analyses:** Identify publicly traded competitors that are similar to the tested party in terms of systematic risk (a qualitative judgement), and use these competitors' betas.
3. **Multiple regression analysis:** When good comparables cannot be identified because independent firms are diversified to a greater or lesser extent than the affiliated company, or diversified in different, albeit overlapping, ways, regress unlevered betas for individual standalone firms against the proportion of assets that the companies devote to each of their lines of business. The coefficients of these weights constitute unbiased estimates of unlevered line-of-business betas.[6]

---

[4] Covariance is a measure of the way in which two random variables move in relation to each other. Variance is a measure of the dispersion of a distribution.

[5] See Copeland, Tom, Tim Koller and Jork Murrin, *Valuation: Measuring and Managing the Value of Companies*, John Wiley & Sons, Inc.: New York, 2005.

[6] As discussed in Copeland et. al., the constant term in this regression equation must be suppressed.

These recommended methods of estimating subsidiary-specific betas for valuation purposes apply equally in a transfer pricing context. It should also be noted that insurance underwriters generally require insurance brokers representing individual companies to perform comprehensive risk assessment analyses of the latter. These analyses are a useful means of identifying key operations-related risks.

As previously discussed, firms that are functionally similar—a somewhat nebulous concept to begin with—may earn widely divergent accounting rates of return, gross margins, gross markups, etc. However, firms with similar systematic risks—a precisely defined concept—should have similar betas. Therefore, the comparability analyses that would be necessary under the proposed required return methodology, absent mutual agreement by taxing authorities to permit the use of industry-wide betas, are more narrowly defined, and more purposeful, than the comparability analyses required under the current transfer pricing regulations.

4.3.1.2 Measures of the Risk-Free Rate and the Price of Risk

The risk-free rate is generally equated with the yield on Treasury bonds, because the U.S. Government is very unlikely to default on its debt. However, some academics and practitioners believe that Treasury yields understate the risk-free rate as a result of several factors, among them (a) the fact that financial institutions are required to hold a certain amount of Treasury bills and bonds to satisfy regulatory requirements, artificially inflating demand for these instruments, and (b) Treasury instruments are not taxed at the state level, whereas other very low-risk investment vehicles are subject to state tax. In view of these considerations, some valuation specialists and market participants favor swap rates over Treasury bond rates as measures of the risk-free rate.[7]

The price of risk (equivalently, the market risk premium) is conventionally measured as the difference between the expected rate of return on the market portfolio and the risk-free rate. The expected rate of return on the market portfolio, in turn, is computed as the long-term historical average realized rate of return.[8]

There is some (albeit limited) room for disagreement about appropriate risk-free rates and market risk premia. For this reason, it would make sense to have tax authorities publish these rates.

4.3.1.3 Fair Market Value of Equity Capital

For the same reason that betas for individual group members cannot be directly estimated, market-determined values of individual group members' equity capital

---

[7] See Hull, John, Mirela Predescu and Alan White, "Bond Prices, Default Probabilities and Risk Premiums," *Journal of Credit Risk*, September 2004, Vol. 1, No. 2, pp. 53–60.

[8] A geometric average, defined as the compound rate of return that equates beginning and ending values, is generally considered preferable to an arithmetic average for this purpose.

do not exist. However, companies periodically require valuations of their assets as a whole, or of individual assets. For example, valuations may be necessary for purposes of:

- Tax reporting (e.g., corporate restructuring for tax purposes, requiring the inter-company sale of individual group members or purchase price allocations);
- Financial reporting (e.g., testing for goodwill impairment); and,
- Contemplated transactions (e.g., fairness opinions, acquisitions and divestitures, going-private transactions, etc.).

To the extent that valuations prepared for these purposes do not reflect intercompany pricing, they may be useful in a transfer pricing context under the proposed required return method. Valuations of individual group members undertaken in connection with contemplated transactions with unaffiliated companies should be given the greatest weight, inasmuch as they will reflect arm's length assessments. (Competent appraisers should adjust for non-arm's length pricing between the subject company and the other group members with which it transacts.) Valuations done for financial reporting purposes may be useful, but only if they do not reflect intercompany pricing. Because goodwill impairment testing is required on an annual basis for financial statement purposes, a more detailed discussion of this requirement, and its potential applicability for transfer pricing purposes, is warranted.

In June 2001, the Financial Accounting Standards Board (FASB) released its *Statement of Financial Accounting Standards No. 142*, relating to the treatment of goodwill and other intangible assets. *Statement of Financial Accounting Standards No. 142* disallows the amortization of goodwill for financial reporting purposes, requiring instead that public companies record goodwill at its fair market value. As such, firms must test goodwill for impairment on an annual basis at the level of individual "reporting units."

Goodwill is defined as "[t]he excess of the fair value of a reporting unit over the amounts assigned to its assets and liabilities ..."[9] Testing for goodwill impairment therefore necessitates that firms establish the fair market value of their reporting units, either by reference to quoted market prices (where feasible) or by means of other valuation techniques, including the "present value technique." The FASB's *Statement of Financial Accounting Standards No. 142* also sanctions the use of earnings multiples "... when the fair value of an entity that has comparable operations and economic characteristics is observable and the relevant multiples of the comparable are known."[10] Reporting units are defined consistently with *Statement of Financial Accounting Standards No. 131, Disclosures About Segments of an*

---

[9] See *Statement of Financial Accounting Standards No. 142*, Financial Accounting Standards Board: Norwalk, CT, June 2001, para. 21.

[10] The FASB's *Statement of Financial Accounting Standards No. 142* also states that the use of multiples "would not be appropriate in situations in which the operations or activities of an entity for which the multiples are known are not of a comparable nature, scope, or size as the reporting unit for which fair value is being estimated." *Ibid*, para. 25.

Enterprise and Related Information. Companies are permitted to equate reporting units with operating segments or "one level below."

Where reporting units are equated with operating segments, valuations for goodwill impairment testing will be unhelpful, because they are likely to require a prior adjustment to transfer pricing. Because the valuation is one step along the analytical road to establishing arm's length transfer prices, the exercise becomes circular in this event.

In view of the difficulties in valuing entity-specific equity capital in a reasonably reliable way, some means of reducing compliance costs under the proposed required return method is quite important. As previously noted, taxing authorities could mutually agree to accept a baseline valuation done at multi-year intervals, absent significant changes in the business, with informed estimates of percentage increases or decreases in value in the interim. The latter should be related to percentage changes in the value of publicly traded companies in the same or similar lines of business.

Alternatively, tax authorities might agree that, for transfer pricing purposes, individual group members' equity capital can be valued by reference to standard valuation multiples that do not have earnings (net income, EBITDA, cash flow, etc.) as their denominator. For example, tax authorities might establish a convention that the equity value of a subsidiary operating in Country X that sells exclusively to third parties will be determined by reference to the median price-to-sales ratio for all publicly traded firms operating in the same, comparatively narrowly defined industry in Country X. If the tested party operates in more than one line of business, a weighted average multiple would have to be used.

4.3.2 Cost of Debt

Individual members of a controlled group may borrow from a centralized internal treasury facility. Taking as given the amount, maturity date, seniority and other features of intercompany indebtedness, one can estimate an individual group member's arm's length, market-determined cost of debt as of a given date by:

- Estimating the group member's credit rating (by reference to financial ratios designed to measure its ability to pay interest and repay principal on a timely basis);[11]
- Assembling a sample of publicly held firms that have similar credit ratings, and have issued publicly traded debt with similar maturities and other characteristics; and,

---

[11] Standardized templates that can be used to estimate credit ratings using simple accounting data are available, and generally produce reasonably accurate results.

- Determining the yield to maturity on this sample of issues, given the prevailing market price and maturity date of each issue.

Alternatively, taxing authorities might agree to utilize a safe harbor range of interest rates, such as the U.S. Applicable Federal Rates (AFRs), published monthly.[12] This alternative would significantly reduce compliance costs.

4.3.3 Non-Cash Charges and Investment

Depreciation, amortization and investment by individual group members are directly reflected on, or easily derived from, consolidating or member-specific financial statements.

4.3.4 Data Requirements

As indicated above, in applying the required return methodology to determine the tax liability of an individual member of a controlled group, and *absent* any agreement among taxing authorities to simplify and standardize the analytical steps, one would need the following data:

1. The affiliated company's estimated beta, along with the risk-free rate and the estimated price of risk;
2. The estimated fair market value of the affiliated company's equity capital;
3. The affiliated company's debt outstanding and borrowing terms, its arm's length cost of debt and its non-cash charges and investment in tangible property, working capital and intangible property; and,
4. The affiliated company's tax credits, deductions, loss carryforwards, etc.

4.3.5 Summary

In summary, a required return transfer pricing methodology has the virtue of building on well-established and widely accepted financial principles. However, estimating a subsidiary's cost of debt and equity, and quantifying the fair market value of its equity capital, are neither easy nor uncontroversial tasks. It also necessitates a degree of subjective judgement. For these reasons, numerical norms have a very important role to play here as well. That is, tax authorities could stipulate to, and publish on a monthly basis, industry-specific betas, as well as risk-free rates of return, the market risk premium and safe harbor loan rates.[13] With regard to the valuation of equity capital, the most labor-intensive and subjective analytical step,

---

[12] See Treas. Reg. Section 1.482-2(a)(2)(iii).

[13] This approach is analogous to the safe harbor contained in the current U.S. transfer pricing regulations, pertaining to the cost of debt on intercompany loans.

tax authorities could require benchmark valuations every 3–5 years absent significant changes in individual group members' business. Estimates of annual percentage
increases or decreases in value, based on observed changes in the value of publicly
held firms operating in the same lines of business and adjusted further for firm-
specific factors, could be used to update the benchmark valuation in the interim.

4.4 Joint Venture-Based Profit Split

As discussed in Chapter 3, the residual profit split method described in the U.S.
transfer pricing regulations incorrectly measures income attributable both to total
assets and to intangible assets. Moreover, U.S. practitioners typically value intangible assets by application of mechanical accounting-based capitalization and amortization rules; the results do not necessarily bear any relationship to the fair market
value of these assets. The comparable profit split method is squarely based on
equally unfounded assumptions. By (a) substituting after-tax free cash flows for
before-tax operating profits, and (b) using more accurate valuation methodologies
to establish the fair market value of tangible and intangible assets (where feasible), or, alternatively, by using arm's length joint venture arrangements to develop
approximations of relative asset values, one eliminates the need to:

(1) Assume a predictable relationship between, or directly equate:

- The functions that independent companies and individual affiliated group members perform and the accounting rates of return (or other profit level indicators)
  that they should realize;
- Affiliated group members' historical R&D, advertising and other "intangibles-
  creating" expenditures and the current fair market value of their respective intellectual property;
- Before-tax operating profits and after-tax free cash flows; and,
- Accounting rates of return and economic rates of return.

(2) Construct hypothetical multinational firms by analytically combining indepen-
      dent companies.

Joint venture companies mimic a multinational firm structure in several analytically important respects, albeit with much more limited incentives to engage in
non-arm's length dealings. Joint venture partners contribute resources to a common
undertaking, make important operational and strategic decisions jointly, and act to
maximize the joint venture's combined profits. At the same time, each joint venture
partner ultimately acts on behalf of its separate shareholders. In marked contrast,
two independent companies that are combined analytically for purposes of applying
the comparable profit split method do not act to maximize their joint profits and
cannot realize the benefits of acting in concert. As such, joint venture partnerships
resemble a multinational group much more closely. Moreover, in any given year,
the distribution of *realized* profits between two independent companies may bear no

relationship to the relative value of assets that they each employ. In contrast, ownership shares in a joint venture company will reflect each entity's relative contributions of tangible and intangible assets over the term of the JV partnership, as anticipated at the outset.

Joint venture arrangements and other types of strategic alliances have proliferated over the past two decades, expanded well beyond high-technology, high-risk undertakings to include more mundane, low-tech ventures, and combined complementary assets and other resources in an enormous variety of ways. As such, the pool of potentially comparable JV arrangements is quite large.

4.5 Financial or Tangible Asset-Based Profit Split

As detailed in Chapter 3, the U.S. regulations reserve the profit split method for situations in which both parties to an intercompany transaction own valuable intangible assets. However, in many respects, a simple profit split is better suited to circumstances in which individual group members engage in an activity that is intrinsically multi-jurisdictional, act in concert, and employ the same types of *tangible* assets.

The global trading of certain physical commodities (e.g., fuel oils) and the provision of content delivery network (CDN) services are examples of activities for which a simple profit split may produce reasonable results. Global trading firms have traditionally employed financial capital primarily (although such capital is generally invested in physical commodities in some form at any given point). Given the prevalence of mark-to-market accounting and the need to monitor and manage risk in global trading, the market value of assets is often readily ascertainable. CDN services providers invest predominantly in high-end servers, which are stationed in proximity to the end-users of digital content in numerous geographic locations. While the book value of these servers will differ from their market value after a comparatively short period of time, the proportional divergence between book and market values will be similar across entities if all group members employ the same types of assets and utilize the same depreciation schedules.

In such instances (where individual group members perform the same functions, act in concert and employ the same types of assets), a division of after-tax free cash flows based on the book or market value of assets employed makes intuitive *and* economic sense. However, if intangible assets are an important element in the activity at issue, and they are not jointly developed and employed, a simple profit split method will clearly not produce reliable results.

4.6 Franchise Model

In Internet-based businesses, multinational groups are often formed sequentially: A start-up firm with operations in only one country will develop a business model, intellectual property and vendor and customer relationships in the first instance.

Geographic expansion takes the form of replicating the same nationally-based business in individual countries. The founding firm transfers rights to its business model, its intellectual property and, if feasible, its vendor and customer relationships, and provides assistance both in the start-up phase and, in some cases, on an ongoing basis. One observes this fact pattern in traditional businesses as well, when physical proximity to customers is important and the economic activity does not require significant investment in fixed assets, so that decentralization is not excessively costly.

Under a conservative interpretation of existing transfer pricing regulations, it may be necessary to establish arm's length charges for each individual transaction (the transfer of a business model, software, trademarks, other intellectual property and services). However, this approach "misses the forest for the trees," and is unnecessarily laborious. An alternative approach would entail using franchise arrangements to determine arm's length fees for the bundle of tangible and intangible assets transferred and services rendered.

4.7 Summary

To summarize briefly, the proposed methods described above reflect certain basic points of reference. First, arm's length pricing data should be used significantly more extensively, and more flexibly, than the U.S. regulations currently provide for. Second, where individual group members perform distinct functions, and a single entity owns and utilizes all of the group's intellectual property, transfer pricing issues lend themselves to the use of simple numerical standards. While obviously imperfect from a theoretical perspective, this approach would greatly reduce compliance costs and the potential for double-taxation, a seemingly worthwhile trade-off. Many traditional transfer pricing issues are of this ilk.

Simplified profit splits may be feasible when the activity at issue is intrinsically multi-jurisdictional and individual group members employ similar assets. In such cases, controlled group members often perform undifferentiated functions, and have jointly developed intangible property in the ordinary course of business. Conversely, in circumstances where the same activity is carried out in multiple, discrete jurisdictions, and there is limited interaction among group members on a day-to-day basis, the franchise model may yield reasonable results. In such cases, a single entity often develops the business model and other intellectual property used by all group members. Lastly, for complex cases involving atypical divisions of functions and risks, and/or where ownership of intellectual property is not concentrated in a single group member and has not been developed jointly, a required return approach may be warranted.

Part III
Case Studies

Chapter 5
Intercompany Sale of Diamonds

This segment contains a series of detailed case studies, each of which is composed of (a) a summary of key facts, (b) a description of the transfer pricing issues raised, (c) an analysis under the existing transfer pricing regime (where feasible), (d) an alternative analysis under one or more of the proposed methods, and (e) a comparison of the methodology and results under existing and proposed methods (where the transactions at issue can be analyzed under both regimes). All of the proposed methods discussed in Part II are illustrated by at least one, and in some instances multiple, case studies.

Our first case study involves a three-member controlled group in the business of purchasing rough diamonds, having a portion of them cut and polished, and reselling stones in both rough and polished forms at the wholesale level. The parent company (FP), based in Belgium, is a sightholder. It purchases parcels of rough diamonds from De Beers, for sale exclusively to a subsidiary in Israel (IS). IS relies on both FP and third parties for its supply of rough stones and owns certain proprietary designs and trademarks. It has some of the rough stones cut and polished by third party cutters, in accordance with its proprietary designs and some generic designs. It sells *generic* polished stones both to FP's U.S. subsidiary (USS) and to third parties in non-U.S. markets. IS sells polished stones cut to its *proprietary designs* exclusively to USS. All of IS' *rough* stone sales are to third parties. USS purchases stones primarily from IS, supplements these purchases with third party purchases when necessary, maintains inventories and resells to high-end jewelry retailers in the United States.

We analyze the various transactions in this case under the resale price method, the comparable profits method, the numerical standards approach and the modified inexact comparable uncontrolled price method. Our analysis under the latter method necessitates a fairly extensive discussion of market structure, competitive dynamics and the pricing of diamonds. Moreover, the trademarking of diamonds is a comparatively recent phenomenon, motivated by a wide range of considerations that go far beyond traditional product differentiation at the consumer level; correspondingly, the funding and ownership of trademarks tend to be more diffuse in the diamond industry than in other luxury goods markets. Because this fact has important implications for our transfer pricing analysis, we address the issue of branding in detail as well.

E. King, *Transfer Pricing and Corporate Taxation*,
DOI 10.1007/978-0-387-78183-9_5, © Springer Science+Business Media, LLC 2009

5.1 Summary of Key Facts

The diamond industry is segmented into a number of distinct market levels, collectively referred to as the "diamond pipeline" by industry participants:

- Diamond mines, located primarily in Angola, Australia, Botswana, Brazil, Canada, Ghana, Guinea, the Ivory Coast, Namibia, the Republic of Congo, Russia, the Sierra Leone and South Africa;
- Dealers of rough stones;
- Cutters and polishers, among them standalone entities that perform cutting and polishing functions on a fee-for-service basis;
- Wholesale distributors; and,
- Retailers.

The number of industry participants operating at each market level progressively increases as one moves along the diamond pipeline toward retailers and end-users. There are comparatively few mines, a relatively limited base of rough stone dealers, a larger number of wholesale distributors and upwards of 40,000 retailers in the United States, 25,000 retailers in Japan and 60,000 retailers in Europe. Industry participants are vertically integrated to widely varying degrees. Moreover, a subset of mines operates through a long-standing cartel that limits the supply of rough stones, both in aggregate and through particular marketing channels. As described in greater detail below, the cartel's modus operandi has largely shaped the structure of downstream market segments, although its influence has diminished significantly in recent years.

5.1.1 Historical Dominance of De Beers

The diamond industry has historically been dominated by De Beers. Together with the Diamond Producers' Association (an association of mine operators), these entities form the nucleus of the DTC (successor to the Central Selling Organization, or "CSO"), the aforementioned cartel. The DTC's primary objective is to maintain high and stable prices for rough (and thereby, polished) stones. It has historically influenced the prices of rough and polished diamonds primarily, albeit not exclusively, through supply-side measures (e.g., production quotas and the maintenance of very large buffer stocks). This has been feasible because the cartel has historically controlled a very high proportion of all rough stone production.

Thus, for example, during the early 1990s, De Beers controlled approximately 70% of all diamond mine production and approximately 85% of rough diamond distribution through the CSO; such control was exercised through a combination of outright ownership, partnerships, structured finance deals and exclusive supply and marketing arrangements. A typical rough diamond supply contract with the DTC involves selling run-of-mine production thereto for cash at a 10.0% discount from the DTC's Standard Selling Values (SSVs). The DTC guarantees to buy producers' entire production and offers a guaranteed minimum price; both features are very effective inducements in down markets. Moreover, the DTC guarantees that purchase prices will not be reduced during the contract term.[1]

The DTC has traditionally selected approximately 95–160 independent rough stone dealers and manufacturers to become "sightholders." This status confers on the selected companies the right, and the obligation, to purchase rough stones from the DTC ten times per annum. The DTC sorts rough stones into approximately 14,000 categories and combines its production and that of its partners (or such portion thereof as it decides to market in a given period) into "series" that contain an assortment of stones, varying widely in quality, size, etc. While sightholders are permitted to view the series, they are, in effect, obligated to purchase the proffered boxes. The DTC unilaterally determines the price of each series and requires payment in cash prior to delivery. Hence, the DTC has historically exercised enormous control over the volume, value and mix of stones sold both up- and downstream.

Until relatively recently, De Beers' role as "custodian" of the rough diamond markets has come at the cost of access to the U.S. market, the world's largest market for polished stones. Because of its dominance and anti-competitive conduct, De Beers was prohibited from operating in the United States for many years. However, in July 2004, De Beers Centenary AG submitted to U.S. jurisdiction and pled guilty to the Department of Justice's charge that it conspired to fix the price of industrial diamonds. Since then, it has operated directly in the United States on a limited scale. De Beers has also been the subject of antitrust investigations initiated by the European Commission (EC) at regular intervals, although the EC has generally ruled in the Company's favor to this point.

5.1.2 The Decline of De Beers' Role and the Emergence of Parallel Primary Markets

Although the DTC continues to operate as it has in the past in certain respects, and still markets a substantial proportion of the total volume of rough stones produced in a given period through its sightholders, its control over the upstream diamond market has waned considerably since the early to mid-1990s for a number of reasons:

- The discovery of several substantial deposits in Canada's Northwest Territories. While the DTC secured a portion (approximately 35%) of the output of the Ekati mine, one of the three Canadian mines, at the outset, the balance was not funneled through the cartel. Moreover, Ekati no longer supplies its rough to the DTC. The decision to bypass the DTC was motivated in part by concerns that exclusive marketing arrangements with the DTC would contravene U.S. antitrust laws.

---

[1] See Even-Zohar, Chaim, "Sierra Leone Diamond Sector Financial Policy Constraints," Management Systems International (under USAID Cooperative Agreement No. 636-A-00-03-00003), June 2003.

- The rapid growth of two diversified mining groups, Rio Tinto and BHP Billiton, that commenced operations in the late 1990s and own the above-mentioned Canadian mines, along with certain important Australian holdings.
- Measures introduced in Russia and a number of less developed countries (LDCs) with diamond mining operations to foster the growth of domestic diamond manufacturing operations, with the resulting diversion of rough stones from the DTC.[2] For example, the Namibian government enacted *The Diamond Act of Namibia* on April 1, 2000, which exempts producers from paying royalties to the government if their rough production is sold to domestic cutters. The South African parliament introduced a *Diamond Amendment Bill* in September 2005, containing the provision that "the state can determine, based on market demand, the percentage of rough diamonds that diamond producers will have to sell to a state diamond trader."[3]
- Increases in state-owned production in Russia and Angola.[4]
- One of the aforementioned EC antitrust investigations into (a) the DTC's sightholder system (now referred to as its Supplier of Choice or "SOC" system), and (b) the DTC's relationship with Alrosa, a large Russian mine. While the EC originally approved the SOC arrangement in January 2003, it re-opened its investigation in response to allegations of collusive conduct formally made by the Belgian Association of Dealers, Importers and Exporters of Polished Diamonds (BVGD) in August 2005.[5] Moreover, the EC required De Beers to reduce its purchases of rough stones from Alrosa by two-thirds of the 2005 level (from $700 million to $275 million) over 6 years. Alrosa accounts for upwards of 98% of all rough diamond production in Russia.
- The termination of the DTC's producer contract with Argyle, a large mine based in Australia, in 1996.[6]
- The decision by Tiffany & Co., Inc., a preeminent jewelry retailer in the United States, to integrate backwards into production through a stakeholding in Diavik Diamond Mines, Inc.[7] This relationship creates a captive market for a substantial

---

[2] See Diamond Bank (Switzerland) Ltd.'s 2004 Annual Report. This institution specializes in the provision of short-term financing of the diamond business on a global basis.

[3] See Mathews, Charlotte, "Way Forward for the SA Diamond Industry," *Business Day*, September 23, 2005.

[4] See Bream, Rebecca and Nicol Degli Innocenti, "The Global Search for New Sparkles of Life," *Financial Times*, August 23, 2004.

[5] More particularly, the BVGD, whose membership consists of approximately 150 wholesalers of cut stones, filed a complaint with the European Commission, alleging that "De Beers misled the European Commission, has abused its dominant position, and has artificially limited the availability of diamonds on the market." See the *National Jeweler*, "DTC Increases Sales to Secondary Market," September 2, 2005.

[6] Fetherston, J.M. and S.M. Searston, "Industrial Minerals in Western Australia: The Situation in 2004," GSWA Record, 2004/21.

[7] This move was motivated in part by the sharp rise in demand for, and prices of, rough stones in 2004 and 2005, and heightened concerns regarding secure access to supplies of rough.

portion of the Diavik Mine's production (25% by value) and reduces Tiffany's demand for rough channeled through the DTC's sightholders.

* The analogous decision by Aber Diamond Corporation (part owner of Diavik Diamond Mines) to purchase Harry Winston, Inc., another prominent U.S. retail jeweler, in 2003, thereby integrating forward from production to retail sales and bypassing the DTC's single marketing channel.

As a result of these developments, the DTC now wields much less control over the supply side of the rough diamond market than previously. In mid-2004, De Beers announced that it controlled less than half of all rough diamond production, down from 70% 10 years ago.[8] In response, De Beers has stepped up efforts to consolidate its influence via several demand-side measures. Such measures include efforts to induce retail jewelers to enter into exclusive supply arrangements with the DTC's sightholders,[9] the creation of the De Beers *Forevermark* brand of diamonds and the subsidization of sightholders' parallel efforts to create valuable brand names and unique proprietary designs.

As De Beers' influence in the rough diamond market has diminished, Rio Tinto, BHP Billiton and the "juniors" (small, independently owned mines) have developed new channels for selling their production. As noted above, Aber Diamond Corporation has integrated forward into retail sales and thereby established an internal, captive market for a portion of its production. Other producers have entered into exclusive marketing arrangements with a single buyer. For example, Kimberley Diamond Company, owner of the Ellendale mine in Australia, entered into an agreement with The Marketing Company, a syndicate of well-known downstream firms with cutting, polishing, manufacturing and retail operations in Japan, China, Thailand, Belgium, New York and Dubai.[10] Striker Resources NL, owner of the Merlin diamond mine in Western Australia, entered into an exclusive supply agreement with Knightsbridge Corporate for the advance sale of its rough diamonds.

Rough diamonds are also sold by tender, whereby the producer provides a small number of prospective buyers with descriptions and preliminary valuations of the parcels on offer for purposes of soliciting bids. The parcels are sold to the highest bidder, typically in a cash transaction. Among others, Kimberley Diamond Company has traditionally sold a portion of its Ellendale mine's production via tender.[11]

Another route to the disposition of rough diamonds entails selling to a group of regular buyers, along the lines of the DTC's sightholder system. For example, Aber Diamond Corporation sells its residual production to approximately 50 designated dealers and manufacturers; these transactions are not governed by a formal sales agreement, in contrast to De Beers' single channel marketing model. Alrosa

---

[8] Bream, Rebecca and Nicol Degli Innocenti, "The Global Search for New Sparkles of Life," August 23, 2004.

[9] This allegation is contained in the antitrust complaint filed by the BVGD.

[10] Ibid.

[11] See, for example, Kimberley Diamond Company's Press Release entitled: "Record US$329/ct Realized From Kimberley's 32nd Diamond Sale," dated April 19, 2005.

also recently announced that it was establishing a new distribution channel that will likewise be modeled after the DTC's sightholder system.

Lastly, rough diamonds can be sold through agents or dealers on a commission basis. Angola has utilized this system in the past, selling primarily through four agents (Jack Lunzer's IDC in London, and George Evens, Beny Steinmetz and Arslanian Brothers in Antwerp). On these transactions, Angola's run-of-mine production was sorted into a number of categories and valued by an Angolan government diamond valuator; each category was divided into four equal parcels, and sold to the four dealers at the previously established price, which was paid up-front. Dealers were compensated on the following basis[12]:

- Premiums of up to 4.0% accrued to the dealer;
- Incremental premiums between 4.0% and 7.0% were split equally between the dealer and the Angolan government;
- Incremental premiums above 7.0% were split 75%/25% between the Angolan government and the dealer.

Because these dealers were privately held businesses, there is no public data on their realized commission fees. However, "there is some anecdotal evidence that the agents/dealers seldom earned more than 4.0%."[13]

5.1.3 Producers' and Sightholders' Branding and Design Development Initiatives

In marked contrast to most other luxury goods markets, branding and other forms of product differentiation are relatively new to the diamond industry, largely because they have been unnecessary given the DTC's historic near-monopoly over the supply of rough stones.[14] Product differentiation also serves several diverse purposes in the diamond industry, whereas in many other luxury goods markets, such as high-end apparel and perfume, its function is more limited. More particularly, branding and the use of proprietary designs in the diamond industry further the following objectives:

1. The identification and authentication of mine origin (to diminish or eliminate trade in conflict diamonds).

---

[12] Even-Zohar, Chaim, "Sierra Leone Diamond Sector Financial Policy Constraints," Management Systems International (under USAID Cooperative Agreement No. 636-A-00-03-00003), June 2003.

[13] Ibid.

[14] Stated differently, given the DTC's ability to exercise virtual monopoly control on the supply side, there has been little or no incremental gain to be had through product differentiation from the consumer's standpoint: Consumer loyalty is unnecessary if the only option is to purchase stones supplied by the DTC.

2. The negotiation and execution of exclusive supply contracts with retailers, thereby ensuring a certain level of demand for cartel members' rough stones.
3. Support of retail jewelers' efforts to differentiate themselves from competitors.

Hence, trademarks and proprietary designs are not solely, or even primarily, a company-specific means of communicating the quality and uniqueness of its products. They serve the broader purposes of certifying the specific origin and authenticity of diamonds (an attribute associated with mines rather than distributors), attesting to the supplier's adherence to a certain code of conduct, and, in some instances, ensuring a certain level of demand. Thus, for example, the World Federation of Diamond Bourses (WFDB), which represents non-sightholder rough diamond dealers, has introduced a Federation-wide trademark that members are permitted to display, provided they sign a document formally committing them to adhere to the World Federation Code of Principles. Similarly, BHP Billiton introduced the *Canadamark*, described as "[a] disciplined, failsafe program of identification and tracking ... to ensure the authenticity of [its] diamonds from the mine through to the consumer."[15]

De Beers' branding initiatives—the first of many such initiatives in the industry—were a cornerstone of its attempts to shore up its market power via demand-side measures. In response to critics' increasingly forceful allegations that the sightholder system was anti-competitive, as well as the EC's formal investigations and findings, the DTC made certain changes to its single channel marketing model in 2000. Among other things, it began providing certain value-added services to sightholders and published a set of criteria that it would use in evaluating prospective sightholders, including

- Financial strength and the ability to finance future growth;
- Market position;
- Distribution strategies and channels;
- Marketing strategies (the applicant's capacity for value-added marketing and branding);
- Manufacturing and technical excellence;
- Compliance with the "DTC Best Practice Principles."

Clearly, certain of these criteria—the market position and marketing strategies of prospective sightholders—are intended to screen out applicants unable to differentiate and adequately promote the DTC's stones. The DTC's value-added services, consisting of both "core services" and "growth services," are similarly designed, in part, to assist sightholders in generating demand, developing marketing plans, building brand recognition and gathering market intelligence.[16]

In addition to the provision of value-added services, De Beers also directly subsidizes its sightholders' advertising and design development activities and invests

---

[15] See http://www.Canadamark.com (viewed December 24, 2005).

[16] Sightholders are obliged to pay a fee for these services equal to 2% of sales.

heavily in its own mark. Thus, for example, in 2006, De Beers invested an estimated $200 million in advertising and marketing programs both to support its own trademark and to underwrite similar investments by its sightholders.[17] Sightholders are also permitted to use De Beers' *Forevermark* trademark on DTC-sourced stones.

In short, the DTC regards sightholders' capacity for, and commitment to, the development of recognized brand names and proprietary designs as being highly important at this juncture, as its control of the supply of rough diamonds has declined. The DTC bears a portion of the costs of developing sightholders' marks, and the latter have rights to use its trademark as well.

As discussed above, De Beers has very successfully bound together the different segments of the diamond pipeline through its captive mines and exclusive rough diamond supply agreements with other producers, its Supplier of Choice program and its active promotion of exclusive polished diamond supply arrangements between sightholders and retail customers. Rio Tinto, Aber Diamond Corporation and BHP Billiton, much newer incumbents, have followed suit to a large degree, with differing combinations of exclusive marketing agreements and acquisitions of prominent retailers; Tiffany & Co. Inc.'s backward integration into production serves the same economic purpose. For this reason, companies all along the diamond pipeline— mines, wholesalers and retailers—benefit from the development and maintenance of the same brand names and designs, as the following observation by a well-known commentator attests to:

> It may well become of utmost importance to the success of a diamond jewelry retailer to choose his polished supplier not only on the merits of price, service and quality, but rather on the basis of the polished manufacturer's affiliation with, and level of support given by, the rough producer. The logos and trademarks of the rough producers will proudly be displayed in the diamond jewelry retail store. ....[18]

In essence, retailers' often-exclusive access to stones cut to proprietary designs and bearing particular laser-inscribed trademarks, whether developed and financed by the manufacturer or the rough stone producer (or a combination thereof), has become an important means by which the retailer distinguishes itself from competing retailers in close physical proximity. This benefit, in turn, creates an incentive for the retailer to co-invest in its supplier's marks, where such investment further enhances the value of the mark. In this sense, brand ownership tends to be more diffuse in the diamond industry, as compared with industries in which individual unaffiliated participants operating at different market levels are not so closely linked, and where branding has been well-established for many years.

---

[17] See the *National Jeweler*, "Israeli Diamantaires, DTC Pledge Cooperation," September 2, 2005.

[18] Even-Zohar, Chaim, "Global Overview of the Diamond Industry Pipeline Today & Tomorrow," Tacy Ltd., September 1, 2000.

5.1.4 Pricing Dynamics: Primary, Secondary and Retail Markets

There are no publicly available price benchmarks for rough diamonds in the primary (direct-from-producer) or secondary markets.[19] As noted, the DTC unilaterally establishes the prices of boxes sold to sightholders, and determines the mix of stones included in each series. The series, and hence their prices, are not uniform, and the method and data used to establish these prices are not publicly available, although the DTC's official selling price is reportedly approximately 10.0% above its buying price.[20] While the DTC sorts its rough stones into 14,000 categories for pricing purposes, "[t]here is still considerable scope for variation. In a given category the DTC varies the overall price paid within a band of about 10%, depending on color, quality, size and shape."[21]

On its sales to Tiffany & Co., Ltd. (primary market transactions), Aber Diamond Corporation reportedly prepares assortments of stones that conform to Tiffany's requirements and sells representative parcels to manufacturers on a small scale to establish their price. Tiffany buys at a discount from this price.[22] Certain other producers obtain independent valuations of representative parcels and sell at a discount therefrom. For example, in Striker NL's aforementioned sale of rough from the Merlin mine, Knightsbridge Corporate is charged the independently assessed value less 16.0%. (Unaffiliated mines may perform such valuations; additionally, WWW International Diamond Consultants Ltd., a London-based firm, offers rough and polished diamond valuation services on a fee-for-service basis.[23])

The pricing of similar-quality rough stones in the primary markets may vary significantly from transaction to transaction, due in part to the intrinsic difficulties in valuing them. This observation is clearly demonstrated by Southern Era Diamonds' News Release dated August 29, 2005, detailing the results of three separate independent assessments of two rough diamond samples mined from the DO-27 pipe in Western Canada. The valuations were performed by Rio Tinto, BHP Billiton and Aber Diamond Corporation. In one of the two samples assessed, the average value ranged from US$77.77 to US$58.54 per carat; hence, the upper-bound value exceeds the lower-bound value by 25%. The other sample values ranged from US$35.36 to US$32.34; the upper-bound value for this sample is 8.5% higher than the lower-bound value. Such discrepancies in fair market valuations are not surprising given the wide range of variables that influence value, among them (a) the rough diamond weight; (b) the estimated weight of the polished stones that the single rough stone

---

[19] Even-Zohar, Chaim, "Sierra Leone Diamond Sector Financial Policy Constraints," Management Systems International (under USAID Cooperative Agreement No. 636-A-00-03-00003), June 2003.

[20] Ibid.

[21] Ibid.

[22] Minews, "Aber Resources Sets Out Stall to Market its Share of Production from the Diavik Diamond Mine," March 20, 2003.

[23] See WWW International Diamond Consultants' website, www.diamondwww.com.

will yield; (c) perceived demand for each category of stones at particular points in time; and (d) the crystalline structure of rough diamonds (octahedron-sawables, flats, wholes and macles), which in turn determines their yield. Moreover, many of these criteria are not susceptible of precise measurement.

The secondary market for rough diamonds has long been centered in Antwerp (although Dubai has become an important trading center as well). It is supplied by mines that have not fully committed their run-of-mine production to specific buyers, and by sightholders that are either pure dealers which perform financing, handling and sorting functions or manufacturers whose allotment exceeds their requirements. In Belgium, diamonds can only be traded legally by members of the Hoge Raad Voor Diamant ("HRD") Diamond Office, and only Belgian and Luxembourg-registered companies can become registered members of the HRD. Many of the DTC's sightholders are based in Antwerp. Most major producers either have their own sales offices in Antwerp or employ independent agents and brokers who are members of the HRD.

In this context, the term "secondary market" does not refer to a competitive and transparent auction market where the same rough stones are concurrently offered for sale to a number of buyers, each of which is capable of assessing their value with some degree of certainty and is privy to the offers made by other parties. Rather, as with primary market transactions, prices in the secondary market are determined largely by negotiation between individual pairs of dealers, wholesalers and manufacturers. For this reason, and because the assessment of rough stone values is subjective to some degree, as noted, secondary market prices for similar-quality rough stones may also vary fairly widely.

In addition to the official secondary market in Antwerp, there are also "grey" and "black" markets, so named because participants are not members of an official exchange and transactions are not officially monitored. A number of producers supply the grey market through independent dealers, among them Namco, Diamond-Works, Southern Era and MIBA (a government agency of the Democratic Republic of Congo). Diamonds are sold or bartered from one dealer to another, or from a manufacturer to a retailer, with little or no accompanying paperwork.[24] Black market transactions are further removed from officially sanctioned markets and may involve conflict diamonds.

Wholesale and retail trades in polished diamonds also tend to be bilaterally negotiated, reflecting the often-exclusive supply arrangements among manufacturers, wholesalers and retailers. While retail polished prices are published on a monthly basis in the *Rapaport Diamond Report*, these prices are high cash-asking prices typically used as a starting point in negotiations, rather than actual transactions prices. As with rough diamonds, polished diamond prices can vary significantly across transactions in similar-quality stones. Additionally, the prices of polished diamonds of a certain cut vary with the crown angle, table percentage, florescence in fine

---

[24] See Smillie, Ian, Lansana Gberie and Ralph Hazleton, "The Heart of the Matter: Sierra Leone, Diamonds & Human Security," Partnership Canada Africa, January 2000.

colors, color, clarity and other factors. Elements other than the physical attributes of the polished stone also enter into the determination of its price, including (a) where the transaction takes place (Africa, Europe, the CIS, the United States or elsewhere), (b) the locale where title passes, (c) the method of payment, and (d) the credit risk posed by the contemplated transaction.

In short, genuinely arm's length prices for fairly closely comparable rough and polished stones may vary significantly across transactions that take place concurrently.

5.1.5 Functional Analysis of FP, IS and USS

The operations of FP, IS and USS collectively, (the "Group"), span the purchase of rough diamonds, the development of designs used by independent cutters and polishers in transforming rough stones into polished diamonds, the assumption of costs and risks associated with the transformation of rough to polished stones, the creation of brand names and the wholesale distribution of polished stones.

FP has been a sightholder for a number of years, and it is the only sightholder in the Group. This status entitles (and obligates) FP to purchase pre-sorted parcels of rough stones from the DTC ten times per annum. It is permitted to view the stones at the DTC's sights in London. Each parcel is valued at approximately $25–$35 million. The DTC requires payment with cash in advance; FP finances its purchases of rough through a combination of credit facilities and equity capital. All of the stones that FP procures from the DTC are sold to IS, and the latter cannot return unsold stones. Hence, FP bears limited market risk.

Broadly speaking, IS is in the business of procuring rough stones from FP and third parties, having a portion of the rough cut and polished by third party cutters, and reselling rough and polished stones to USS and third party dealers, wholesalers and retailers. (More particularly, as previously noted, IS sells proprietary polished stones exclusively to USS, rough stones exclusively to third parties and generic polished stones to both USS and third parties.) The performance of these broad functions, in turn, entails:

1. Assessing the rough to determine which individual stones should be sold in rough or polished form, and marking the subset of rough stones destined to be sold as polished diamonds;
2. Arranging for the cutting and polishing of stones by third party manufacturers in Israel and elsewhere;
3. Sorting polished stones by color, quality and size;
4. Maintaining stocks;
5. Performing complex logistical functions related to the shipment, stocking, importation and exportation of rough and polished diamonds; and,
6. Marketing and selling stocks of rough and polished stones to USS and third parties.

IS also owns all of the Group's intangible property, consisting of trademarks and proprietary designs. IS has borne all expenses relating to the development of proprietary designs, and the majority of expenses relating to the development of its trademarks. However, USS has borne a portion of the latter expenditures also, as has the DTC. IS' trademarks and designs are quite valuable. (Only proprietary stones are trademarked.)

IS employs 50 people in its Rough Department, who collectively perform the assessment and generic marking functions described above, 16 people who mark stones to be cut to one of the proprietary designs owned by IS, 35 people in its Sorting Department who are responsible for the sorting of polished stones into color, quality and size categories, 35 individuals who perform sales and marketing functions, 30 individuals who perform logistical and stocking functions and 18 people in an administrative capacity (finance/export, administration, IT and reception).

IS purchases as many rough stones as it anticipates being able to resell in rough, generic polished or proprietary polished form. As previously noted, IS cannot return rough (or polished) stones to FP. It supplements its intercompany supply of rough via third party purchases as necessary. IS retains all right, title and interest in the rough and polished diamonds throughout the cutting and polishing processes. Hence, it bears all related risks, other than shipment shortages or damage to the stones caused by the cutter. Cutters, in turn, are responsible for (a) cutting and polishing the stones in accordance with specifications provided by IS, (b) packaging the polished stones for shipment, (c) maintaining an agreed-on standard of quality, and (d) maintaining comprehensive "all-risk" insurance (including fire, theft and product liability). IS compensates cutters at a fixed fee per carat.

IS purchases most rough diamonds from FP at a stated percentage discount from the published price lists contained in the *Rapaport Diamond Report* ("RAP"). The magnitude of the discount is revisited on a quarterly basis. The pricing of stones that IS purchases from third parties is determined by negotiation at the time of sale.

As noted, IS sells all of its proprietary polished diamonds to USS. In a typical year, it sells approximately 40% of its generic polished diamonds to independent companies and the balance to USS. Consistent with industry norms, IS sells a certain percentage of its polished inventory to USS on a consignment (or "memo") basis (whereby the customer has the option of returning or purchasing the merchandise after a stipulated period). IS provides stones to third parties on memo as well, in approximately the same proportions. On memo transactions, IS bears the costs and risks of carrying inventory, regardless of whether the inventory "sits" in its own facilities or in those of its related or unaffiliated customers. Moreover, even where IS sells stones outright, it retains a measure of inventory risk, inasmuch as USS and third party customers have generous return privileges. IS' terms of sale (encompassing payment terms, return privileges, etc.) are comparable, on average, on sales to USS and third parties. Payment terms are variable and can be as long as 180 days. (The diamond industry is notorious for its very extended terms, which, in combination with consignment practices, greatly increase producers' funding requirements and interest expense.)

USS is in the business of purchasing polished stones primarily from IS and secondarily from third parties, for resale to U.S. retailers. (USS generally procures 85%–95% of its polished stones from IS and the balance from third parties.) USS has royalty-free rights to use the trademarks owned by IS. The return to IS' intangible assets is reflected in the premium pricing of proprietary stones. Consistent with the function of intellectual property in the diamond industry more generally, USS has built on IS' trademarks and proprietary designs to secure exclusive marketing arrangements with certain key U.S. retailers. These arrangements benefit both IS and USS by ensuring a certain level of demand for polished stones.

Broadly speaking, USS' employees present inventory to customers on a regular basis, ascertain the combination of stones (distinguished by color, quality and size) that customers want to take into their own inventory, negotiate which of these stones will be purchased outright and which will be provided on memo, and negotiate price and terms on the former transactions. As with IS, USS sells a substantial percentage of polished stones on memo and offers its customers extended terms on outright sales. Therefore, USS' inventory-carrying costs are quite high relative to distributors of other luxury goods, although its inventory risk is low. USS also employs gemologists, a shipping staff of 10 and a staff of 22 who collectively perform accounting HR, IT, marketing, memo reconciliation and office management functions.

As with IS' purchases of rough diamonds from FP, USS purchases generic polished diamonds from IS at a percentage discount from the published price lists contained in the *Rapaport Diamond Report*. The discounts from RAP on IS' pricing to USS are smaller (and the prices are therefore higher) than FP's discounting on sales to IS. IS sells proprietary stones at a fixed price.

5.2 Transfer Pricing Issues

The fact pattern described above gives rise to several transfer pricing issues:

- FP's pricing of rough diamonds on sales to IS;
- IS' pricing of generic polished diamonds on sales to USS; and,
- IS' pricing of proprietary polished stones to USS.

5.3 Analysis Under Existing Regime

For purposes of analyzing FP's sales of rough stones to IS, and IS' sales of generic polished stones to USS, the CUP method is unlikely to be considered a viable approach under the current transfer pricing regime. First, with regard to FP's intercompany sales, there are obvious data limitations: FP does not sell rough stones to third parties, and market prices for rough are not published. Moreover, as described in detail above, no two rough or polished stones are identical, and adjustments for salient differences would be both difficult to make in principle and exceedingly burdensome in practice.

While the resale price method, as applied to FP, has certain notable shortcomings, it will likely produce more reliable results than any other method under the current regime. Conversely, although IS acts as a reseller of rough stones, it does not sell rough stones to affiliated companies, and its arm's length resale margin on polished stones should exceed its resale margin on rough stones. Reliable third party resale data on polished stones are also unavailable. As such, the resale price method is not applicable to IS (where IS serves as the tested party). Moreover, although the cost plus method would appear to be a logical means of establishing IS' arm's length prices on sales of generic polished stones to USS, IS commingles its inventory of rough stones across sources and therefore cannot determine markups on stones sourced from independent and affiliated suppliers, respectively.[25] The same difficulties arise with respect to profits-based methods. As such, under the current transfer pricing regime, USS is the only viable tested party on transactions with IS. In principle, one can utilize either the resale price method or the comparable profits method (applied to USS) to evaluate the pricing of IS' intercompany sales of generic polished stones to USS, depending chiefly on whether one can assemble closely comparable companies or only distantly comparable firms. We apply the comparable profits method.

5.3.1 FP's Intercompany Sales of Rough Stones to IS

FP functions as a pure dealer: It purchases DTC boxes of rough diamonds for resale on an "as is" basis (that is, without substantial transformation) and bears very limited risk. Hence, FS' principal contributions to the Group's operations consist of (a) preferential access to rough stones by virtue of its status as a DTC sightholder, and (b) the financing of rough stone purchases.

The DTC has appointed other pure dealers as sightholders as well. If these entities were publicly held, they would constitute comparable companies, from which one could derive arm's length resale margins. However, rough diamond dealers are uniformly closely held businesses, and information on their results of operations is therefore not publicly available. Accordingly, we approximate the gross margins that these entities earn by reference to the differential in pricing of rough stones in the primary and secondary markets, respectively.

On its purchases of rough diamonds from other producers for resale to sightholders, the DTC functions essentially as a dealer. As noted, the DTC's official selling

---

[25] Although in principle one could use IS' commingled supply of rough to determine its arm's length cost-plus markup (after adjusting FP's selling prices), any miscalculation of FP's arm's length selling prices will be compounded using this approach.

price is reportedly approximately 10.0% above its buying price.[26] Inasmuch as the DTC's sales of rough to sightholders are considered primary market transactions, the primary/secondary market spread is presumably somewhat higher than 10.0%. It was also reported, circa mid-2005, that "[c]urrent premiums [are] 15% on DTC-sourced boxes in the secondary market ... Many sightholders ... are not cutting their rough at this point in time, but re-selling their boxes with immediate profit."[27]

The above information is indicative of the gross margin that FP should earn (and, therefore, the selling price it should charge) on its resale of rough diamonds to IS. Because secondary market prices for rough diamonds are not published, more precise estimates of the primary/secondary market price differential are difficult to come by. However, the Group is able to assess this differential with a high degree of accuracy, given its substantial and continuous presence in the primary and secondary markets. Hence, FP's gross margin on sales of rough to IS in a given period should be equated to the prevailing primary/secondary market price differential for DTC boxes in that period. It is also important that FP maintain documentation that substantiates the magnitude of the price differential in each period, for purposes of supporting its transfer prices to the satisfaction of the relevant taxing authorities.

5.3.2 IS' Sales of Generic Polished Stones to USS

As previously noted, we utilize the comparable profits method to establish IS' pricing on sales of generic polished stones to USS (with USS serving as the tested party). As is often the case, the rub lies in identifying quasi-comparable companies. Most firms operating as wholesale distributors of diamonds are privately held. Lazare Kaplan, the one publicly held U.S. firm that performs functions similar to those of USS, is also a sightholder (as is FP) and manufactures polished diamonds (as does IS); as such, Lazare Kaplan's results of operations do not provide any basis for determining the arm's length division of income among FP, IS and USS.[28]

Moreover, the unique structure of the diamond industry, the fact that participants are overwhelmingly family-owned businesses where personal relationships are centrally important, and the practices of providing product to retailers on memo and offering very extended payment terms distinguish diamond wholesalers from many other wholesalers of luxury goods. Furthermore, even if such distinctions

---

[26] Unofficially, the DTC's gross margin on stones procured from other producers might be somewhat higher than 10.0%.

[27] Slegers, Paul, "The Diamond Industry in 2005 – Halfway Review," *Pricescope Diamond Journal*, July 29, 2005.

[28] While we identified two arm's length distribution agreements, between Stuller Settings and Charles & Colvard, Ltd., and Rio Grande and Charles & Colvard, Ltd., respectively, all pertinent pricing information was redacted from these documents. Stuller Settings and Rio Grande are two of the largest wholesale distributors of loose stones and finished jewelry in the United States; both are privately held.

were not problematic, there are virtually no publicly held U.S. distributors of luxury goods, broadly defined. For example, only four firms are listed under U.S. *Standard Industrial Classification Code* 5094 (consisting of firms in the business of distributing jewelry, watches, precious stones and precious metals). None of these entities function purely as wholesale distributors and are therefore not suitable comparables.

Given the paucity of information that we obtained through our narrowly defined search for luxury goods distributors, we expanded our search parameters to include independent distributors of high-end personal care products of any kind. We identified such firms through the following searches:

- Keywords = "Distribution, Distributor or Distributes" and "Jewelry"; Industry/Market Segment = Unspecified (4 hits).
- Keywords = "Distribution, Distributor or Distributes" and "Designer"; Industry/Market Segment = Unspecified (9 hits).
- Keywords = "Distribution, Distributor or Distributes" and "Luxury"; Industry/Market Segment = Unspecified (28 hits).
- Keywords = "Distribution, Distributor or Distributes" and "Prestige"; Industry/Market Segment = Unspecified (12 hits).
- Keyword = "Distribution, Distributor or Distributes" and "Perfume"; Industry/Market Segment = Unspecified (44 hits).
- Keywords = "Distribution, Distributor or Distributes" and "High-End"; Industry/Market Segment = Unspecified (2 hits).

After reviewing descriptions of business for all companies identified by means of the above searches, we eliminated those that (a) were integrated backwards into manufacturing; (b) were engaged primarily in direct selling (i.e., through individuals to end-users); (c) operated retail establishments (stores or salons) in lieu of, or in addition to, distribution operations; (d) were engaged principally in the development of personal care products; (e) were engaged primarily in the performance of services; (f) were in the development stage; or, (g) distributed significantly dissimilar products (e.g., pre-recorded music and video game hardware and pharmaceutical compounds).

Following this process of elimination, the following companies constituted our distributor sample:

1. **Signature Eyewear, Inc.**: Designs, markets and distributes prescription eyewear frames and sunglasses, primarily under exclusive licenses with well-known retailers (*Laura Ashley*, *Eddie Bauer*, *Hart-Schaffner & Marx* and others). Sells to independent optical retailers in the United States through own salesforce and independent representatives and through exclusive distributors in foreign markets. Procures frames from independent contract manufacturers. Performs design function internally.
2. **Orange 21, Inc.**: Designs, develops and markets premium products, primarily sunglasses and goggles, under the self-developed *Spy Optic* brand and other brands. Targets active sports markets (surfing, skateboarding, snowboarding,

motocross, etc.). Utilizes patented, engineered optical lens technology. Sells to key multi-store action sport and youth lifestyle retailers in the United States and internationally. Design, marketing and branding handled by in-house staff. Sources finished product inventory from independent contract manufacturers.

3. **Helen of Troy, Ltd.**: A global designer, developer, importer and distributor of brand name consumer products. Operates in two segments: Personal Care and Housewares. Personal Care products include straighteners, curling irons, hairsetters, mirrors, footbaths and hair accessories; housewares include kitchen tools, cutlery, tea kettles and trash cans. Relies exclusively on outside manufacturers. Sells products to mass merchandisers, warehouse clubs, drug chains, grocery stores, specialty stores and beauty supply retailers and wholesalers. Utilizes own and licensed brands.

4. **CCA Industries**: Imports and sells health and beauty aids and cosmeceutical products (skin care, oral care, nail care, hair care and sun care products, depilatories, fragrances, etc.). Sources all products from contract manufacturers. Provides the latter with formulations and color selections. Markets and sells to major drug and food chains, mass merchandisers and wholesale beauty-aid distributors. Certain of the company's products are sold under its own trademarks; others are sold under licensed marks. CCA Industries also licenses rights to certain manufacturing technologies from third parties.

5. **Prestige Brands Holdings, Inc.**: Sells well-recognized brand name healthcare, household cleaning and personal care products, including nail polish remover, shampoo, pain relief sprays and liquid bandages. Carries 14 well-known brands. Performs marketing, sales, customer service and product development functions. Relies on external manufacturers and logistics services providers. Sells to mass merchandisers, drug, grocery, dollar and club stores.

Clearly, there are significant shortcomings with our sample companies. Most notably, they are very few in number, and, in addition to distribution, certain of the "comparables" perform product development functions and own valuable trademarks, as distinct from USS. Moreover, our sample distributors sell principally to mass merchants and major drug and food chains, whereas USS sells primarily to independent retail jewelers. Furthermore, USS carries substantially higher inventories, incurs lower inventory risk, has higher accounts receivables per dollar of sales (due to the extended terms it offers) and pays much higher insurance premiums, relative to the sample companies. It should be noted that the lack of meaningful functional and product comparability in this case is typical of applications of the comparable profits method. Hence, in addition to lacking a theoretical foundation, this method is generally wanting from an empirical vantage point as well. There is simply a limited number of publicly held distributors operating in the United States in total at present.

Because the (largely unstated) theory underlying the comparable profits method is that profit level indicators represent a return on invested capital, and that this return on investment will be equalized across distributors of various stripes, adjustments for some of the differences noted above are generally considered unnecessary.

For the same reason, this is *not* the case when sample distributors are distinguishable from the tested party by virtue of the fact that they employ more or fewer assets per dollar of sales. In this instance, the fact that some sample companies have developed (or license) intangible assets, and all carry far lower inventories and have far lower accounts receivables per dollar of sales than the tested party, is problematic even under the comparable profits method. As such, under the current transfer pricing regime, one should adjust for these differences to the extent possible.

U.S. practitioners routinely adjust standalone sample companies' results of operations for differences in inventory, accounts receivables and accounts payables (per dollar of sales or assets, depending on the profit level indicator), relative to the tested party, by means of the "asset intensity adjustment." Conceptually, this adjustment presupposes that higher-than-normal inventories or accounts receivables reflect strategic decisions on the part of firms to better serve their customers by providing just-in-time delivery and/or extended payment terms. As such, the argument goes, firms adopting such strategies build the added financing costs into their product pricing.[29] Quantitatively, the asset intensity adjustment entails:

- Imputing to each sample company the tested party's ratio of (i) inventories plus accounts receivables less accounts payables (an approximation of working capital) to (ii) sales or assets (depending on the profit level indicator used);
- Applying a reasonable cost of capital thereto; and,
- Adjusting the sample companies' profit level indicators upward or downward to reflect differences between their imputed cost of working capital and their actual cost of working capital.

To the extent that one can estimate the per-period income generated by particular intangible assets employed by the sample distributors in this case, their profit level indicators should also be reduced by this income (less the associated development costs).

In the instant case, we compute asset intensity adjustments (which reflect differences in both (a) inventories and accounts receivables, and (b) USS' lower inventory financing costs), but do not attempt adjustments to reflect intangible asset values and costs. (The margin of error on such adjustments probably exceeds the adjustments themselves.) We find that USS should earn an operating margin of approximately 5.5%–8.0% on its resales of generic polished stones. Given this arm's length margin, coupled with FP's resale margin on the sale of rough stones to IS, the latter's arm's length income on generic polished stones sold to USS is determined as a residual. (In the event, USS' operating margin is less than 5.5%, indicating that IS' pricing of non-proprietary stones exceeds arm's length prices.)

---

[29] While true in the instant case, in many other instances, higher inventories and accounts receivables may simply reflect overly optimistic sales projections, adverse economic conditions or customers' difficulties in paying their bills. Upward adjustments in margins in these instances, to reflect suppliers' intentionally higher cost of capital, would not be warranted. I would like to thank Joseph Boorstein, Ph.D., for his insights on this point.

5.3.3 IS' Pricing of Proprietary Polished Stones Sold to USS

It remains to determine the price premium that IS should charge USS on its sales of proprietary polished stones. This price premium should be established so as to ensure that IS earns all income attributable to its designs, and a reasonable share of income attributable to its trademarks (reflective of its share of the associated development expenditures). Because USS sells both generic and polished stones to the same third parties on the same terms, the premium that is *jointly* attributable to IS' designs and trademarks at this market level can readily be calculated, in both dollar and percentage terms. The price premium per dollar of sales to retailers can also readily be translated into a price premium per dollar of sales to USS by multiplying the former ratio by the ratio of retail to wholesale selling prices.

As noted above, a portion of the total price premium represents a return to designs owned exclusively by IS, and should be allocated solely thereto. The balance of the price premium should be divided between USS and IS based on their relative advertising expenditures in prior years. This allocation methodology requires estimating the relative values of designs and trademarks. However, this determination cannot be made on a systematic basis, because only proprietary designs are sold under the Group's trademarks. (Stated differently, the intangible assets are only used in combination, as previously noted.) Absent a more systematic method, we make the admittedly arbitrary assumption that 50% of the price premium represents a return to designs, and 50% to trademarks.

In sum, in computing IS' prices on sales of proprietary polished stones to USS, its pricing of generic stones should be increased to reflect its share of intangible income, consisting of (a) 50% of the price premium, which we ascribe to the designs that it owns, and (b) 65% of the remaining price premium (or 32.5% of the total price premium), which we ascribe to trademarks. The latter division reflects the fact that IS has historically borne approximately two-thirds of the combined advertising expenditures of IS and USS.

5.4 Analysis Under Alternative Regime

Under the proposed alternative transfer pricing regime, we utilize numerical standards to establish FP's arm's length pricing of rough stones to IS, and the modified inexact CUP method to establish IS' arm's length prices on sales of generic polished stones to USS. Our analysis of IS' pricing of proprietary polished stones to USS under the alternative regime is the same as our analysis under the current regime.

5.4.1 FP's Intercompany Sales of Rough Stones to IS

FP has very limited below-the-line expenses (other than interest, a non-operating expense), and its resale and operating margins differ by a relatively small magnitude.

The uniqueness of its business points up the importance of establishing numerical standards on an industry-by-industry basis. For purposes of discussion, we assume that an annual benchmarking study indicates that FP should earn a resale margin of 10.0%–12.0% in the year at issue.

5.4.2 IS' Sales of Non-Proprietary Polished Stones to USS

As previously noted, IS sells a substantial percentage of its non-proprietary polished stones to third parties. We utilize these transactions as CUPs. However, the CUP method is necessarily applied somewhat differently to firms in the diamond industry than it would be applied in other industries.

As discussed above, arm's length prices for polished (and rough) diamonds vary across transactions to some degree, even where they take place on the same date and the stones are closely similar, because such pricing is generally the outcome of bilateral negotiations. Moreover, individual polished stones often have certain idiosyncracies that detract from or enhance their value, and frequently vary to some extent along one or more quality dimensions (e.g., color or clarity). These variables also contribute to price differentials across transactions. Furthermore, the assessment of individual stones' physical attributes is a somewhat subjective process, further contributing to variations in arm's length pricing.[30] Lastly, external factors unrelated to the physical attributes of the stones themselves can influence their value, such as location and the creditworthinesss of the counterparty. Therefore, there is not a "market price" as such for diamonds, but numerous individually negotiated arm's length prices for similar, albeit not identical, stones. Moreover, transactions prices are not published. Accordingly, the only feasible means of applying the CUP method is by reference to internal CUPs and ranges of arm's length prices. These shortcomings aside, the CUP method will very likely produce more reliable results than the resale price method in this instance.

In applying the CUP method, we utilize a data set consisting of IS' pricing on its intercompany and third party sales of non-proprietary polished diamonds, aggregated into categories in accordance with the Group's internal grading system. More particularly, within each calendar quarter and category, IS identified all transactions involving sales of the same-sized non-proprietary stones to affiliated and unrelated companies, respectively. Only transactions that could not be paired were excluded from our sample. It should be noted that IS does not consistently sell stones in the same category on precisely the same date to both USS and third parties. For this reason, we necessarily compare prices on transactions that are not concurrent. Because our comparisons are within calendar quarters, the difference in transactions dates cannot exceed 3 months, and is generally significantly less. (In contrast to

---

[30] Such variability in the physical attributes of diamonds is presumably the reason that diamonds are not traded on an electronic exchange.

many commodities, diamond pricing is not exceptionally volatile over comparatively short periods.)

The Group's categories are defined by certain ranges of color, quality and cut. Within categories, quality gradations are generally moderate, albeit clearly in evidence. Thus, for example, variations of 5%–15% in IS' prices for stones included in the *same* internal category, sold to the *same* third party on the *same* date, are common. However, in limited instances, there are significant variations in quality (and hence, price) within grades, as evidenced by the fact that IS' prices for stones sold to the same third party on the same date and in the same category periodically differ by as much as 40%–50%.

We interpret the CUP methodology, as applied to IS, as follows:

- We postulate that, within the Group's internal grades, pricing on the *majority* of matched intercompany and third party transactions (75%–80%) should not differ by more than 10%–15% in either direction (and not consistently in only one direction). These comparatively limited differentials in price may be attributable to (a) limited variations in quality within categories, (b) the fact that prices are established through bilateral negotiations, (c) the differing dates of the transactions being compared or (d) a combination thereof.
- Wider disparities in prices on the remaining 20%–25% of IS' matched transactions can reasonably be attributed to significant differences in the diamonds' physical properties, widely differing assessments of value, material changes in market conditions (within quarters) or a combination thereof.
- If the above observations are borne out, IS' percentage discounts from RAP, used to establish its intercompany prices on sales of generic stones to USS, are consistent with arm's length prices. Hence, under this set of facts, IS' transfer pricing practices vis-a-vis non-proprietary diamonds would satisfy the arm's length standard.
- Disparities in excess of 10%–15% in the pricing of matched transactions, on more than 25% of such transactions, would indicate that IS' intercompany pricing of generic polished diamonds is not arm's length.

Our quantitative analysis of IS' matched transactions entails (a) computing the absolute value of the difference in intercompany and third party prices on individual paired transactions, expressed as a percentage of the higher price, (b) determining the percentage of the total sample transactions for which this difference was less than or equal to 10% and 15%, respectively, and (c) quantifying the percentage of transactions, within each of these thresholds, for which the intercompany price was higher than the third party price, and conversely.

Our findings are as follows:

- For close to 90% of all paired transactions, IS' third party and intercompany prices differed by 15% or less.
- The intercompany price exceeded the third party price in 46% of paired transactions meeting the 15% threshold, and the third party price exceeded the intercompany price in 54% of paired transactions meeting the 15% threshold.

- Applying the more restrictive 10% upper bound, IS' intercompany and third party prices differed by no more than this magnitude in 78% of all paired transactions.
- The intercompany price exceeded the third party price in 42% of paired transactions meeting the 10% threshold, and the third party price exceeded the intercompany price in 58% of paired transactions meeting the 10% threshold.

Based on these findings, we conclude that IS' percentage discounts from RAP, used to establish its intercompany prices on sales of generic stones to USS, produce arm's length results.

5.5 Comparison

Under the existing transfer pricing regime, we analyze FP's sales of rough stones to IS by means of a variant of the resale price method. Under the alternative regime, we would rely on published numerical standards. While the use of numerical standards would greatly reduce compliance and dispute resolution costs, it would only improve the reliability of results (within the inherent limits of transfer pricing methods that utilize accounting measures of profit) if the studies used to establish such standards were sufficiently comprehensive and industry-specific.

Under the existing regime, we analyze IS' sales of generic polished stones to USS by application of the comparable profits method. Under the alternative regime, we would rely on the modified inexact CUP method. The former method produces an adjustment in this case, while the latter does not. In view of the substantial differences between our sample of standalone distributors and USS, respectively, and given that operating profits expressed as a percentage of sales or book assets are *not* equalized across distributors, the comparable profits method produces distinctly unreliable results. In contrast, our CUP application is based only on the uncontroversial proposition that similar stones will sell for similar prices. As such, it is more compelling.

Chapter 6
Intercompany Sale of Medical Devices

Our second case study involves a medical device company headquartered in the United States that recently acquired one of its opposite numbers in Germany. The U.S. parent company has begun to import certain products in small volumes from its German affiliate, and anticipates exporting other devices to the latter in the near future. We analyze the various transactions in this case under the resale price method, the comparable uncontrolled price method, the comparable uncontrolled transactions method and the numerical standards approach, and consider the merits and shortcomings of existing and proposed methods, respectively, in this context.

6.1 Summary of Key Facts

The U.S. parent company in this case study ("USP"), a relative newcomer in its market, has rapidly developed a portfolio of best-in-class inpatient and outpatient monitoring devices and systems. It initially specialized primarily (albeit not exclusively) in the design, marketing and sale of monitoring devices for use in outpatient settings. These products are manufactured by a third party subcontractor ("Company X") on a fee-for-service basis. USP also designs and sells a limited range of in-hospital patient monitoring systems. It fabricates these products internally.

USP recently expanded its product offerings substantially through third party licensing arrangements and acquisitions of established companies. It entered into licensing and distribution agreements with two unaffiliated companies, which granted USP certain global development, sales and distribution rights to a proprietary gas analyzer used to measure the concentration of anesthetic agents during surgery, and a system designed to measure lung function during ventilation. One of the acquired companies, based in Germany, designs, manufactures and sells state-of-the-art multi-parameter monitoring systems for use in surgical and critical care venues. It also manufactures and sells a small number of outpatient monitoring devices, most of which have essentially the same functionality as certain of those offered by USP. The acquired German company has been organized as a wholly owned subsidiary of USP, and is henceforth referred to as "FS".

E. King, *Transfer Pricing and Corporate Taxation*,
DOI 10.1007/978-0-387-78183-9_6, © Springer Science+Business Media, LLC 2009

USP was recently organized into two separate business units (A and B), corresponding to specific product lines and target markets (products for use in hospital settings and outpatient care, respectively).

6.1.1 Business Unit A: In-Hospital Monitoring Systems

USP's Business Unit A encompasses products used in hospital settings. To date, USP has sold its pre-acquisition in-hospital monitoring devices exclusively in the United States, through a network of agents and distributors. It relies much more heavily on agents than distributors. U.S. agents maintain ongoing contact with end-users (primarily hospitals) and negotiate sales on terms that USP establishes. USP's agency agreements typically provide for a commission rate of 10%–12% of net sales. Its twenty agents do not carry stocks or take title to product, and have very limited responsibility for advertising and promoting USP's products. USP, for its part, provides sales agency training and education, promotes its products through physician education and advertisements in medical journals, carries stocks, and invoices end-users. USP's six independent U.S. distributors of in-hospital devices carry stocks, take title, bear inventory, credit and collections risk and have primary responsibility for advertising and promoting USP's products in their respective territories. In 2007, USP instituted a standardized distributor pricing policy (i.e., a standardized discount from list price equal to 40%).

Certain of FS' in-hospital monitoring systems received FDA approval prior to its acquisition by USP.[1] USP began selling several of these systems in the United States in the latter half of 2007, and it is in the process of determining which of FS' other in-hospital monitoring devices would find a home in the U.S. market. USP sells FS' products under its own brand name. Accordingly, the packaging and other cosmetic features of these products have been (and are being) redesigned. However, the basic functionality of FS' products has not been, and will not be, modified. By the same token, the head of Business Unit A anticipates working closely with physicians and other health care providers to determine the necessary minor modifications to FS' products as they are introduced in successively larger-scale rollouts.

Given (a) the physical distance between USP and FS, (b) uncertainties as to how rapidly FS' products will be accepted in the United States, (c) USP's limited experience in procuring product from FS, and (d) the potential for delays arising from FDA oversight, USP plans to maintain substantial local stocks of FS' in-hospital monitoring devices. More particularly, at the outset, USP will carry stocks equal to 6 months' projected requirements. After observing FS' manufacturing processes,

---

[1] Approximately 5 years prior to its acquisition by USP, FS attempted to sell in-hospital monitoring systems and products in the U.S. market on a limited scale. It obtained FDA approval for these products at that time. However, FS was unsuccessful in its efforts to establish a foothold in the U.S. market, principally because it had not built up a distribution network of sufficient depth, did not have the mechanisms in place to monitor distributors' performance, and did not promote its products sufficiently heavily.

the degree of support that it receives from its own vendors, the efficacy of FDA oversight, etc., USP's inventories of FS' in-hospital monitoring devices may be reduced.

It is anticipated that FS will market and sell a small number of USP's in-hospital patient monitoring products in European markets as well. It will sell these products directly to end-users in Germany and to stocking distributors elsewhere in Europe. The products will bear USP's trademarks and names.

6.1.2 Business Unit B: Outpatient Monitoring Devices

USP's Business Unit B encompasses products designed for use in outpatient settings. These products are already well-established in the U.S. market. Because FS has historically specialized in the design, manufacture and sale of in-hospital monitoring systems, and has few products that would compete directly with USP's outpatient product lines, it will likely import such products in significant volumes. FS will resell these products directly to end-users in Germany and to stocking distributors elsewhere in Europe, in both cases under USP's trademarks and names.

USP has historically sold approximately 80% of its outpatient monitoring devices in its domestic market (principally through agents) and 20% outside the United States (primarily in Europe, Australia and Japan). It has relied on stocking distributors to market, promote and maintain inventories of these products in foreign markets and has gradually built up an extensive distribution network. At the outset, USP encountered significant difficulties in building up its distributor base in certain foreign markets. In most cases, its products were (and remain) a comparatively small part of foreign distributors' overall business. Additionally, reimbursement rates in many European countries are lower than U.S. reimbursement rates and reimbursement policies are applied more unevenly. For these reasons, European distributors have historically been charged lower prices than U.S. distributors. USP's foreign distributors typically seek discounts of 45%–50% from list price; as previously noted, U.S. distributors are given a standard discount of 40% from list price.[2]

FS also has an extensive network of stocking distributors throughout Europe (although it sells direct in Germany, as noted). In most instances, individual countries are not large enough to support two distributors. Hence, USP will need to consolidate the Group's established base of European distributors.

As previously noted, USP relies on Company X, an independent subcontractor, to manufacture its outpatient monitoring products. USP provides Company X with product specifications; the latter procures raw materials, performs fabrication functions and delivers the finished product. Company X requires a fairly long lead time, ranging from 8 to 16 weeks, in part due to its ongoing commitments to other

---

[2] This does not necessarily translate into resale margins of 45%–50% and 40%, respectively, in that the distributors' actual selling prices may be higher or lower than their list price, and cost of goods includes other items, in addition to the purchase price of product.

customers and its "first-come first-served" policy. Therefore, USP routinely plans around a 16-week lead time, and builds in an additional cushion of 1 month. While carrying excess stocks is undesirable, the more important objective is to avoid the worst-case scenario, in which a physician would like to use USP's product, but none are available and he or she resorts to a competitor's product.

With regard to outpatient monitoring devices destined for non-U.S. markets, USP will formally engage Company X. However, the latter will ship product directly to FS, and FS will bear the costs and risks associated with ocean and inland transport. Moreover, it will not have return privileges. With FS interposed between USP and independent foreign distributors outside of Germany, the latter will not be required to carry exceptionally large stocks. Rather, FS will carry sufficient inventories to ensure that demand for USP's outpatient products in European markets can be met on a timely basis, taking into account both Company X's comparatively long lead time and the additional time required to ship product. FS will also be primarily responsible for advertising and promoting USP's products in Europe, and will oversee the performance of independent European distributors.

FS manufactures three outpatient monitoring devices that USP could potentially sell in the United States. At present, none of these products are FDA-approved. Two of the three products serve the same medical purpose as certain of the products already manufactured and sold by USP. Both have certain design features that are not well-accepted in the United States.[3] Thus, USP will probably not market and sell these two products domestically. If USP ultimately decides in favor of doing so, it would have to obtain FDA approval. Because these products would likely be considered Class II medical devices, and there are substantially equivalent predicate medical devices currently on the market, USP could obtain such approval relatively quickly and at limited expense.[4]

USP does not currently manufacture or market a product that would compete directly with FS' third outpatient monitoring device. However, by virtue of certain design features, this product may be considered a Class III device, requiring a much more arduous FDA approval process. The approval process for Class III medical devices, referred to as "PMA," requires extensive clinical trials to demonstrate safety and efficacy. If the product is manufactured with new materials, animal tests are also required.

---

[3] A competing product with similar design characteristics was previously sold in the United States; as a result of unacceptably high failure rates, the product was ultimately withdrawn from the market some years ago.

[4] Medical devices not used in applications that can potentially be life-threatening may be approved under a process known as "5–10(k)"; the supplier of such a device is only required to demonstrate that its product is substantially equivalent to a device currently on the market, which has been shown to be safe and effective.

6.2 Transfer Pricing Issues

As the discussion above indicates, USP and FS will engage in the intercompany purchase and sale of tangible property. FS will also assist USP in developing and enhancing the value of its trademarks and names in Europe.

6.3 Analysis Under Existing Regime

Under the current transfer pricing regime, our analysis and recommendations regarding USP's transfer pricing policies distinguish between the following types of intercompany transactions:

- Products manufactured by Company X for export to FS, and sold by FS to end-users in Germany;
- Products manufactured by USP internally for export to FS, and sold by FS to end-users in Germany;
- Products manufactured by Company X for export to FS, and sold by FS to European stocking distributors;
- Products manufactured by USP internally for export to FS, and sold by FS to European stocking distributors;
- Products manufactured by FS, exported to USP, and sold by USP to end-users in the U.S. market; and
- Services rendered by FS.

Our transfer pricing analysis under the existing regime differentiates among the transactions in tangible property listed above because, under our application of the *Best Method Rule* (contained in the U.S. transfer pricing regulations), we have concluded that each type of transaction is most reliably analyzed under a different method. Our analysis of services rendered by FS to USP is incorporated into our analysis of intercompany transactions in tangible property.

6.3.1 FS' Sales of Tangible Property to USP

Consider first FS' sales of in-hospital monitoring systems and, potentially, outpatient monitoring products to USP. While FS attempted to sell certain in-hospital systems in the U.S. market through independent distributors some years ago, these efforts were unsuccessful, and the company has not sold to independent U.S. distributors during the past 5 years. Hence, there are no internal CUPs to use in establishing FS' arm's length prices on sales to USP. Moreover, data on competitors' pricing practices are not publicly available, and their products are not sufficiently comparable to FS' products in any event. As such, we do not utilize the CUP method to establish FS' intercompany selling prices.

In lieu of the CUP method, we designate USP as the tested party and utilize the resale price method. We consider this approach to be the best method, given our fact pattern, principally because we are able to draw on internal resale margins. The U.S. transfer pricing regulations clearly favor such internal data (for good reason), relative to resale margins reported by unrelated companies:

> [C]omparability under [the resale price] method is particularly dependent on similarity of functions performed, risks borne and contractual terms, or adjustments to account for the effects of such differences. If possible, appropriate gross profit margins should be derived from comparable uncontrolled purchases and resales by the reseller involved in the controlled sale, because similar characteristics are more likely to be found among different resales of property made by the same reseller than among sales made by other resellers.[5]

As noted, USP will function as a stocking distributor on products sourced from FS, selling directly to end-users in the U.S. market (with the assistance of agents). As such, USP should earn its standardized U.S. stocking distributor discount of 40%, before adjustments. To the extent that USP performs incremental marketing and minor re-engineering functions that U.S. stocking distributors do not typically perform, it should be reimbursed by FS.[6] Correspondingly, if USP carries proportionately larger inventories of FS' products than USP's independent U.S. stocking distributors are generally expected to carry, USP should be compensated for the incremental carrying costs. Lastly, because USP will sell FS' products under its own name, the standard distributor margin should be increased to reflect the income attributable thereto.

The U.S. transfer pricing regulations generally do not favor adjustments to resale margins for differences in trademark values.[7] However, in this instance, we identified closely comparable uncontrolled trademark licensing arrangements, involving trademarks that are similar to USP's marks in terms of field of use, term, etc. This sample indicates that USP's trademark and name would command a royalty rate of 2.0%–4.0% of net sales on an arm's length basis. In keeping with the *Commensurate with Income* standard, we take these arm's length royalty rates to be a measure of *all* income attributable to USP's trademark and name (and, hence, the amount by which USP's standardized distributor discount should be increased).

---

[5] Treas. Reg. Section 1.482-3(c)(3)(ii)(A).

[6] The U.S. services regulations promulgated in 1968, in combination with the Business Judgment Rule contained in the Temporary Regulations issued in 2006, jointly determine whether a cost-based intercompany services fee is warranted in 2007 (unless a taxpayer elects to apply the Temporary Regulations in their entirety). Under these rules, a markup over cost for marketing and minor re-engineering services rendered on a small scale should not be required.

[7] Example 7 under Treas. Reg. Section 1.482-3(c)(4) has a similar fact pattern in some respects. In this example, three of five potentially comparable uncontrolled distributors are excluded from the sample of comparable firms, for purposes of applying the resale price method, because they distribute unbranded widgets, while the controlled distributor at issue resells branded widgets. The rationale given for this sample selection criterion is that the products distributed by the excluded companies are not sufficiently similar in value to the products distributed by the controlled distributor. Moreover, "because in this case it is difficult to determine the effect the trademark will have on price or profits, reliable adjustments for the differences cannot reliably be made."

As noted, the subset of FS' in-hospital patient monitoring devices and systems that USP will sell domestically over the next 1–2 years are already FDA-approved. Hence, adjustments for the costs of obtaining FDA approval for these products are not necessary. However, as discussed above, FS' limited offerings of outpatient products have not yet been approved by the FDA for sale in the United States. If USP does in fact import such products for resale in its domestic market, it should be compensated by FS for facilitating the FDA review process. More particularly, if a third party Contract Research Organization (CRO) is engaged to conduct the necessary clinical trials and prepare the requisite submissions to the FDA, these costs should be passed through to FS (without a markup).[8] However, if USP performs these functions internally or devotes significant resources to overseeing an unaffiliated CRO, it should mark up its internal direct and indirect costs, in that facilitating FDA approval does, arguably, "contribute significantly to key competitive advantages, core capabilities or the fundamental chances of success or failure in one or more businesses" of the controlled group.

6.3.2 USP's Sales of Tangible Property to FS

Consider next USP's sales of monitoring devices to FS. The matrix below shows the categories of such transactions that we analyze separately.

	Products Mfg'd. by Company X	Products Mfg'd. by USP
Products sold w/in Germany	CASE A	CASE B
Products sold o/s Germany	CASE C	CASE D

6.3.2.1 Recommendations: Case A

In Case A above, USP outsources the manufacture of certain outpatient products for export to FS, which the latter resells in the German market. Our analysis of this case is based on the CUP method. As previously noted, USP has sold its outpatient devices in foreign markets through independent distributors for a number of years. One such distributor was based in Germany ("Company Y"). (This relationship was recently terminated, pursuant to USP's acquisition of FS.) FS will carry most of the

---

[8] In principle, FS could contract directly with a CRO, and would not be willing to pay a fee over and above the CRO's standard fees on an arm's length basis unless USP, acting as an intermediary, added significant value.

products that Company Y previously purchased from USP, for resale in the same geographic market and to customers at the same market level. It will also have the same advertising, marketing and inventory-carrying responsibilities. Hence, USP should charge FS the same prices that it previously charged Company Y. (To the extent that FS bears incrementally higher advertising and promotional expenses, it should be compensated for marketing services rendered.)

6.3.2.2 Recommendations: Case B

Case B is analogous to Case A, except that USP manufactures these (in-hospital) monitoring devices internally. We cannot use the CUP method to establish USP's arm's length prices on sales of in-hospital monitoring systems to FS, because USP has historically sold these products exclusively in its domestic market.

However, FS should earn approximately the same gross margin on products sourced from USP, for resale in the same geographic market and to customers at the same market level, whether USP manufactures the subject products internally or engages an independent subcontractor to manufacture the products. Hence, USP's intercompany selling prices for products covered by Case B should be established by (a) calculating FS' gross margin on the resale of products covered by Case A, and (b) deriving USP's transfer prices such that FS earns the same gross margin on products covered by Case B.

The following example illustrates this approach: Assume that FS earns an average gross margin of 48% on the sale of products covered by Case A, and sells products covered by Case B at a price of P_B to German customers. USP's transfer price on the latter products, denoted by x, should solve the following equation: $(P_B - x)/P_B = 0.48$, or $x = P_B \times 0.52$. Hence, if P_B is equal to $600.00, USP's selling price to FS should be $312.00. As with Case A, to the extent that FS bears incrementally higher advertising and promotional expenses, it should be compensated for marketing services rendered.

6.3.2.3 Recommendations: Case C

FS will act as a master distributor in European markets other than Germany, reselling to smaller independent distributors in these local markets (Case C in the above matrix). While USP previously sold outpatient monitoring devices to third party distributors in some of the same European markets, such transactions took place at a different market level than USP's prospective sales of outpatient products to FS, for resale outside Germany. Relatedly, in its capacity as a master distributor, FS will assume certain of the functions that USP and its independent European stocking distributors, respectively, previously performed (e.g., oversight of distributors in the case of USP, and the maintenance of local stocks, advertising and promotion in the case of European distributors). For these reasons, we do not utilize the CUP method to analyze Case C transactions.

On Case C transactions (where product is manufactured by Company X for export to FS and resold by FS to distributors outside of Germany), USP's substantive contribution consists exclusively of its intellectual property (the proprietary product specifications that USP provides to Company X, and its trademarks and names, which FS will use). USP does not manufacture these products internally, bear any responsibility for logistics, carry inventories of raw materials or finished products destined for European markets, or bear the associated price and quantity risks. Moreover, USP has no marketing responsibilities vis-a-vis European sales. As such, FS should compensate USP on these types of transactions as follows:

1. The payment of arm's length royalty fees for USP's contributions of intellectual property; and,
2. The reimbursement of Company X's manufacturing and logistical fees, borne in the first instance by USP.

We establish USP's arm's length royalty rate for rights to its manufacturing and process technologies by application of the CUT method. More particularly, USP should charge FS a royalty fee equal to 7%–9% of FS' net sales to European stocking distributors. This recommendation is predicated on USP's internal arm's length licensing transactions (referenced in the summary of key facts), augmented by a sample of ten third party technology licensing arrangements. USP should charge FS a royalty rate of 2%–4% of the latter's net sales to European distributors for rights to use its trademarks and names (see discussion above).[9]

The following simplified example illustrates these recommendations: Assume FS' selling price of Product Q to European distributors is $475.00 (converted from Euros). USP's royalty fees for manufacturing and marketing intangible assets combined are therefore equal to $42.75–$61.75 (with an average of $52.25). Manufacturing and logistics services fees payable to Company X, for which USP is fully reimbursed, are equal to $150.00. Consequently, in total, FS should pay USP approximately $202.25 per unit.

Because FS bears advertising and promotional expenses vis-a-vis USP's names and marks in Europe, and does not retain income attributable to these marketing intangible assets under our proposed transfer pricing policy, it should be compensated for these outlays (or, more precisely, the outlays in excess of those made by USP's third party stocking distributors in Europe). Based on a sample of third party marketing services providers, the markup over cost should be approximately 8.0%–10.0%.

6.3.2.4 Recommendations: Case D

Lastly, consider the intercompany pricing of product that USP manufactures internally for export to FS, and FS resells to European stocking distributors (Case D in

---

[9] An analogous trademark royalty payment is not warranted under Cases A and B, because USP's arm's length pricing on transactions with Company Y, used to establish USP's selling prices to FS, would have enabled Company Y to earn a return on its distribution functions alone.

the gross matrix above). In its role as master distributor, FS should earn the same gross margin on products sourced from USP, regardless of whether USP manufactures such products internally or subcontracts out their manufacture to Company X. Therefore, if and when USP begins to export to FS the in-hospital devices that it manufactures internally, it should price these products so as to leave FS with the same resale margin as in Case C transactions, analyzed above.

The following example illustrates this recommendation: FS' selling price of Product Q to distributors is $475.00, its royalty fees approximately $52.25, and its reimbursement of USP's subcontract manufacturing and logistics costs, $150.00. Therefore, FS' approximate resale margin is equal to ($475.00 − $52.25 − $150.00)/$475.00 = 57.42%. If Product M (a "Case D" product) sells for $525.00 in European markets, USP's arm's length selling price to FS should be equal to $525.00(1 − 0.5742) = $223.55.

As in Case C above, FS also requires compensation for the services that it renders with regard to developing and enhancing the value of USP's trademarks and names in Europe.

6.4 Analysis Under Alternative Regime

One of the alternative transfer pricing approaches proposed in Chapter 4 entails establishing numerical norms vis-a-vis the returns that certain routine activities and relatively common intangible assets, such as trademarks, should command. As applied to distributors, tax authorities might agree on a safe harbor range of (a) resale margins, (b) advertising-to-sales ratios, (c) inventory-to-sales ratios and (d) SG&A-to-sales ratios. Where individual affiliated distributors' results deviate from these norms, adjustments would likely be warranted.

Given this simplified "numerical norms" framework, the five distinct cases analyzed above can be collapsed down to two cases: FS' imports of devices and systems from USP for resale in Europe, and USP's imports of devices and systems from FS for resale in the United States. As previously noted, the five separate analyses are necessary under the current transfer pricing regime because each category of transactions is most reliably analyzed under a different transfer pricing method. Under the proposed simplified approach, both USP's and FS' results on their respective intercompany purchases would be evaluated by reference to published benchmarks, inasmuch as both entities function as distributors with respect to these transactions. If USP sought to obtain FDA approval for FS' outpatient monitoring devices at its own expense, its SGA-to-sales range would presumably exceed the stipulated safe harbor range, prompting a more detailed analysis. Similarly, if FS, in its capacity as a master distributor in European markets, carries larger-than-normal inventories or expends more on advertising and promotion than independent European stocking distributors, its inventory-to-sales and advertising-to-sales ratios would fall outside the safe harbor norms, necessitating further analysis (and adjustments).

6.5 Comparison

As discussed in Chapter 3, there is no market mechanism at work that would equal-ize gross margins across standalone distributors operating in the same geographic market, but sourcing "similar" products from different suppliers. Correspondingly, there is no real justification for comparing an affiliated distributor's resale mar-gin with the gross margins reported by its unaffiliated counterparts in the same geographic market, sourcing similar, albeit not identical, products from various suppliers.

However, for purposes of our analysis under the current transfer pricing regime, we assume in this instance only that:

- An individual supplier would charge two unaffiliated distributors operating in the same geographic market, with the same obligations regarding advertising and promotion, the maintenance of adequate local stocks, etc., the same price for the same products; and,
- The two distributors would resell these products at approximately the same price.

While the circumstances that legitimately permit gross margin comparisons rarely arise, in this case, where the multinational group is transitioning from unaf-filiated to captive distributors, this more valid comparison of gross margins is fea-sible. Hence, the current transfer pricing regime produces reasonable results in this instance. The virtue of the simplified alternative approach is that it is vastly less time- and resource-intensive.

Chapter 7
Performance of Intercompany Services

Our third case study involves a multinational group consisting of two legal entities in different taxing jurisdictions (the United States and Indonesia). Collectively, the foreign parent (FP) and its U.S. subsidiary (USS) develop, manufacture and market thin-film disks (thin film magnetic media on rigid disk platters) for incorporation into disk drives. FP performs engineering and manufacturing functions, is the contract party on all transactions with third parties, and owns all of the Group's technology and other manufacturing-related intellectual property. USS performs R&D/engineering and customer relationship management functions.

Disk drives are composed of magnetic media, a spindle assembly powered by a spindle motor, read/write heads mounted onto an arm assembly and a base casing. Magnetic disks and heads are the most technologically demanding of these components and perform the core functions of digital storage (in the case of disks) and the recording and retrieval of data (in the case of heads). Disk suppliers sell their output on an OEM basis to disk drive manufacturers. The latter, in turn, sell primarily on an OEM basis to computer manufacturers. While both disk and disk drive suppliers were once plentiful, both demand and supply sides of the market for thin film disks have consolidated dramatically over the past decade, despite rapidly increasing demand for digital storage. The need for extremely rapid technical improvements, the high cost of R&D programs and exceedingly high fixed manufacturing costs have been the impetus behind such consolidation.

As one often observes in industries with a small number of incumbent suppliers and customers, high fixed manufacturing costs and high switching costs, individual magnetic disk producers have long since paired up with individual magnetic disk customers. This feature, in addition to high fixed costs per se, makes entry virtually impossible. Because established customer relationships are a very significant, if not insurmountable, barrier to entry, a fairly extensive analysis of market structure is necessary in this case to determine whether USS should earn above-normal returns, given its key role in establishing and maintaining customer relationships.

We analyze the intercompany transactions between USS and FP under both the comparable profits method and our alternative numerical standards approach.

E. King, *Transfer Pricing and Corporate Taxation*,
DOI 10.1007/978-0-387-78183-9_7, © Springer Science+Business Media, LLC 2009

7.1 Summary of Key Facts

USS engages in the following principal activities: Product and process development services, product prototyping services and customer relationship management services. USS' research facilities are located in close proximity to its customers' design centers. Broadly stated, the objective of the Group's research is to increase areal (or storage) density. Over the past two decades, storage density has increased at a rate of approximately 40% per annum. Storage density is determined jointly by:

1. Flying height (the minimum distance at which read/write heads can reliably pass over the surface of a disk to detect a change in magnetic polarity when reading from the disk);
2. Signal-to-noise ratio (the ability of the head to discriminate a signal from background media noise); and,
3. Coercivity (the strength of the magnetic field required to change the polarity of a bit of data on the magnetic layer of a disk when writing).

USS' research team of approximately 300 individuals works on projects in each of these areas. As the above determinants indicate, increases in storage density are accomplished through technological improvements in both disks and heads, and the two components must remain "in sync." As such, one-sided improvements in heads (or disks) generally have to be accompanied by corresponding changes in disks (or heads). Additionally, independent suppliers' disks must work in conjunction with the relatively wide range of heads used by their customers. For these reasons, research activities are highly collaborative, involving thin film disk suppliers, head suppliers and disk drive suppliers.

Given the structure of the market for magnetic disks (described below), and the fact that FP supplies disks to only three principal customers, there is a limited role for sales and marketing in the traditional sense. Instead, USS is engaged predominantly in maintaining already-established customer relationships. Its account managers and customer service specialists collectively deal with order placement, delivery scheduling and addressing customers' day-to-day concerns. They are also responsible for sales forecasting on a Group-wide basis. Individual staff members are dedicated to individual customers.

FP has volume purchase agreements in place with all three of its customers, although the latter do not make binding commitments through these vehicles. Two of these customers have internal disk manufacturing capacity, and look to the Group as a secondary supplier. Therefore, these suppliers' volume "commitments" to FP are honored only insofar as their own disk manufacturing capacity falls short of their requirements by the full amount of such commitments. Customers are not penalized for the cancellation of orders, and only individual purchase orders are regarded as firm for production planning purposes.

FP owns all of the Group's manufacturing facilities and intangible assets, performs all manufacturing functions, acts as the principal in transactions with customers, bears all associated risks and engages in extensive process and equipment development and testing. More concretely, FP enters and processes orders, and schedules production accordingly. It sources raw materials, handles all aspects of inbound and outbound logistics, manufactures all magnetic disks, invoices customers, collects receivables and contributes very substantially to the development and implementation of new processes, manufacturing equipment and testing equipment. As the principal on all sales of magnetic media, FP bears the associated market, inventory, credit and collections, foreign exchange and environmental liability risks.[1]

The manufacture of thin film magnetic disks is an exceedingly precise and complex process. It entails converting aluminum substrates into finished data storage media through the deposition of uniform, microscopic layers of magnetic film. The finished product is manufactured to nano-level specifications. The disk manufacturing process consists of five stages, most of which are conducted in Class 100 (or more restrictive) clean room environments. These five stages are summarized below.

1. **Substrate machining and grinding**: A raw aluminum blank substrate is machined for edge and surface preparation prior to nickel alloy plating. This process sets the ultra smooth surface finish for the aluminum substrates. The substrates are annealed to relieve stress in the material and to temper the parts for the next steps in the manufacturing process.
2. **Nickel alloy plating**: Through a series of chemical baths, ground aluminum substrates are plated with a nickel phosphorus layer in order to provide support for the magnetic layers.
3. **Nickel polishing and cleaning**: The nickel phosphorus layer is polished to a mirror finish and cleaned to enable the read–write heads in the disk drives to fly at low and constant heights over the disks.
4. **Sputtering and lubricating**: Magnetic film is deposited onto the polished substrate by means of a technically demanding vacuum deposition process. During the sputtering process, microscopic magnetic layers are successively deposited on the disk. These layers ultimately provide the magnetic storage capacity for data. The disk is finished with an ultra-thin carbon overcoat. The properties of this final overcoat barrier are equivalent to laying a fine film of diamond over the surface. After sputtering, a monolayer of lubricant is applied to the disk's surface to improve durability and reduce surface friction.
5. **Testing and certification**: In robotically controlled test cells, disks are optically screened for surface defects. Read/write heads are then positioned over the surface to identify microscopic imperfections and ensure superior magnetic properties, which directly influence the storage capacity of the disk. Additional tests may also be run, as required by individual disk drive manufacturers. (Disks are also subjected to numerous tests at various phases of the manufacturing process.)

---

[1] Environmental liability risks relate to the use, storage, discharge and disposal of hazardous materials, the treatment of water used in the disk manufacturing processes and air quality management.

7.2 Transfer Pricing Issues

As the above description suggests, USS renders both R&D/engineering and customer relationship management services to FP. Under U.S. and foreign transfer pricing regimes, it should be paid arm's length fees for these services. However, inasmuch as USS is responsible for establishing and maintaining customer relationships, we must also ascertain whether it has developed a valuable intangible asset, on which it should earn a return separate and apart from its services fees. This is our analytical starting point.

7.3 Value of Customer Relationships

Demand for digital storage has increased at an annual rate of approximately 60% over the first half of this decade, for a variety of reasons. First, progressively more information is stored in digital form (e.g., hospital records and library collections). Demand for mobile computing products (notebook computers) is also increasing markedly, and firms have turned to new data management technologies, such as dedicated storage area networks. Moreover, certain new consumer electronic and imaging products require much more storage capacity than traditional consumer products, among them high-definition television, digital video recorders, digital music players and video game consoles. This sharply increasing demand for digital storage necessitates increases in both magnetic disk production capacity and the number of bits that can be stored on individual disks.

The extremely rapid growth in demand for digital storage notwithstanding, disk and disk drive suppliers' end-use markets rise and fall with broad macroeconomic trends. Discretionary consumer spending and firm investment in capital equipment (including computers and storage systems) decline when the economy is weak, and with it, demand for magnetic media and other components used in the manufacture of disk drives. Hence, demand for disks has historically been highly volatile, and will continue in this pattern unless and until disk drives are incorporated into non-discretionary products. Independent magnetic disk producers face greater volatility in demand for their products than captive suppliers (disk suppliers that are vertically integrated into the manufacture of drives), in that the latter will cease to purchase disks on the external market if their internal capacity suffices.

As previously noted, the supply sides of the markets for magnetic disks and heads are extremely concentrated. There is only one independent supplier of heads worldwide at present (TDK), and a handful of independent suppliers of magnetic disks (Showa Denko KK, Fuji Electric and Hoya Corp.). Similarly, the demand sides of the markets for magnetic disks and heads (composed of disk drive manufacturers) are highly concentrated. Seagate Technology, Western Digital Corporation and Hitachi Global Storage Technologies are the largest disk drive manufacturers in the world. All of these major consumers of magnetic disks have internal disk manufacturing operations, which they naturally attempt to keep fully utilized.[2] Seagate Technology produces approximately 85% of its disk requirements internally, and outsources the balance to a combination of vendors. Hitachi manufactures most of its glass-based media requirements internally, while independent suppliers manufacture the majority of Hitachi's aluminum disk requirements. With its acquisition of the Komag Group, Western Digital Corporation now manufactures a large proportion of its magnetic disk requirements internally. Samsung Electronics, Inc., Toshiba Corporation and Fujitsu are substantially smaller disk drive suppliers. While they do not produce disks, they are integrated forward into the manufacture of computers.

The number of firms on both sides of the markets for disks and heads has progressively declined over the past two decades, despite the recent, dramatic annual increases in demand for digital storage capacity. Disk drive manufacturers numbered 77 in the mid-1980s; there are now only 8 such firms worldwide.[3,4] The number of magnetic disk and head suppliers has likewise diminished sharply over the same period. Consolidation on both sides of the markets for magnetic media and read-write heads has been driven largely by the capital-intensive nature of disk and head manufacturing processes and the need for enormous investments in R&D on an annual basis. Read–write heads, which most disk drive suppliers now produce internally, are manufactured with thin film and photolithographic processes similar to those used to produce semiconductor integrated circuits. The manufacturing process entails more than 300 steps, virtually all of which take place in clean room environments. Disk drive customers, such as Dell, IBM and Hewlett-Packard, demand constant improvements in storage capacity, spindle rotation speed (which in turn influences the speed of data access), average seek time (the amount of time needed to position a head over a selected track on a disk surface), etc.

Magnetic disk manufacturing equipment is highly automated, facilities consist largely of clean room environments, and manufacturing technologies are extremely sophisticated, a necessity in view of the fact that finished disks are made to

---

[2] There are advantages and disadvantages to having internal magnetic disk manufacturing capabilities. Disk drive manufacturers without internal capacity have a lower overall cost structure, in that they do not incur costs associated with the research, development and manufacture of magnetic disks, much of which are fixed. Conversely, if a firm relies entirely on internal capacity, it may not remain cost-competitive and its disk technology may evolve in ways that are not consistent with the industry as a whole. IBM found itself in this position, and was motivated thereby to sell its disk operations to Hitachi. Seagate attempts to avoid this dilemma by using independent suppliers as a benchmark to ensure that its internal operations remain competitive in terms of both yield and technology.

[3] See Wong, Nicole C., "Seagate: The Big Fish in the Shrinking Hard-Drive Pond," *Mercury News*, April 15, 2007.

[4] Moreover, consolidation is still ongoing. At present, Toshiba and Fujitsu are likely targets. Additionally, Hitachi has reportedly been suffering large losses on its disk manufacturing operations, acquired from IBM. (These losses are in part attributable to the fact that Hitachi has not integrated the acquired operations into its existing operations or rationalized its disk manufacturing facilities as a whole.) These losses have prompted speculation that it too may sell off its disk manufacturing operations.

extraordinarily precise nano specifications. (Read–write heads fly over thin film disks with fly heights of less than 0.20 millionths of an inch.) A new entrant would have to invest approximately $1 billion to construct manufacturing facilities comparable to incumbent magnetic disk suppliers' existing facilities, leaving aside the investments necessary to develop the requisite technology and know-how. The magnitude of these outlays, coupled with incumbent disk suppliers' established relationships with disk drive customers, constitutes formidable barriers to entry.

There are a number of important structural parallels between the markets for magnetic disks and disk drives. Such parallels include (a) the use of advanced manufacturing technologies with very high fixed costs, (b) a small base of large suppliers and customers, (c) customers' dual role as competitors vis-a-vis their suppliers, (d) industry standards regarding technical form, fit and function that effectively preclude product differentiation to any significant degree, and (e) the volatility of demand. Several notable dynamics common to both magnetic disk and disk drive markets flow from these structural characteristics:

- Despite the limited number of competitors, suppliers compete fiercely in price, and prices have historically eroded over time;
- Despite declining prices, suppliers invest vast sums in RD&E, as noted, and innovate extremely rapidly[5]; and,
- Close relationships with customers are a *sine qua non* of participation on the supply side of the market and constitute a formidable barrier to entry, as noted. At the same time, established customer relationships do *not* enable suppliers to earn above-normal returns.

Each of these points is addressed in greater detail below.

7.3.1 Declining Average Prices

Over an individual disk drive product's life cycle, its price steadily declines. Moreover, aggressive pricing of new disk drive products is standard practice, as the following quote by Seagate Technology attests to:

> Our competitors have historically offered new or existing products at lower prices as part of a strategy to gain or retain market share and customers, and we expect these practices to continue. Even during periods when demand for disk drives is growing, our industry is price competitive and vendors experience price erosion over the life of a product.[6]

The same observation applies equally to magnetic media. There are certain general reasons for this trend. First, both disk drive suppliers and magnetic disk suppliers sell a relatively standardized and substitutable product to *individual*

---

[5] For example, Western Digital Corporation's R&D expenses were $297 million, $240 million and $202 million in 2006, 2005 and 2004, respectively. Seagate Technology's R&D expenses were $805 million, $645 million and $666 million in FY 2006, 2005 and 2004, respectively.

[6] See page 10 of Seagate Technology's Form 10-K filing with the Securities and Exchange Commission, covering its 2006 fiscal year.

customers (although disks and drives are customized). This is necessarily the case in part because customers routinely dual-source. Moreover, firms must comport with certain industry standards, as noted.[7] Additionally, disk drive suppliers' and magnetic disk suppliers' extremely high fixed costs make it imperative to produce at the highest volume possible, in order to exploit economies of scale. The need to gain and maintain market share further contributes to intense price competition; it is in individual firms' interest to produce at any price that covers its variable costs and some fraction (even a very small fraction) of its fixed costs. While incurring a loss at such prices, firms will nonetheless reduce the loss (equal to fixed costs) that they would otherwise bear.

The factors discussed above—homogenous products and high fixed costs—are widely recognized and relatively generic factors contributing to price competition. Additionally, a variety of industry-specific factors heighten competition in the markets for magnetic disks and disk drives. In both markets, certain suppliers are vertically integrated or horizontally diversified, as noted. More specifically, certain manufacturers of disk drives also manufacture other computer components and/or sell computers; certain manufacturers of magnetic disks also manufacture disk drives. Integrated suppliers are able to price disk drives or magnetic disks very aggressively and recoup profits on other components or complete systems. Moreover, those disk drive suppliers (and computer manufacturers) that both manufacture and externally source disks (or disk drives), and have underutilized capacity, will only purchase externally if the purchase price is lower than their own manufacturing costs.

The volatility of demand for magnetic disks and disk drives further contributes to price competition. As noted, demand for computer and storage systems and consumer electronics products is closely correlated with broad, macroeconomic trends, and demand for magnetic disks and disk drives is derived therefrom. As such, it rises and falls with business cycles. The cycling of demand for magnetic disks and disk drives is exacerbated on the upside by manufacturers' practice of hoarding core components in anticipation of shortages, and on the downside by the rapid buildup of excess inventories and firms' efforts to liquidate these stocks. The introduction of new operating systems or semiconductor improvements can also exaggerate swings in demand.

As discussed below in greater detail, the rate of technological change is extremely rapid in the computer, disk drive and magnetic media industries. As a corollary, the rate of obsolescence is similarly high. As disk drives and disks held in stock become obsolete, firms price these products extremely aggressively. Finally, highly concentrated customer bases are another important factor contributing to price competitiveness in the disk drive and magnetic disk markets.[8] This state of

---

[7] As such, suppliers are unable to differentiate their products significantly, one common means of ameliorating pricing pressures by circumventing head-to-head competition.

[8] As Seagate Technology puts it, "[s]ome of our key customers, including Hewlett-Packard, Dell, EMC, Microsoft and IBM, account for a large portion of our disk drive revenue." See Seagate Technology's Form 10-K filing with the Securities and Exchange Commission for its fiscal year 2006.

affairs, coupled with the fact that suppliers intermittently have excess capacity, means that customers can exercise a significant amount of market power vis-a-vis their suppliers. As expressed by Western Digital Corporation, "[c]ustomers have a variety of suppliers to choose from and therefore can make substantial demands on us, including demands on product pricing and on contractual terms ...."[9]

7.3.2 Rapid Rates of Technological Change

The introduction of new products is a common form of non-price competition. If a given firm is first to market with a new disk drive or magnetic disk with expanded functionality, it will make substantial gains in market share and realize the associated scale economies. New product introductions are also a means of counterbalancing declining prices over the life cycle of a product. At any point in time, a supplier's revenue stream is a volume-weighted average of revenues earned on the sale of products at various phases of their respective life cycles.

There are also several factors specific to the computer industry that motivate very large investments in R&D throughout the supply chain. Demand for computers is driven in large part by new functionality (greater storage capacity, faster computing speed, faster access to data, higher screen resolution, greater reliability, etc.). Such improvements render installed systems obsolete. Stated differently, the economically useful lives of computers must be significantly shorter than their physical lives to sustain the current level of demand for computers. The functionality of computers depends principally on the functionality of disk drives (and certain other componentry). The functionality of disk drives, in turn, is highly dependent on the areal density of magnetic media (the number of bits that can be stored per square inch of disk), as is evident in a general sense from Western Digital Corporation's commentary:

> [T]he success of our [disk drive] products depends on our ability to gain access to and integrate parts [magnetic media and heads] that are "best in class" from reliable component suppliers.[10]

This technological interdependence throughout the supply chain induces computer manufacturers and disk drive manufacturers to exert a great deal of pressure on their respective suppliers to innovate continuously. Moreover, because components (e.g., disks and heads) must be compatible, technological innovations must be synchronized. Such alignment of "product roadmaps" requires very close collaboration between computer manufacturers and disk drive suppliers, on the one hand, and disk drive suppliers and magnetic media (and head) suppliers, on the other.

---

[9] See Western Digital Corporation's Form 10-K filing with the Securities and Exchange Commission, covering its 2006 taxable year.

[10] Ibid, p. 26.

7.3.3 Established Customer Relationships

Relationships with key customers are very important to disk drive suppliers and magnetic disk suppliers alike. As Western Digital Corporation expresses it, "[o]ur ability to maintain strong relationships with our principal customers is essential to our future performance. If we lose a key customer [or] if any of our key customers reduce their orders of our products or require us to reduce our prices before we are able to reduce costs, ... then our operating results would likely be harmed."

To a significant extent, close customer relationships are a natural outgrowth of technical collaboration:

> [The] ability to have our design teams work in ... close proximity to our customers has, in part, facilitated the strong and collaborative customer relationships that we have established with these large disk drive manufacturers. We devote significant time working with our customers to produce disks that are highly specialized and customized for our customers' particular technological requirements, and these close relationships provide added insight into our customers' product and technology roadmaps.[11]

Long term contracts between suppliers and customers are the norm in both magnetic disk and disk drive markets. However, they are largely for the benefit of customers, as Seagate Technology observes in the following commentary:

> OEM customers typically enter into master purchase agreements with us. These agreements provide for pricing, volume discounts, order lead times, product support obligations and other terms and conditions. The term of these agreements is usually 12 to 36 months, although our product support obligations generally extend substantially beyond this period. These master agreements typically do not commit the customer to buy any minimum quantity of products, or create exclusive relationships. ... In addition, with limited lead time, customers may cancel or defer most purchase orders without significant penalty. Anticipated orders from many of our customers have in the past failed to materialize or OEM delivery schedules have been deferred or altered as a result of changes in their business needs.

Correspondingly, independent magnetic disk suppliers generally have volume purchase agreements with their major customers. However, as with disk drive suppliers' OEM customers, buyers of magnetic disks (disk drive suppliers) do not make binding commitments through these vehicles, as previously noted, and are not penalized for the cancellation of orders.

Therefore, while constituting a formidable entry barrier, established relationships with customers do not enable magnetic disk suppliers to earn above-normal rates of return. More particularly:

- Established customer relationships do not enable magnetic disk suppliers to innovate less rapidly or to charge constant (or increasing) prices for their disks. To the contrary, as previously described, suppliers' dependence on a small number of customers that (a) have internal disk manufacturing capacity, (b) must themselves contend with steady declines in their disk drive selling prices, (c) are

---

[11] See Komag, Incorporated's Form 10-K filing with the Securities and Exchange Commission, covering its 2006 taxable year.

forced by their OEM customers to deliver constantly improving disk drives, and
(d) depend on their disk suppliers to enhance their own products' functionality,
generates extreme pressure on independent magnetic disk suppliers to innovate
continuously and steadily reduce disk prices.

- Established customer relationships do not enable independent magnetic disk suppliers to realize marketing cost savings. Although disk suppliers have no need
(or real opportunity) to solicit new customers, their existing customers demand
an extremely high level of interaction and service. Hence, while disk suppliers'
customer-related expenditures are more in the nature of customer service than
selling per se, they are not lower by virtue of their established customer base.
- Independent magnetic disk suppliers do not benefit from their respective established customer bases by means of a reduction in the volatility of their earnings.
Individual customers' volume "commitments" do not constitute a guaranteed
stream of income. Despite the fact that such commitments are part of long-term,
written contracts, they are not legally binding, as noted, and disk suppliers do not
penalize customers for the cancellation of orders or reductions in order volumes.

Based on this analysis of market structure and dynamics, we conclude that USS
should *not* earn a return, over and above its services fees, in consideration for its
development of customer relationship intangible assets.

7.4 Analysis Under Existing Regime

Consider next USS' arm's length consideration for services rendered to FP, as determined under the existing transfer pricing regime.

7.4.1 Application of Best Method Rule

The R&D and engineering services that USS renders to FP are integral to the latter's
business and "contribute significantly to its key competitive advantages, core capabilities [and] fundamental chances of success or failure." As such, USS' R&D and
engineering services fees should include a profit element, in addition to the recovery
of its associated costs.

The customer-related services that USS renders to FP consist predominantly of
liaison functions and sales forecasting. These activities are routine, and companies
in a broad range of industries perform them. However, given the importance of customer relationships in this industry, we conclude that a markup is warranted on these
services as well. (Moreover, a reasonable argument could be made that the services
at issue are included on the U.S. Temporary Regulations' "black list" of services.)

To the end of applying the comparable uncontrolled services price method to
establish USS' arm's length fees for R&D and engineering services, we identified
a number of engineering services agreements between unrelated parties. Some of
these agreements were attached to one (or both) of the parties' Form 10-K filings

with the Securities and Exchange Commission. However, in most instances, the filing companies requested confidential treatment of the agreements, and all pricing information was redacted. As such, we were unable to use the comparable uncontrolled services price method to establish USS' arm's length R&D and engineering services fees. The same issue arose with respect to USS' customer relationship management services.

The cost of services plus method does not apply to USS' performance of R&D and engineering services or to its customer relationship management services. USS does not render either of these services to third parties. USS' customer relationship management activities could reasonably be characterized as liaison services rendered on behalf of FP, and, in principle, the gross services margin method may therefore apply. However, as illustrated by certain of the examples given in the U.S. Temporary Regulations, this method is intended to address situations in which the tested party functions as a commission agent. Standalone commission agents typically perform liaison functions in relation to comparatively small prospective customers rather than current customers with very large-scale operations and correspondingly high-volume purchases. Accordingly, commission agents are not sufficiently comparable to USS, and the gross services margin method would not produce reliable results in this instance.

As described in Chapter 3, the residual profit split method is ordinarily reserved for controlled transactions that involve "a combination of non-routine contributions by multiple controlled taxpayers." USS does not make non-routine contributions of significant value in rendering services to FP. While it manufactures prototypes as part of its R&D services, all of the proprietary intellectual property utilized in the development and manufacture of disks is owned by FP. While the Group has long-standing relationships with disk drive suppliers, these relationships do not enable it to earn above-normal returns, as discussed at length above. Stated differently, established customer relationships are "routine intangibles," and do not generate residual income.

Given that the safe harbor services cost method, the comparable uncontrolled services price method, the gross services margin method, the cost of services plus method and the residual profit split method do not apply, we utilize the comparable profits method to establish USS' arm's length fees for the R&D, engineering and customer relationship management services that it renders to FP. Because several of the companies included in each of our samples reported only segment revenues and segment operating profits, as discussed below, we utilize reported markups over total cost as our profit level indicator. (The alternatives would have entailed working with significantly smaller samples.)

7.4.2 Application of Selected Method: CRM Services

As noted, we establish arm's length fees for USS' customer relationship management services by application of the comparable profits method. We identified independent companies in the business of rendering CRM and other business process outsourcing services by means of the following keyword and industry segment searches:

1. Keyword = Customer Care; Industry Segment = Business Services
2. Keyword = Business Process Outsourcing; Industry Segment = Business Services
3. Keyword = Liaise; Industry Segment = Business Services
4. Keyword = Customer Relationship Management; Industry Segment = Business Services

Upon reviewing descriptions of business for all firms identified through the above searches, we screened out those that (a) received rather than rendered customer relationship management services; (b) provided CRM services in combination with a host of other services, and did not provide segmented results; (c) were start-up companies whose results could not be taken as indicative of arm's length results for established services providers; or (d) reported losses in consecutive years. Following this process of elimination, eight companies remained in our CRM sample. While these firms deal with a much larger base of customers than USS, and in some instances they perform a broader range of intermediary functions, their core role as liaison between end customers and manufacturers is effectively the same. Moreover, both USS and our comparable CRM services providers render back-office functions as part of their role (e.g., order processing, tracking of shipments, the handling of claims and billing issues).

The eight customer relationship management services providers included in our sample reported markups over total cost ranging from a high of 12.64% to a low of (5.54)% in 2007, a high of 16.24% to a low of (5.76)% in 2006 and a high of 14.84% to a low of (2.24)% in 2005. The median markup for this sample amounted to 5.89% in 2007, 3.82% in 2006 and 2.11% in 2005. Based on these results, USS should charge FP a markup over total associated costs of 5.0%–6.0% for CRM services rendered.

7.4.3 Application of Selected Method: R&D Services

As noted above, we establish arm's length fees for USS' R&D and engineering services by means of the comparable profits method as well. To the end of identifying standalone high-end engineering services providers, we undertook the following keyword and industry segment searches:

1. Keyword = "Process Engineering"; Industry Segment = "Business Services"
2. Keyword = "Mechanical Engineering"; Industry Segment = "Business Services"
3. Keyword = "Engineering Services"; Industry Segment = "Business Services"
4. Keywords = "Engineering" and "Materials"; Industry Segment = "Business Services"
5. Keyword = "Magnetic"; Industry Segment = "Business Services"

6. Keyword = "Nano"; Industry Segment = "Business Services"
7. Keyword = "Materials Science"; Industry Segment = "Business Services"
8. Keywords = "Engineering" and "Molecular"; Industry Segment = "Unspecified"
9. Keyword = "Deposition or Sputtering"; Industry Segment = "Unspecified"
10. Keywords = "Engineering Services" and "Materials Science"; Industry Segment = "Unspecified"
11. Keyword = "Process Engineering Services Agreement"; Industry Segment = "Unspecified"
12. Keyword = "Engineering Services Fees"; Industry Segment = "Unspecified"
13. Keywords = "Engineering Services" and "Nano"; Industry Segment = "Unspecified"

We reviewed descriptions of business for all of the companies identified by the above keyword and industry segment searches. Firms were excluded from our sample for four principal reasons:

- Firm specialized in construction-related design–build–operate engineering services, which differ significantly from the product and process development engineering services that USS renders;
- Firm offered services unrelated to engineering and product development (e.g., storage services, bank card payment processing services, marketing services, grading and authentication services, drug development and clinical testing services, network services and testing and inspection services);
- Firm engaged in activities other than services (e.g., the auctioning of transportation and industrial equipment; the manufacture and sale of apparel; R&D relating to hybrid engines for commercialization; the design, development, manufacture and sale of ceramic components; the development of lithium batteries and fuel cell components; the development of applications software; and, the operation of a semiconductor foundry); or,
- Firm was in a start-up phase.

Following this process of elimination, six engineering services providers remained in our sample. These companies reported markups over total cost ranging from a low of 0.91% to a high of 14.78% in 2007, a low of (0.24)% to a high of 16.64% in 2006 and a low of 1.64% to a high of 16.11% in 2005. The median markup for our engineering services sample was 6.84% in 2007, 7.59% in 2006 and 6.18% in 2005. Based on these results, USS should charge FP a markup over total associated costs of 7.0%–8.0% for engineering services rendered.

7.5 Analysis Under Alternative Regime

As with our second case study, we would analyze this case by application of the numerical standards approach under the proposed alternative transfer pricing regime. With two distinct types of services, which differ significantly with respect to the degree of specialized skills required, we would look to different services safe harbors. It should be noted, that an analysis of market structure and dynamics would still be necessary to establish whether, in the course of providing CRM, R&D and engineering services, USS had developed a valuable customer-based intangible asset, on which it should earn a separate return.

7.6 Comparison

Our analysis of this case under the current services regulations is rather burdensome, and there is no assurance that the IRS and other taxing authorities would accept our choice of methods and sample selection procedures. Moreover, considering the vast number of multinational firms that must establish arm's length fees for intercompany services of various kinds, the burden, viewed from a broader perspective, is enormous. The numerical standards approach, which would provide a number of safe harbor ranges for services requiring different skill levels, would eliminate much of this work.

In contrast to the dwindling number of standalone U.S. distributors, independent services providers have proliferated over the past decade, as firms have increasingly outsourced non-core functions. As such, taxing authorities would have considerable data on which to draw in establishing safe harbor ranges. However, even with such safe harbor ranges in place, it would still be important to ascertain whether individual services providers developed valuable intangible assets, such as established customer relationships, in the course of rendering services, and, if so, to determine how much income should be ascribed to these assets.

Chapter 8
Replication of Internet-Based Business Model

Despite the fact that national boundaries do not exist in cyberspace, customers in different countries are clearly more adept at navigating and transacting on websites designed by domestic companies, with a "look-and-feel" and user interface features with which they are familiar. Moreover, legal restrictions vis-a-vis e-commerce vary to some degree by country, making firms similarly more comfortable dealing with customers in their own geographic "backyard". (For example, the treatment of proprietary customer data is more highly regulated in European countries, as compared with the United States.)

As a result of these national differences, many e-commerce businesses have expanded through a process of replication, beginning in one geographic market and sequentially expanding to other geographic markets (with certain market-specific modifications as needed). This method of expansion poses certain difficulties vis-a-vis transfer pricing, because a unique (and potentially patented) business model is generally among the intangible assets transferred intercompany. However, business models per se are generally not transferred or sold individually, absent the sale of a going concern or the license of a franchise.

Our fourth case study involves a U.S. parent company ("USP") and a European subsidiary ("FS"). USP has developed a novel e-commerce business in its domestic market, which has proven to be very successful, and is in the process of expanding into Europe. We analyze this case, which typifies the difficulties noted above, under the franchise model. It is not amenable to analysis under the existing regime.

8.1 Summary of Key Facts

USP is an online marketing services company that enables its customers—web-based firms and traditional retailers with a presence on the Internet—to target email advertisements to relatively small subsets of consumers, based on detailed statistical analyses of purchasing patterns by gender, age, geographic location, level of educational attainment, home ownership and value, and other pertinent variables. More particularly, USP performs extensive data analysis (utilizing both internal and external data sources), develops creative content and formulates highly customized

E. King, *Transfer Pricing and Corporate Taxation*,
DOI 10.1007/978-0-387-78183-9_8, © Springer Science+Business Media, LLC 2009

marketing strategies. USP currently has a customer base of 475 clients, all of which operate websites in North America.

As noted, USP draws on both public data (e.g., census data and credit histories) and information obtained directly from customers in the course of rendering its marketing services. Its data analysis, based on standard statistical methods, is not proprietary. However, key aspects of its business model, such as the rewards-based process by which it elicits private data from customers, are proprietary and have proven to be exceptionally effective. USP is compensated for its services by commission, based on certain metrics designed to measure success (i.e., the increase in sales attributable to its marketing programs), as negotiated with individual clients.

From an organizational standpoint, USP is composed of the following four core groups: Business Development, Account Management, Marketing and Information Technology (IT). Additionally, USP performs a number of support functions, including customer service, human resources (HR), legal, finance, tax and internal audit. Each of these functions is described briefly below.

8.1.1 USP: Business Development Group

USP's Business Development Group is responsible for developing new client relationships. It makes initial contact with prospective clients through a number of different channels, among them email, trade shows, cold calls, etc. If prospects express interest during these initial contacts, USP's Business Development staff will meet face-to-face at the prospective client's location. At this first meeting, members of the Business Development Group will describe USP's marketing programs, walk through the process by which individual customers' private information is solicited and how they are rewarded, illustrate USP's analytical and creative contributions and the economic benefits to prospects through case studies, and briefly review certain metrics of success that it has used with other clients.

This initial meeting is followed by discussions with client constituencies who were not represented at the meeting, negotiations over the economics of the program to be offered, technical and other discussions with the prospective client's IT and marketing staffs, etc. The sales cycle ranges from 90 days to a full year and is completed with the execution of a contract. USP concludes contracts with approximately 30%–35% of prospects that express an interest in implementing a highly customized direct marketing program during their initial contact.

8.1.2 USP: Account Management Group

USP's Account Management Group is responsible for managing all aspects of client relationships once clients have entered into a contract with the Company. At the outset, the Account Management Group works with clients to develop and launch an initial campaign. Among other things, this step entails (a) providing clients with USP's data solicitations page, (b) implementing data feed protocols and procedures such that information obtained through the solicitations page is provided to USP in a secure and timely fashion, and (c) ensuring that all legal and client-specific disclosure requirements are fully satisfied.

After the initial launch, the Account Management Group handles all technical, financial, marketing, customer service and other aspects of ongoing relationships with clients. Payment or fee issues may arise, for example, if clients and USP have different assessments of the increase in sales volume attributable to the direct marketing program (although both assessments will be based on the same negotiated metric). USP's Account Management Group is also in regular contact with its clients' marketing staffs to assess the effectiveness of its direct marketing campaigns, determine how to modify the program or its presentation so as to optimize response rates, etc.

8.1.3 USP: Marketing Group

USP's Marketing Group is divided into two subgroups. The first of these subgroups is responsible for testing and maximizing response rates to the data solicitations page. It does so by varying the format of the page and the range of information requested, and developing and evaluating specific rewards. The other subgroup consists of copy writers, graphic artists and production teams. These individuals are responsible for designing and producing USP's data solicitations pages and customized direct marketing messages.

8.1.4 USP: Information Technology Group

USP's IT Group has developed all of its core software internally, which has the following functionality:

1. IT tools that support the Marketing Group's online data solicitation and testing procedures, parse response rates by page design, content and reward, and estimate the volume of purchases attributable to USP's direct marketing programs;
2. Software that resides on USP's server; and,
3. Software that facilitates online communications with clients' customers.

USP's IT Group is constantly in the process of maintaining, testing and upgrading its systems and building in new functionality. The Company's IT infrastructural and maintenance costs include Oracle license fees, hardware, hosting and telecom costs, voice/data systems costs, network engineering, etc.

8.1.5 USP: Customer Service

USP has a large Customer Service Group, which responds to clients' and customers' inquiries regarding safeguards in place to maintain the confidentiality of personal data, the use of such data, rewards, measures of program effectiveness, etc.

8.1.6 USP: Legal

USP's Legal Group handles a wide range of issues, among them (a) drafting contracts with clients, (b) handling contentious employment matters, (c) reviewing and approving data solicitations pages, marketing materials and copy, (d) managing compliance issues, and (e) handling litigation.

8.1.7 USP: Finance, Tax, Internal Audit and Back-Office

USP performs financial planning and analysis, prepares financial statements, budgets and forecasts, assesses the adequacy of financial controls, and reviews technical accounting issues as needed.

8.1.8 FS

FS was established in late 2007. The Managing Director of FS, who was hired at about the same time, spent several months at the facilities of USP to familiarize himself with its business model and organizational structure. FS has effectively replicated USP's business model in one European country, although certain support functions that are not customer-facing have remained centralized in USP. More particularly, FS has Business Development, Account Management and Marketing Groups. USP performs customer service, legal, finance, tax, internal audit and back-office services on behalf of FS.

The Managing Director of FS has weekly conference calls with his U.S. counterpart and monthly calls with the Senior Vice Presidents of USP. These discussions are largely for purposes of providing status updates and to obtain advice on operational issues that have arisen.

8.2 Transfer Pricing Issues

USP and FS engage in intercompany transactions in intangible assets and services. More particularly, USP has transferred the following intellectual property to FS:

1. <u>An established business model</u>. Elements of USP's business model are patented, and FS has replicated this model.
2. <u>Proprietary software</u>. To a large extent, USP's internally developed software is directly transferable to the European market, although its IT Group has made certain minor modifications, and anticipates having to further customize elements of its software for the European market as FS' operations grow.
3. <u>Trademark and name</u>. FS will have rights to use USP's trademark and name in the European market.

4. Data solicitation and marketing tools. USP utilizes "control pages" (or base pages) in developing different data solicitation and direct marketing formats and content. FS will use these control pages, along with the basic graphics and layout, testing methodologies and other know-how that USP's marketing staff have built up. However, we are advised that both solicitations and direct marketing formats and content have to be adapted to the European market for cultural and legal reasons.

The transfer of this bundle of intangible assets is akin to a business format franchise, which "includes not only the product [or] service and trademark, but the entire business format itself—a marketing strategy and plan, operating manuals and standards, quality control, and continuing two-way communication."[1]

USP's legal, HR and financial planning staffs have also provided, and will continue for some time to provide, certain start-up services to FS. For example, the European Union imposes significantly more stringent controls vis-a-vis consumers' confidential data than the U.S. Government at present. As such, FS was required to register as a Data Controller and to provide the necessary assurances regarding its protocols for the protection of confidential data. USP's legal staff assisted FS in this process. The legal staff has also assisted FS in structuring and drafting its contracts with clients. USP's HR Group developed an employee contract template, with input from the Legal Department. USP's financial planning staff developed an initial budget and projections for FS, based on input from the latter's senior staff and its own results during its ramp-up period.

Lastly, in addition to the above start-up services, USP's IT Group will perform routine software and hardware maintenance on an ongoing basis, provide customization services to FS, and make all software upgrades available to it. USP's legal staff will provide routine legal support for the foreseeable future. Financial planning documents and statements will be prepared by USP's personnel, and payroll, the processing of transactions, and receivables and payables functions will be handled by USP's personnel. Both the President and the CEO of USP will provide high-level advisory services to the Managing Director of FS for some period.

8.3 Analysis Under Existing Regime

Arm's length services fees, payable by FS to USP, can be established under one of several specified transfer pricing methods. However, none of the specified methods under the existing transfer pricing regime can be used to analyze USP's transfer of intangible assets to FS (unless one interprets the franchise model as an application of the inexact comparable uncontrolled transactions (CUT) method).

The CUT method, as currently drafted and applied, requires a higher level of comparability than broadly similar franchise arrangements would satisfy. The resale

---

[1] U.S. Department of Justice, *Franchising in the Economy*, 1988.

price and cost plus methods presuppose a particular division of labor that is not characteristic of USP and FS. The comparable profits method would require identifying quasi-comparable companies in the same start-up stage, and would presumably yield no residual profits (and, therefore, no royalty fee payable to USP). While one might argue that an independent licensor would not require the payment of royalties until its licensee moved beyond its start-up phase and began to earn positive accounting profits, this position is likely to be challenged on audit. Hence, our analysis of this case is solely based on the proposed franchise model.

8.4 Analysis Under Alternative Regime

As described above, FS will replicate USP's operations, with the exception of certain support functions that will remain centralized. This duplication requires that USP transfer its proprietary business format (inclusive of its proprietary IT, its trademarks and its successively refined Internet-based data collection and marketing tools).

In principle, one can analyze each of these intercompany transfers of intangible assets and the performance of services separately. However, business models as such are only transferred as part of a franchise arrangement or an acquisition, not in isolation. This fact makes it difficult to apply the CUT method to individual transactions. Conversely, by bundling USP's intercompany transfers of intellectual property and the performance of certain services, we can apply the inexact CUT method, because the relationship between USP and FS in its totality is akin to that of a franchisor and franchisee:

> Business format franchising is a method by which one business entity expands the distribution of its products and/or services through independent, third party operators. Franchising occurs when the operator of a concept or system (the franchisor) grants an independent businessperson (the franchisee) the right to duplicate its entire business format at a particular location and for a specified period, under terms and conditions set forth in the contract (franchise agreement). The franchisee has full access to all of the trademarks, logos, marketing techniques, controls and systems that have made the franchisor successful ... It is important to keep in mind that the franchisor and franchisee are separate legal entities. Ongoing services [rendered by the franchisor] include research and development, marketing strategies, advertising campaigns, group buying, periodic field visits, training updates [and other forms of support].[2]

The bundling of intellectual property and services is permitted under the IRC Section 482 regulations when it will improve the reliability of one's results:

> The combined effect of two or more separate transactions (whether before, during or after the taxable year under review) may be considered, if such transactions, taken as a whole, are so interrelated that consideration of multiple transactions is the most reliable means of determining the arm's length consideration for the controlled transactions.[3]

---

[2] See Bond, Robert E., *Bond's Franchise Guide*, CA: Source Book Publications, 2006.

[3] See Treas. Reg. Section 1.482-1(f)(2)(i).

Hence, for purposes of our transfer pricing analysis, we liken USP to a franchisor and FS to a franchisee and determine the former's arm's length consideration on this basis. However, despite our aggregation of most intercompany transactions, USP should be *separately* compensated for certain ongoing services that it will render to FS, but that franchisors do not routinely provide to their franchisees. Such services include accounting, tax, HR and legal support services. In contrast, USP's Marketing and IT Groups' activities serve primarily to enhance and refine its proprietary business model and systems, and USP should not charge FS a separate fee therefor. Stated differently, USP will be fully compensated for most of these activities through its franchise fee.[4] Moreover, the regular meetings that USP's senior executives hold (via conference call) with FS' Managing Director are similar to the meetings, conferences and newsletters that independent franchisors utilize to transfer know-how and disseminate information on an ongoing basis to their franchisees. As such, USP will be compensated for these latter contributions by means of its franchise fee as well.

In sum, given the range of intangible assets that USP has transferred to FS, the fact that third parties do not typically license or buy and sell business concepts and systems in isolation, and the fact that USP's relationship with FS closely resembles that of a franchisor with a franchisee, we conclude that bundling transactions will yield the most reliable results under the Best Method Rule in this instance. In analyzing these bundled transactions, we therefore look to arm's length franchise arrangements.

Bond's Franchise Guide, an annual publication, is widely considered to be the most comprehensive source of information on U.S. franchises.[5] We developed our sample of comparable arm's length franchise arrangements through a review of all franchises included in this *Guide* and listed in the following categories:

- Business: Advertising & Promotions
- Business: Internet/Telecommunications/Miscellaneous

Through this process, we identified five broadly comparable franchise arrangements, summarized briefly below.

1. **Coupon Cash Saver:** A direct mail Internet coupon company. Specializes in designing ads for customers that increase their sales. Franchisor instructs franchisees on system, customer acquisition and customer retention. Provides site selection assistance, cooperative advertising, central data processing, centralized purchasing (at additional cost), field operations evaluation, field training and inventory control. Established in 1984. Has ten company-owned units and two franchised units. Franchisees are required to pay an up-front fee of $9,500 and a royalty of 6.0% of net sales on an ongoing basis.

---

[4] However, USP should be separately compensated for the relatively generic IT maintenance and support services that it will render and for the customizaton of its software for the European market.

[5] Bond, Robert E., *Bond's Franchise Guide* (2007 Edition), California: Source Book Publications, 2007.

2. **RSVP Publications:** A direct mail operation that targets upscale consumers. Publications reach approximately 8 million homes. Has over 11,000 clients. Offers extensive training to franchisees. Also provides central purchasing and field training, organizes regional meetings, and operates an 800 hotline number. Established in 1985. Has no company-owned units and 80 franchised units. Franchisees pay an up-front fee of $30,000 and a royalty of 7.0% of net sales on an ongoing basis.

3. **Impressions on Hold:** An advertising company tied to the telecommunications industry. Franchisees enable businesses to use the "on-hold" time of their phone system as a marketing tool. Franchisor provides central data processing, central purchasing, field operations evaluation and field training, publishes a franchisee newsletter, organizes regional meetings (at additional cost) and operates an 800 hotline number. Franchisees are required to pay an up-front fee of $47,000 and a running royalty of 4.0% of net sales. Franchisees must also contribute 1.0% of net sales to an advertising fund.

4. **Netspace:** Consults with companies to help build their business. Utilizes technology available through the Internet. Assists clients to increase sales, reduce costs and improve customer communications. Provides initial and quarterly training, central data processing, central purchasing, field operations evaluation and field training, assistance with initial store opening and inventory control (at additional cost); publishes a franchisee newsletter, organizes regional meetings and operates an 800 hotline number. Established in 1996. Has 40 franchised units and 1 company-owned unit. Franchisees are required to pay an up-front fee of $39,500 and a running royalty of 10.0% of net sales. Franchisees must also contribute 1.0% of net sales to an advertising fund.

5. **WSI Consulting and Education:** Franchisees assist clients (small and medium-sized businesses) to assess their Internet needs and develop a customized Internet marketing solution. Provides at additional cost central data processing, central purchasing, field operations evaluation and assistance with initial store opening; provides at no additional cost an 800 hotline number, publishes a franchisee newsletter and organizes national meetings. Has 1,998 franchised units and 2 company-owned units. Franchisees are required to pay a one-time fee of $49,700 and a running royalty of 10.0% of net sales.

The above sample of comparable B2B arm's length franchise arrangements indicates that running royalties range from 4.0% to 10.0% of net sales, and entitle franchisees to (a) initial training, (b) access to an established business model, (c) rights to use franchisors' other intellectual property, and (d) certain limited ongoing support services. One-time fees range from $9,500 to $49,700.

USP's operations most closely resemble those of *Coupon Cash Saver*, *Netspace* and *WSI Consulting & Education*, in terms of both mandate and medium. In contrast, *Impressions On Hold's* direct marketing activities are tied to the telecommunications industry, and *RSVP Publications'* activities are tied to traditional hardcopy publishing. Based on these considerations, we conclude that USP should charge running royalty fees of 8%–10% of FS' net sales.

USP should also be compensated for the costs that it incurred in rendering start-up assistance during the first 6 months of FS' operations. Under the franchise model, a markup over these start-up costs is not called for. The above-mentioned one-time franchise fees are generally considered to be the means by which franchisors recoup their costs in rendering start-up assistance:

> [Initial lump-sum] franchise fees are often understood in the franchise community as 'payment to reimburse the franchisor for the incurred costs of setting the franchisee up in business – from recruiting through training and manuals.'[6]

It remains to determine whether USP's fees for accounting, general and administrative, tax, legal and HR services should include a profit factor, over and above the associated direct and indirect costs. These services do not contribute to the "key competitive advantages, core capabilities or fundamental risks of success or failure" of FS. Moreover, accounting and auditing, budgeting, tax, general and administrative, HR, routine IT, general legal and related services are "specified covered services" (in the terminology of the U.S. Temporary Regulations). For these reasons, we conclude that USP is permitted to charge FS at cost (without a profit element) for such services.

8.5 Conclusions

The franchise method, which may also be construed as an application of the modified inexact CUT method, is the only feasible means of analyzing certain of the intercompany transactions at issue in this case (i.e., bundled intangible assets). The current transfer pricing regime does not clearly contemplate or provide for this type of analysis.

It should be noted that our analysis of this case is not based on unfounded assumptions regarding market structure. Rather, we base our analysis on the empirically evident fact that franchisors almost always utilize standardized contracts:

> ... [I]f the franchisor is to maximize its profit, economic theory generally suggests that it should tailor its franchise contract terms for each unit and franchisee in a chain. In practice, however, contracts are remarkably uniform within chains and thus insensitive to variations in individual, outlet and specific market conditions. Indeed, a business-format franchisor most often uses a single business-format franchising contract – a single royalty rate and franchise fee combination – for all of its franchised operations that join the chain at a given point in time.[7]

---

[6] See Blair, Roger D. and Francine Lafontaine, *The Economics of Franchising*, New York: Cambridge University Press, 2005, p. 57.

[7] Ibid.

Chapter 9
Sale of Assets with Embedded Intellectual Property

Our fifth case study involves a foreign parent based in Japan (FP) and its U.S. subsidiary (USS). FP has developed, manufactures and sells key elements of an electronic toll collection (ETC) system, certain of which incorporate proprietary technology. USS purchases these ETC system components and assets, and, in some instances, resells them to tolling authorities and performs ongoing program implementation and maintenance services. In other instances, USS retains ownership of the ETC equipment and infrastructure assets, and is responsible for maintaining these assets and implementing the toll collection program. We analyze this case under the resale price method and the required return method.

9.1 Summary of Key Facts

In the United States and elsewhere, the private sector has played an increasingly important role in the provision of public works and services, traditionally the purview of federal, state and municipal governments. This trend is evident in:

- The private construction and ownership of Internet backbones and other core assets that enable the Internet to function;
- The sale of major infrastructure assets that were formerly government-owned in numerous countries (e.g., gas and electric utilities, telephone systems, railroads, seaports and water and wastewater systems);
- Long-term franchises, whereby the private sector provider, or concessionaire, undertakes a large infrastructure project for public use, pays a substantial fee to the governmental authority for the franchise, and retains user fees (or other revenue sources); and,
- The outsourcing of certain services to the private sector that governmental agencies previously performed (e.g., the management of welfare programs, garbage collection, food services, etc.).

The construction and/or operation of private toll roads and electronic toll collection systems are additional examples of governmental authority being ceded to the private sector. ETC systems (e.g., E-Z Pass in much of the Northeastern

E. King, *Transfer Pricing and Corporate Taxation*,
DOI 10.1007/978-0-387-78183-9_9, © Springer Science+Business Media, LLC 2009

United States and FasTrak on the West Coast) have been in place in certain locations for many years,[1] and continue to be installed in new locations.

Simply put, the ETC system automatically collects tolls by establishing a wire-less communication between an electronic roadside device (an antenna) installed in a tollgate and a vehicle unit (a transponder). The motorist's identification number is read from the transponder by the antenna and fed into a computer that debits the vehicle owner's prepaid account. The ETC system also identifies toll violators. ETC software, equipment and infrastructure consist of:

- Automatic vehicle identification (AVI) technology that determines the owner-ship of the vehicle (by means of the aforementioned wireless communication between an antenna installed in the tollgate and connected to a computer and vehicle-mounted transponders). ETC systems generally utilize dedicated short range communications (DSRC) radio frequency to effect the wireless communi-cation.
- Automatic vehicle classification (AVC) technology that permits toll authorities to levy differential tolls on different types of vehicles. Lower-end systems rely on information stored in customer records to make this determination. However, inasmuch as some motorists periodically tow a trailer or a boat, for example, or may affix the ETC tag to different vehicles as needed, such a system will not always be accurate. More sophisticated systems use advanced inductive loop sen-sors embedded in the road surface that can determine vehicle length and number of axles, and light-curtain laser profilers to record the shape of the vehicle.
- Transaction processing hardware and software that permits operators to maintain customer accounts, post toll transactions, handle customer inquiries and send out notices of violation. (Certain firms, such as VESystems, sell or license an ETC software suite to tolling authorities, or provide customer service, violations pro-cessing, video billing, toll operations and program management on an outsourced basis.)
- Video enforcement systems (VES) that identify motorists seeking to evade tolls by passing through the ETC lanes. Inasmuch as these vehicles do not have transponders, stored customer data do not exist. While traditional enforcement methods, such as police patrols and physical barriers (e.g., a gate arm), con-tinue to be used, many VES use digital cameras to collect a series of images that enable violations processing personnel to identify the vehicle's license plate and, in some instances, the motorist.

Toll agencies generally purchase ETC equipment, infrastructure and software. However, the costs of these system components and assets, coupled with installation expenses, can be prohibitively high in certain instances. By the same token, there are well-documented benefits to ETC, among them congestion reduction, substantially increased capacity and throughput, fuel savings, time savings, enhanced data collec-tion and better emission control. ETC's high costs and substantial benefits, and toll

---

[1] The first ETC system in North America was installed on the Dallas North Tollway in 1989.

authorities' limited budgets, have motivated certain suppliers to enter into long-term leases with tolling authorities to operate and maintain roads and install ETC infrastructure and equipment, in return for rights to retain toll revenues. (As noted, these arrangements have involved substantial up-front payments by the concessionaires to the governmental authorities, as with other large-scale infrastructure projects.) On a smaller scale, tolling authorities may negotiate arrangements with suppliers in which the latter retain ownership of the ETC equipment and provide program implementation services, while the tolling authority retains ultimate responsibility for operating the highways, tunnels, bridges and other transportation-related infrastructure under its mandate.

FP develops, manufactures and sells certain ETC equipment and infrastructure assets that embody proprietary technology. The preponderance of FP's sales are to USS, although it also sells in low volumes to local governments in the Middle East and Asia.

FP has developed and funded all proprietary intellectual property embodied in the Group's equipment and infrastructure assets. It also licenses off-the-shelf software to debit customers' prepaid accounts, view violation files and document that data bits have not been changed. FP is likewise the holder of all patents, whether filed in Japan, the United States or elsewhere. Although certain innovations have come about as a result of tolling authorities' requests for specific system modifications, FP retains ownership of all such intellectual property as well.

The elements of ETC systems produced by the Group include the following:

- Antennas;
- Transponders;
- Industrial and commercial cameras (used to take video clips of each alleged violation);
- Camera and flash enclosures (large metal units that house the camera systems on-site); and,
- A site deployment control module (SDCM) that utilizes in-road sensors (loops embedded in the road) to detect vehicle weight and number of axles.

FP sources certain standard, commercially available components from third parties. Core third party-sourced items include the industrial and commercial cameras and lenses incorporated into the Group's system, and all system enclosures. However, FP substantially modifies the components sourced externally to conform to specifications developed for particular applications. The SDCM is built internally, as are the antennas and transponders.

FP's manufacturing operations are located in its domestic market. The Company employs a 175-person production staff responsible for manufacturing control modules, antennas and transponders, as well as customizing and assembling ETC components. In addition to these functions, FP's production staff is responsible for testing and calibrating the completed systems. Such testing is quite extensive because accuracy is extremely important. Certain performance criteria are established internally; others are established by governmental regulation.

In contrast to many foreign markets, toll collection functions are highly decentralized in the United States, with individual tolling authorities bearing both the responsibility for, and the costs of, toll collection and enforcement programs for specific bridges, tunnels, highways, etc. For example, in the New York area, the Lincoln Tunnel and the Triborough Bridge are each operated by a separate toll authority. The E-Z Pass Interagency Group is made up of the New York State Thruway Authority, the Port Authority of New York and New Jersey, the New Jersey Highway Authority, the Pennsylvania Turnpike Commission and the South Jersey Transportation Authority. The Bay Area Toll Authority oversees the operation of the region's seven state-owned bridges, while other tolling authorities in California, such as Transportation Corridor Agencies and the Orange County Transportation Authority, have responsibility for specific infrastructure assets outside of the Bay area.

USS markets and promotes ETC systems in the United States, procures infrastructure, equipment and software exclusively from FP, and enters into contracts with U.S. tolling authorities to provide electronic toll collection on an outsourced basis. In some cases, USS retains ownership of the equipment and infrastructure. On other important contracts, USS resells the equipment and infrastructure outright, but retains an obligation to perform engineering and maintenance, along with ongoing program implementation services.

In implementing and administering ETC programs, USS is called upon to perform construction, maintenance and operations. In the first phase after being awarded a contract, USS obtains "as-built" drawings of toll plazas and, where relevant, intersections, showing the placement of existing utilities, right-of-way restrictions and other details. For the most part, the Company outsources construction work to independent contractors. The latter are responsible for boring under the street, performing all electrical work, placing sensors and other equipment in the road or on pole mounts, etc.

Along with its construction and installation functions, USS is responsible for maintaining its installed base of equipment and infrastructure in good working order. More particularly, it is responsible for carrying out proactive maintenance on installed equipment on a scheduled basis, and responding promptly to complaints. Proactive maintenance encompasses regular physical checks of the equipment. For example, with respect to cameras, USS ensures that the lenses and housing units are clean, verifies that voltage levels, grounding and basic connections remain intact, conducts diagnostics, and reviews test images to ensure that violators' license plate images are sufficiently sharp. Installed cameras are subject to extensive vibration, and gradually shift over time. Moreover, light, precipitation and temperature levels vary by time of year, and there is a degree of system degradation as a result of the constant movement and auto-focusing of the camera systems. Analogous maintenance issues arise vis-a-vis other elements of installed ETC systems.

USS' Operations Group is responsible for ensuring that non-violators' accounts are debited in the appropriate amounts, in accordance with usage records and data, notifying non-violators when additional funds must be deposited in their accounts, reviewing evidence of infractions, determining whether a violation has in fact occurred, enhancing photos, operating help desks for both violators and non-violators, printing and mailing citations and preparing court evidence packages (consisting of duplicate copies of the citations mailed to violators, several full-size, unmodified photographs and a checklist of these items).

9.2 Transfer Pricing Issues

There is only one transfer pricing issue in this case: USS' purchases of components, equipment and infrastructure assets from FP.

9.3 Analysis Under Existing Regime

In this segment, we establish arm's length prices for FP's components, equipment and assets on sales to USS under the current transfer pricing regime. In applying the Best Method Rule, we first considered the CUP method, a logical possibility in that FP sells ETC system components, equipment and assets to third parties as well. However, we conclude that these transactions are not suitable CUPs for the following reasons:

- FP sells to USS in *much* higher volumes than it sells to third parties;
- FP's third party customers are located primarily in the Middle East and Asia, whereas USS is domiciled in the United States. The U.S. market differs from these other markets in a number of respects (degree of decentralization, the rate at which ETC technology has been adopted, etc.);
- The system elements that FP sells to USS are generally customized to a significantly greater extent than the standardized system elements that it sells in other markets; and,
- In most cases, FP sells directly to governmental entities, whereas USS is interposed between FP and tolling authorities.

In short, application of the CUP method would require adjustments for differences in equipment attributes, market conditions, market level and volume. While the effects of different physical attributes and volumes on price can be quantified with reasonable accuracy, the same cannot be said of differences in market level and market conditions. Therefore, we do not use the CUP method to establish FP's arm's length prices on sales of ETC system elements to USS.

In determining whether the resale price method can be utilized in this case, we distinguish between USS' role as a services provider, on the one hand, and an importer/reseller of equipment, on the other. As previously noted, many toll authorities purchase systems from USS outright on a one-time basis and rely on USS to perform ongoing program implementation and maintenance services. USS does not transform the systems materially, or otherwise add significant value to the components or components and equipment, prior to resale. Therefore, in relation to the sale of equipment per se, USS functions as a distributor. The services fee income that USS earns on an ongoing basis vis-a-vis these types of transactions is not a function of intercompany pricing, but, rather, of its own cost of services, operating expenses, and revenues received from third parties. As such, USS' services fees are not properly subject to analysis under IRC Section 482.

Consequently, the resale price method can be applied to establish USS' arm's length gross margin on the resale of ETC system elements to those tolling authorities that purchase equipment outright. This gross margin, in turn, implies a certain transfer price. The resale price method *cannot* be used to establish USS' arm's length gross margin on transactions where it retains ownership of ETC system elements. However, FP should charge the *same* transfer price regardless of whether USS resells the ETC system elements or retains ownership thereof, because FP's contributions are the same in both instances.

We establish USS' arm's length gross margin on the sale of ETC system components and equipment to certain toll authorities by reference to the gross margins earned by functionally comparable wholesale distributors. More particularly, we apply the resale price method in the following steps:

- Step 1: Adjust USS' bundled pricing of systems and services (on transactions with toll authorities that purchase equipment outright) to net out the following elements: (i) embedded site analysis and construction costs, (ii) embedded program implementation services fees, and (iii) the value of components that USS sources locally and adds to the systems prior to resale.
- Step 2: Develop a sample of third parties that distribute broadly similar equipment and perform the same range of selling, marketing and other distribution functions that USS performs in connection with equipment sales.
- Step 3: Compute the arm's length range of resale margins reported by the sample companies.
- Step 4: Apply the median arm's length resale margin to USS' unbundled selling price of equipment and infrastructure assets.
- Step 5: Determine the implied arm's length transfer price for tangible property, payable by USS to FP.

We develop a sample of functionally comparable U.S. wholesale distributors by means of several Standard Industrial Classification (SIC) Code- and keyword-based searches of publicly held U.S. companies. Our searches are summarized below.

- All firms included in SIC Code 504 (*Professional and Commercial Equipment and Supplies—Wholesale Trade*);
- All firms with the terms "wholesale distributor" and "government" in their Form 10-K filings with the Securities and Exchange Commission;
- All firms with the terms "wholesale distributor" and "toll collection" in their Form 10-K filings;
- All firms with the terms "wholesale distributor" and "infrastructure equipment" in their Form 10-K filings;
- All firms with the terms "wholesale distributor" and "ETC" in their Form 10-K filings;
- All firms with the term "systems installation" in their Form 10-K filings;

- All firms with the terms "resell" and "equipment" in their Form 10-K filings; and,
- All firms with the terms "transportation" and "distribute" in their Form 10-K filings.

We reviewed descriptions of business for all companies identified through these searches to ascertain which firms are functionally comparable to USS. We initially eliminated from our sample those firms that (a) were in a start-up mode, (b) engaged in activities unrelated to the wholesale distribution of equipment used in commercial applications, or (c) reported losses in sequential years, were in receivership or otherwise evidenced significant financial difficulties.

After this first "cut," wholesale distributors of large-scale IT products remained in our sample, among others. However, upon calculating resale margins for these companies, it became apparent that distributors of commercial computer products utilized a much more expansive definition of above-the-line costs than distributors of other types of commercial and industrial equipment, and generally reported very meager gross margins (in the range of 5%–10%). Hence, in our second round of eliminations, we excluded distributors of commercial computer products.

Our final sample consists of 18 firms, all of which are in the business of sourcing equipment and parts from independent suppliers for resale to commercial, industrial and governmental end-users. In all cases, these firms also supply consumables or render ongoing maintenance or other services. Most of the sample companies separately report revenues, above-the-line costs and gross profits on (a) the sale of equipment, and (b) the sale of consumables, the provision of maintenance and other services and/or equipment rentals. Because our objective is to establish USS' arm's length gross margin *only* on the distribution of equipment, we do not include the sample companies' consumables revenues, services fees or rental income and costs in their resale margins. The resellers included in our sample reported gross margins on the sale of equipment ranging from 28.5% to 44.8% in 2007, 29.5% to 39.0% in 2006, and 30.7% to 36.9% in 2005. The median gross margin amounted to 34.8% in 2007, 34.5% in 2006 and 34.7% in 2005. Hence, USS should earn a gross margin of 34%–35% on the resale of equipment, and retain all associated services fee income.

To further confirm the reasonableness of these results, we also reference the pricing provisions contained in an arm's length distribution agreement between Image Sensing Systems, Inc. and Wireless Technologies, Inc., dated January 1, 2001.[2] Wireless Technologies, Inc. is in the business of designing and manufacturing video camera systems and wireless video, audio and data communications equipment

---

[2] We identified one additional arm's length distribution agreement, between GVI Security Solutions and Samsung Electronics, granting the former exclusive rights to sell, market, lease, license and distribute Samsung security products throughout North, Central and South America. While the agreement is attached to GVI Security Solutions' Form SB-2 (No. 33-11321), filed with the Securities and Exchange Commission, the document stipulates only that prices will be "established by mutual agreement." Hence, it contains insufficient data to use in establishing arm's length resale margins on USS' sale of equipment.

used in enforcement, surveillance and security applications. Under the terms of its distribution agreement, Image Sensing Systems, Inc. is granted exclusive rights to distribute Wireless Technologies' products in the transportation, retail and banking markets, and non-exclusive rights in the security, military and law enforcement markets. Image Sensing Systems, Inc. agrees to (a) use its best efforts to promote, market and distribute Wireless Technologies' products, (b) commit the financial, intellectual and human resources necessary to grow the market for these products, (c) provide appropriate training to its salesforce, and (d) provide Wireless Technologies with a detailed business plan, inclusive of marketing and strategic plans. With regard to pricing, "[t]he parties agree that the prices to Image Sensing Systems for Wireless Technologies' products shall be 50% of Wireless Technologies' list price . . .."[3]

Inasmuch as Image Sensing Systems, Inc. likely offers discounts from list price to its customers, and presumably incurs certain above-the-line costs other than the purchase price of product, its gross margins on the resale of Wireless Technologies' products are likely within the range of our sample companies' results, as summarized above.

As noted, we determine USS' arm's length gross profits on its equipment sales by applying the median resale margin reported by our sample companies to the adjusted selling price of FP's equipment to U.S. end-users. USS' cost of goods sold (per unit) is therefore readily quantifiable. The purchase price of product constitutes 85% of USS' cost of goods on equipment. Therefore, FS' arm's length price on sales of equipment to USS is also readily quantifiable. As previously noted, USS should pay the same transfer price for all ETC systems sourced from FP, regardless of whether USS resells the equipment or retains ownership thereof, because FP's contributions are the same in both cases.

9.4 Analysis Under Alternative Regime

We utilize the "required return" method to analyze this case under the proposed alternative transfer pricing regime. As discussed in Chapter 4, to apply the required return methodology, we require the following data:

1. USS' estimated beta, along with the risk-free rate and the estimated price of risk;
2. The estimated fair market value of USS' equity capital;
3. USS' arm's length interest costs, outstanding debt, principal repayments, non-cash charges and investment in tangible property, working capital and intangible property; and
4. USS' tax credits, deductions, loss carryforwards, etc.

For purposes of our analysis, we assume that taxing authorities have agreed to, and publish, industry-specific betas, the risk-free rate, the market risk premium and

---

[3] See Image Sensing Systems, Inc.'s Form 10QSB, filed with the Securities and Exchange Commission on August 13, 2001. We do not include Image Sensing Systems, Inc. in our sample of comparable wholesale distributors because it does not function purely as a distributor.

safe harbor loan rates. Moreover, we assume that tax authorities require a comprehensive valuation only every three years, rather than annually.

9.4.1 USS' Estimated Cost of Equity Capital

While the user fees collected by toll authorities may fluctuate somewhat with discretionary travel by motorists, commuter traffic should correlate fairly closely with
broad, macroeconomic trends. For purposes of establishing USS' beta, we utilize
the unlevered industry beta for traffic management systems in the United States,
published (by assumption) by the IRS. Suppose this beta is 0.87. After relevering to
reflect USS' financial structure, we obtain a beta of 0.92. We utilize a risk-free rate
of 3.5% and a market risk premium of 6.00%, consistent with the IRS' published
rates. Hence, USS has a required return on equity capital of 9.02%.

9.4.2 Estimated Value of USS' Equity Capital

USS would either have commissioned a valuation within the prior two years or it
would have to prepare a comprehensive valuation in the current year. Suppose it
was in the latter position. USS could not use a discounted cash flow methodology
for valuation purposes, inasmuch as its cost of goods is heavily influenced by the
intercompany pricing of transponders, antennas, etc. One potential alternative is to
compute price-to-revenue and/or price-to-book equity ratios for all companies in
similar lines of business. If these ratios fall within a reasonably narrow range, a
multiples-based analysis, using revenues or the book value of equity as the base,
may yield reasonable results. (While not theoretically compelling, this approach to
establishing value may be empirically valid.)

Another possible approach (either as a supplement to, or in lieu of, the multiples
approach) would entail valuing USS' assets directly. A number of appraisal companies maintain large databases that include the pricing of used equipment in the
secondary market, which may contain relevant data.[4] In principle, USS could also
be valued by reference to the fair market value of the Group as a whole (composed
of two entities in this case), with the Group-wide value parsed between USS and FP
based on informed guestimates of their relative asset values. (If the Group utilized
this approach, FP should be required to "live with" the implied value of its assets for
purposes of determining its tax liability in Japan.) More generally, over the course
of a three-year period, there may be windows of transparency into the value of USS'
assets, for one reason or another, and these data points should be exploited. (In this

---

[4] As a general proposition, if the tested party owns valuable intellectual property, the direct valuation of assets may be infeasible (although it is required under the 2005 proposed cost-sharing
regulations and the Coordinated Issue Paper on cost-sharing released in 2007). However, the market for financial instruments backed by intangible assets is growing rapidly and may in the future
constitute a useful source of data on the value of such assets.

context, assets should include intangible and off-balance sheet assets, among them goodwill and going concern value, in addition to tangible assets.)

Given the inherently inexact nature of valuation, it would make sense to establish USS' equity value in several ways and utilize a weighted average of these values based on the reliability of the individual methods. Moreover, to the extent that one can establish objective upper and lower bounds, this should be done, and any valuations that fall outside these ranges should be discarded. For example, if an independent company in the same line of business as USS, albeit with a larger installed base and superior technology, was acquired in the past several months, the acquisition price would exceed USS' fair market value. Similarly, the fair market value of USS' current and tangible assets cannot exceed USS' value as a whole (inclusive of potentially valuable intellectual property).

If the valuation method utilized yields the value of USS' assets rather than its equity capital, the value of its debt should be subtracted from the valuation as a whole.

If USS had prepared a comprehensive valuation of its equity capital in the past two years, it would be in the position of updating this valuation currently. As noted, percentage changes in the values of publicly traded companies in the same line of business would be a good indicator of the requisite adjustments. In this way, the effects of industry-wide factors (e.g., the development of superior, satellite-based toll collection technologies) would be captured. It would also be necessary to identify developments specific to USS that would favorably or adversely affect its value.

For purposes of discussion, we assume that USS as a whole has a fair market value of $200 million, debt of $145 million, and, therefore, an equity value of $55 million.

9.4.3 Cost of Debt

Again, we assume that the IRS and other taxing authorities have agreed to permit the use of Applicable Federal Rates (and their equivalents) for purposes of applying the required return methodology. Alternatively, we could determine USS' current cost of debt by (a) developing a sample of publicly traded bonds with similar maturities and other characteristics as USS' debt, issued by firms with similar credit ratings (as estimated either by the Company's treasurer or the transfer pricing economist), and (b) determining the yield to maturity on these issues. For purposes of illustration, we assume that the current before-tax cost of USS' debt is 4.46%.

9.4.4 Required Return on Capital Assuming Statutory Tax Rate Applies

As reviewed above USS' required return on equity, r_e, is 9.02%, the fair market value of its equity capital, E, is $55 million, its before-tax cost of debt, r_d, is 4.46%, and the value of its debt, D, is \$145 million. We assume a combined federal and state statutory tax rate, t, of 0.40. Therefore, under the required return method, USS' after-tax free cash flows, FCF, are equal to \$8.841 million:

$$FCF = r_e \times E + r_d(1 - t) \times D \qquad (9.1)$$
$$FCF = 0.0902 \times 55 + 0.0446(1 - 0.4) \times 145 = 8.841 \qquad (9.2)$$

Using the after-tax free cash flows of \$8.841 million computed above as a starting point, USS' before-tax net income can be determined as follows:

- Add the tax shield on debt (0.4 × 0.0446 × \$145 million), or \$2.587 million.
- Deduct interest expense of (0.0446 × \$145 million), or \$6.467 million.
- Add USS' actual investment in tangible and intangible assets and changes in working capital (\$15.5 million) and deduct its non-cash charges (\$12.8 million).
- Divide by $(1 - t)$, the statutory tax rate.

If USS repaid any principal or borrowed additional monies during the relevant period, these amounts should be factored into the analysis. (We assume that it did not.) USS' arm's length before-tax net income, *prior* to factoring in any firm-specific carryforwards, credits, etc., is equal to \$12.8 million.

9.4.5 Adjustments to Reflect Loss Carryforwards, Other Firm-Specific Factors

Finally, it remains to adjust USS' estimated before-tax net income for any additional tax-reducing factors. USS has certain loss carryforwards that reduce its taxable income by \$2.5 million. Therefore, under the required return methodology, USS should report taxable income of \$10.3 million.

9.5 Comparison

For the reasons discussed in Chapter 3, the resale price method often has significant shortcomings in terms of the reliability of results (relative to actual arm's length allocations of income). While conceptually more compelling, the required return method necessitates a hefty dose of subjective judgment in practice, absent taxing authorities' consensus on certain simplifying conventions regarding the valuation of equity capital and the use of published industry betas, risk-free rates, market risk premia and safe harbor loan rates. If this framework is not put in place, the required return methodology may not significantly enhance the consistency of results across tax jurisdictions, and between corporations and individual tax authorities.

Moreover, the required return methodology is more labor-intensive than the resale price method. To some degree, this feature can be reduced by mutual agreement on various valuation conventions, but it cannot be entirely eliminated.

(However, this downside is not an issue in those instances where a tested party has been valued recently in the normal course of business for non-tax purposes.)

In short, from a practical perspective, the required return methodology represents an improvement over existing methods only under certain circumstances, as summarized below:

Scenario A

- The tested party has recently been valued in the normal course of business for non-tax purposes, and the valuation is not potentially distorted by intercompany pricing; and,
- Tax authorities agree on the use of industry betas, safe harbor loan rates, risk-free rates and the market price of risk, and publish all of the latter on a monthly basis.

Scenario B

- Taxing authorities accept a baseline valuation done at multi-year intervals (e.g., every three years), absent significant changes in the business, with informed estimates of percentage increases or decreases in value in the interim; and,
- Tax authorities agree on the use of, and publish, industry betas, safe harbor loan rates, risk-free rates and the market price of risk.

Scenario C

- A sufficient number of comparable companies can be found to calculate valuation multiples, and these multiples fall within a reasonably narrow range; and,
- Tax authorities agree on both (a) industry-specific valuation multiples, and (b) the use of industry betas, safe harbor loan rates, risk-free rates and the market price of risk, and publish all of the latter on a monthly basis.

Chapter 10
Provision of CDN Services to Third Parties

This case study involves a U.S. parent (USP) and multiple foreign subsidiaries. The Group's business is multi-jurisdictional by its nature, and its infrastructure is geographically dispersed. Foreign affiliates own all the Group's infrastructural assets in non-U.S. markets, which USP is permitted to utilize on a fee-for-service basis. As a point of departure, we illustrate why it is difficult to analyze this case under traditional transfer pricing methods. In lieu of such methods, we utilize both (a) a simplified version of the required return method, and (b) the simplified profit split method (under a modified set of assumptions).

10.1 Summary of Key Facts

The public Internet has grown exponentially in its brief history, albeit not in an overly structured or organized fashion. It consists of a large number of private networks that interconnect, allowing data packets to traverse the Internet through a complex system of servers, routers, switches, agreed-on protocols and other elements. While the Internet's current architecture was adequate to handle traditional forms of use and volumes of traffic, demand for Internet-delivered content, particularly rich media content, has ballooned in recent years as a result of several factors:

1. A high and progressively increasing percentage of North American households have broadband Internet access. Broadband Internet penetration was nearly 50% in 2006 and is expected to reach 73% by 2010. European households are not far behind. Such access is a prerequisite to streaming or downloading rich media content onto personal computers and mobile devices.
2. Consumers increasingly expect on-demand access to a broad range of media content (videos, games, music, etc.).
3. In response to increased consumer demand, consumer electronics manufacturers have developed new mobile devices that are capable of connecting to the Internet.

As presently constituted, the Internet is not well-suited to accommodate high-volume demand for the delivery of rich media content. From an infrastructural standpoint, the public Internet is divided into four segments: (a) the connection

E. King, *Transfer Pricing and Corporate Taxation*,
DOI 10.1007/978-0-387-78183-9_10, © Springer Science+Business Media, LLC 2009

between origin servers and the Internet (the "First Mile"); (b) the "hosting" segment, consisting of data centers and the network infrastructure that is housed in these centers; (c) the "backbone" segment, which consists of the fiber connections that link data centers to points of presence ("POPs") and both public and private peering points; and, (d) the connection between end-users and the Internet (provided by Internet Service Providers, or ISPs, and referred to as the "Last Mile").[1] At each of these junctures, latency and reliability problems can and often do arise.

If a content provider chooses to manage its own Internet-facing infrastructure and does not have sufficient bandwidth, the First Mile can cause significant delays, particularly during periods of traffic surges (for example, in response to short-term Internet marketing campaigns). Data centers, while generally better equipped with bandwidth, also suffer from traffic congestion on a regular basis. The Internet backbone is another common source of delays in data transmission, in part because of the complexity of its pathways. Data packets are routed from point to point on the public Internet, and each such "hop" requires router processing to determine the subsequent destination. The number of hops and the potential for sub-optimal routing increases latency. Moreover, Internet traffic may exceed the capacity of routing equipment. The Last Mile likewise has its own infrastructural shortcomings. Here, too, bandwidth constraints may be a problem. Moreover, peering points between ISPs may be inefficient or non-functioning.

CDN services providers came into being in response to shortcomings in the public Internet. In essence, they have knitted together parallel, private Internets, consisting of a large number of edge and storage servers, routers, switches, enabling software and connectivity. These private networks have sufficient capacity and bandwidth to comfortably handle normal loads associated with rich media content, and to manage traffic spikes. CDN services providers also attempt to reduce latency and bypass congestion entirely by caching (or storing) commonly requested objects (that is, various kinds of rich media content) on servers located in comparatively close physical proximity to end-users. Firms in the business of developing rich media content utilize these alternative methods of delivering such content because customer satisfaction turns on a positive viewing or listening experience, without delays, freezes and other interruptions.

First-generation CDN services providers built systems that were less-than-well-suited to handle rich media content, which requires the transfer of very large data files. Instead, they were built to handle the less data-intensive files initially transmitted over the Internet (e.g., web pages). Second- and third-generation CDN services providers, such as Akamai, Limelight Networks, Level 3 Communications, Mirror Image, VitalStream (acquired by Internap Network Services Corporation) and Panther Networks, designed systems that could handle a more diverse range of file sizes. To varying degrees, this mandate is manifested in:

---

[1] See Mirror Image, *Powering Your Web Strategy with CDN Services*, April 2007.

- The particular configuration of individual CDN services providers' edge and storage servers;
- The lease of private line backbone capacity from independent companies, such as Global Crossing, Inc.;
- Individual providers' proprietary, internally-developed software that manages the delivery of content objects, storage and retrieval of customer content libraries, activity logging and information reporting; and,
- Individual CDN services providers' peering relationships with broadband ISPs.

Akamai is currently the largest North American CDN services provider, with over 22,000 servers deployed globally. However, competing providers are growing rapidly, and count some of the largest multinational content providers among their customers (e.g., Disney, Apple, Amazon.com, eBay, myspace.com, facebook, Microsoft and others). CDN services are marketed via webinars, newsletter sponsorships, trade shows, banner campaigns, cold calls, etc.

The Group in this case employs approximately 220 people in sales and marketing, 85 people in network engineering, 40 people in research and development (consisting predominantly of software engineers), and 35 people in general and administrative capacities. Almost all of these individuals (with the exception of 15–18 people) are employed by USP, and are based in the United States. The remaining individuals are employed by foreign affiliates, and are based overseas. The Group has numerous servers, routers and switches deployed throughout North America, Europe and Asia. As noted, foreign affiliates own all infrastructure assets located outside North America (albeit not the proprietary software incorporated into these assets), while USP owns all infrastructure assets within North America (and all proprietary software used worldwide).

As a starting point in our analysis (under both the current and proposed regimes), it is necessary to determine whether USP and its foreign affiliates *collectively* provide CDN services to third parties, or USP *alone* provides these services, albeit with the use of servers, routers and switches owned by its foreign affiliates. We conclude that USP simply accesses network infrastructure assets owned by its foreign affiliates and is the sole provider of CDN services as such. This conclusion is premised on the following facts:

1. The performance of CDN services requires network engineers, software engineers and administrators, and these individuals are, and will continue to be, employed solely by USP;
2. In addition to hardware and enabling software, connectivity is a *sine qua non* of CDN services. USP is the contract party on, and bears the cost of, its arm's length lease of dedicated backbone network assets. It has also negotiated peering agreements with numerous ISPs, and bears the associated settlement costs; and,
3. USP is the contract party on all transactions with third party content providers.

10.2 Transfer Pricing Issues

As noted, given the facts outlined above, we conclude that the Group's foreign affiliates simply permit USP to utilize their network infrastructure assets (servers, routers and switches) in rendering CDN services to third parties. Hence the transfer pricing issue: What is an arm's length fee for exclusive access rights to these assets?

10.3 Analysis Under Existing Regime

As reviewed in Chapter 3, two of the transfer pricing methods governing intercompany transactions in tangible property presuppose that ownership rights to such property are transferred in their entirety. More particularly, both the resale price and cost plus methods presuppose that tangible property is sold outright and used or resold by the recipient. These methods do not apply where the transactions at issue are not structured in this way. As such, only the comparable uncontrolled price (CUP) method and the comparable profits method (CPM), which are able to accommodate more diverse types of transactions in tangible property, can in principle be applied in this case.

At first blush, the transactions in tangible property between USP and its foreign affiliates resemble lease arrangements. However, under a lease, the lessee is effectively treated as the owner of the leased assets, and has all of the associated rights and responsibilities during the lease term. This is *not* true of USP's access rights to its foreign affiliates' infrastructure assets. Rather, the latter retain legal ownership of their infrastructure assets, along with all of the attendant obligations and risks. Therefore, if, under the CUP method, one were to look to arm's length lease fees for dedicated servers to establish the foreign affiliates' pricing of access rights to their servers, these lease fees would have to be adjusted to reflect the differing allocations of legal rights, risks and responsibilities. Such an adjustment would depend on the specific features of the comparable arm's length lease arrangements, including:

- The duration of the lease relative to the useful life of the equipment;
- The right of the lessee to terminate the lease before its stated term expires; and,
- Rights to sublease.

These factors influence the degree of risk assumed by an arm's length lessee. Quantifying the monetary effects of such differences in risks is both challenging and inexact. Moreover, the use of lease arrangements as CUPs, even if adjusted as required, may incline taxing authorities to treat USP as having permanent establishments in all countries in which its foreign affiliates operate.

Under the comparable profits method, one would establish USP's arm's length fees, payable to its foreign affiliates, by reference to standalone firms in the business of providing access to their network infrastructure assets.[2] For example, standalone data centers are logical "candidate" comparables, inasmuch as they permit firms without their own Internet-facing infrastructure to utilize data center infrastructure to host their websites. Data centers ordinarily provide additional support services as well, for which one would have to adjust before comparing data centers' profit level indicators with those of USP's foreign affiliates. However, most data centers are either privately held or part of much larger, vertically integrated or horizontally diversified firms. As such, financial results on data center operations per se are very hard to come by.

The alternative under the comparable profits method, again, is to wander further afield in search of quasi-comparable firms. However, this will render one's results much less reliable. Accordingly, the current regime does not provide a satisfactory means of analyzing the transactions between USP and its foreign affiliates.

10.4 Analysis Under Alternative Regime

As described in detail in Chapters 4 and 9, the required return methodology would often be extremely laborious absent certain conventions to which tax authorities would agree in advance. However, a much simpler variant of the required return method is applied in this case.

One can view USP's use of hardware owned by its foreign affiliates as being economically equivalent to the following series of transactions: (a) foreign Group members borrow capital for purposes of purchasing edge and storage servers, routers and switches (with the latter serving as collateral); (b) individual foreign affiliates permit USP access rights to their equipment; and, (c) USP compensates its foreign affiliates both for the cost (or value) of their equipment and for their cost of capital.

The U.S. transfer pricing regulations contain safe harbor provisions as applied to loans. Safe harbor loan rates (or "Applicable Federal Rates") for short-term, mid-term and long-term loans are published on a monthly basis by the Internal Revenue Service. Short-term rates apply to loans with maturities of 3 years or less, mid-term rates apply to loans with maturities of between 3 and 9 years, and long-term rates apply to loans with maturities of more than 9 years. For purposes of our analysis, we utilize the mid-term rate of 4.46% published in February 2008.

We assume that the Group's foreign members would have to pay back their respective loan principal in equal monthly installments over their terms (equal, in turn, to the useful life of the network infrastructure equipment that they purchase with the loan proceeds). Assuming that the servers (and other equipment) at issue

---

[2] While USP's foreign affiliates permit third parties to access their network infrastructure assets, this is done purely through informal barter (or peering) arrangements with owners of complementary infrastructure assets, which in turn provide connectivity. These reciprocal rights cannot readily be valued.

have a useful life of T months, and a value of V_s, individual foreign Group members would repay the following amount in principal per month:

$$\frac{V_s}{T} \tag{10.1}$$

Additionally, in month 1, individual foreign Group members would pay an interest charge equal to $V_s\,(i/12)$, in month 2, $V_s\,(T-1/T)(i/12)$, and in month t:

$$V_s\left(\frac{T-(t-1)}{T}\right)\left(\frac{i}{12}\right) \tag{10.2}$$

Therefore, the total amount that USP would pay in intercompany fees to individual foreign affiliates over T months (or $T/12$ years), equal, in turn, to the foreign affiliates' interest fees and repayments of principal, is given by:

$$V_s + V_s \sum_{t=1}^{T}[T-(t-1)]\left(\frac{i}{12}\right) \tag{10.3}$$

The monthly equivalent of Equation (10.3) (that is, the amount that USP would pay each of its foreign affiliates per month for access rights to their respective infrastructure assets) is given by:

$$\frac{V_s}{T} + V_s\left(\frac{T-(t-1)}{T}\right)\left(\frac{i}{12}\right) \tag{10.4}$$

The foreign affiliates' monthly infrastructure-related operating expenses are approximately equal to the depreciation of servers, V_s/T. Therefore, dividing the above equation by this magnitude (equivalently, multiplying through by T/V_s), we obtain the foreign affiliates' markup over associated costs in month t:

$$1 + [T-(t-1)]\left(\frac{i}{12}\right) \tag{10.5}$$

For purposes of our transfer pricing analysis, we assume that T is equal to 36 months (the period of time over which the Group depreciates its servers). Substituting $T = 36$ and $i = 4.46\%$ (the relevant Applicable Federal Rate) into Equation (10.5), we obtain a markup, in month 1, of 1.1338, or 13.38% over depreciation expenses. The markup in month 12 is equal to 1.0925, or 9.25% over depreciation expenses. (This figure declines over time because the interest cost component diminishes as the principal is repaid.) On average during the first year, USP should pay its foreign affiliates a markup of 11.32% over the latter's depreciation expenses.

In the second year of the 3-year loan term, USP's foreign affiliates should receive an average markup of 6.85%,[3] and in the third year, 2.41%.[4] Therefore, averaging over the 3-year period, USP should pay its foreign affiliates a markup over depreciation expenses of approximately 7.0% per annum. This compensates the foreign affiliates for both their expenditures on capital equipment and their cost of capital.

10.5 Additional Analysis Under Alternative Regime

Because USP is the contract party vis-a-vis all domestic and non-domestic content providers in this case, and it bears the costs of co-location agreements,[5] peering arrangements with ISPs, backbone leases, software development, etc., we concluded that foreign Group members did not possess all of the resources necessary to provide CDN services per se, and, therefore, were simply permitting USP to utilize their network assets. However, if (a) foreign Group members were the counterparties on CDN services contracts with non-U.S. content providers, (b) each foreign entity bore the costs of peering and co-location agreements and backbone leases in its territory, and (c) all foreign Group members compensated USP for software development services rendered to them, an entirely different methodology would be indicated.

Under the existing U.S. transfer pricing regime, a profit split methodology would probably not be warranted, given these postulated facts, because intangible assets (in the form of proprietary software) are not an overly significant factor in the provision of CDN services.[6] More generally, U.S. transfer pricing rules provide very limited guidance as to how a group's consolidated income should be allocated among taxing jurisdictions when (a) these members cooperatively provide a service to third parties, (b) there is limited or no division of labor among group members, and (c) group members do not engage directly in intercompany transactions.

However, USP and its foreign affiliates would be excellent candidates for the proposed simplified profit split methodology. Under the modified fact pattern, all Group members (a) contribute the same tangible and intangible assets; (b) require similar levels of working capital; and, (c) bear the same risks. While the book value of each entity's tangible assets would generally differ from their fair market value, the divergence between book and market values would be similar for both USP and its foreign affiliates (provided that they acquired their servers, routers and switches at approximately the same time and utilized the same depreciation schedule). As

---

[3] In month 13, the markup is 8.88%, and in month 24, 4.81%.

[4] In month 25, the markup is 4.44%, and in month 36, 0.37%.

[5] Under a co-location agreement, a third party provides space, power and maintenance services *vis-a-vis* servers owned by a CDN services provider or other independent company.

[6] One could legitimately argue, however, that peering arrangements, an indispensable element of a CDN network, constitute intangible assets.

such, in this instance, it would be reasonable to divide combined after-tax free cash flows among Group members based on each party's relative contributions of tangible assets, valued at book.

10.6 Comparison

The traditional transfer pricing methods are difficult to apply in analyzing this case, in part because the transactions in tangible property involve only the transfer of access rights, not of the property as a whole. Therefore, neither the resale price method nor the cost plus method applies. Additionally, the most intuitively logical CUPs, consisting of lease transactions, require difficult and inexact adjustments and may raise misplaced permanent establishment issues. The comparable profits method is difficult to apply as well, due in part to data limitations.

At bottom, the foreign affiliates in this case have invested in network assets, and must recoup both the cost of these assets and their cost of capital through USP's payment of access fees. Our alternative methodology is based on this more fundamental view of the foreign members' contributions, and does not suffer from the theoretical weaknesses of, or give rise to the data constraints associated with, the existing transfer pricing regime.

Chapter 11
Global Trading of Commodities

This case study involves a Swiss parent company (FP), and subsidiaries in the United Kingdom (UKS), China (CHS), the United States (USS) and Canada (CAS).[1] Collectively, FP, UKS, CHS, USS and CAS engage in the global trading of natural gas, aluminum and alumina (primarily physicals and secondarily derivatives). These markets are representative of commodities trading in general, and have many features in common with trading in financial products as well.

We analyze this case under both (a) the formulary approach described in *Notice 94–40* and the proposed global dealing regulations, and (b) the simplified profit split method. The summary of key facts, below, is lengthy, because it contains a description of individual commodities markets and an overview of the trading function. Those readers familiar with these contextual details are advised to skip Section 11.1.

11.1 Summary of Key Facts

We begin this segment with a discussion of the markets for natural gas, alumina and aluminum. Following this description, we identify the core assets and skills used in physicals trading, and consider how and why these key elements have shifted in relative importance over the past 3–5 years.

11.1.1 Description of Natural Gas Markets

Natural gas is consumed by cogeneration plants (to produce energy), industrial companies (to power production equipment), commercial end-users (to heat offices, schools, hotels, etc.), and individual consumers. Gas is extracted from natural reservoirs through a "wellhead," a mechanism that controls the flow of gas to the surface, and is transported along a pipeline system from supplying regions to consuming

---

[1] Portions of this chapter originally appeared in the *Tax Director's Guide to International Transfer Pricing*, and are being reprinted here with permission of the publisher, Global Business Information Strategies, Inc.

regions throughout the United States and other countries. The pipeline system consists of small-diameter pipelines, or gathering systems, feeder pipelines, large-diameter pipelines for long-distance transport, storage facilities along the system, and receipt or delivery points. Mineral rights and the wellhead and pipeline systems are generally owned, and natural gas is produced, by separate and independent companies.

Natural gas producers generally contract directly on a long-term, firm basis with large end-users and intermediaries (e.g., utilities). However, an individual utility or other long-term customer may require more or less natural gas than it has directly contracted for, or a producer may have committed to deliver more or less natural gas than it has available at a point in time. Analogously, pipeline operators generally contract directly on a long-term, firm basis with large end-users for most of their capacity. However, the amount of capacity leased out on a long-term basis is somewhat less than total capacity, to allow for peak usage. Long-term users, for their part, want the flexibility to lease out their temporarily excess capacity, or obtain additional capacity on a short-term basis, which their long-term leases with the pipeline owners do not provide.

Natural gas traders take positions and trade in natural gas and pipeline capacity. More fundamentally, they provide an outlet for producers' excess production and assume their market risk, constitute a source of incremental supply to end-users, and take advantage of arbitrage opportunities (or "basis differentials") across markets and over time. Moreover, traders buy and use or resell the incremental capacity that pipeline companies do not lease out on a long-term, firm basis. They obtain such capacity through leases with the latter, and with end-users, on daily, weekly or monthly bases. Traders typically obtain "interruptible" service, which is less costly than firm service. However, as the term implies, such service is not guaranteed. Rather, one can be displaced by a firm user, and trading strategies must allow for this eventuality through "park and loan" arrangements (permitting traders to draw on pools of natural gas located near their customers).

Traders hedge their physical positions by entering into offsetting positions in the same or a related commodity, thereby mitigating the resulting price exposure and eliminating the open position in whole or in part.[2] Some hedges are done on exchanges (e.g., standardized, tradable futures entitling the buyer to claim physical

---

[2] In principle, hedges are entered into as an offset to underlying physical trades. However, the latter may not materialize (due to non-performance of one kind or another) or they may be significantly delayed (due, for example, to production or shipping problems). When the physical trade is delayed, the hedge itself becomes an open position and carries with it substantial risk. Moreover, futures markets are much more volatile than physicals markets. While one clearly bears a measure of price risk on open positions in physicals, in that the price of a particular commodity is quite likely to fluctuate over time, the potential for backwardation on hedges (where the commodities price in the future is lower than the current price), coupled with the potential for non-performance or delayed performance in the physicals market, poses substantially greater risks. While outright non-performance has historically been relatively uncommon, in part because few contracts are fixed to the day, delays in production and/or shipping, unacceptable variations in quality or volume, and other similarly smaller-scale adverse developments are relatively common.

delivery at the contract delivery point and at the specified date, and similarly entitling the seller), and others are done over-the-counter (e.g., swaps negotiated bilaterally and providing for the exchange of the commodity, or a derivative, at some
specified future point).

Not all natural gas traders enter into physicals transactions, and not all traders
entering into such transactions have to make or take delivery. In some instances,
traders deal solely in derivative, or financial, instruments, such as futures and swaps.
Others buy natural gas into, or sell out of, a hub, involving the transfer of title in a
ledger, but no physical movement of product as such. In general, customer-driven
business entails the physical movement of product, and the accompanying expertise
in pipeline systems. Proprietary trading may also involve physicals business, but has
a larger financial component.

11.1.2 Description of Alumina and Aluminum Markets

Alumina and aluminum markets have always been closely linked, because alumina
is the key raw material used in the manufacture of aluminum. It is not unusual for
alumina end-users and aluminum smelters to be one and the same firm, or to be part
of the same multinational group. Despite this linkage, a number of metals trading
firms traded aluminum exclusively prior to the 1990s. However, with the collapse of
the Soviet Union, pre-financing arrangements increasingly became a prerequisite to
assured supplies of aluminum from formerly government-owned Russian producers
with limited financial resources. Thus, Glencore, Trafigura, Gerald Metals, Noble
and others began prepaying for aluminum under long-term offtake arrangements
circa the second half of the 1990s, and agreed to supply aluminum producers with
their alumina requirements.

Aluminum and alumina traders in the physicals market generally have relationships with a number of major suppliers. In addition to Russia, these suppliers are
based in Australia, Venezuela, China, India, Mexico and Brazil. Traders source
product both in the spot market (i.e., tendered business put out for bid by the large
producers) and under long-term contract.

Counterparties on the buy side of the alumina markets consist primarily of aluminum producers; counterparties on the buy side of the aluminum markets consist
primarily of major commercial and industrial end-users, and, to a lesser extent,
independent distributors and small merchants. On transactions with large aluminum
producers, traders' roles entail correcting imbalances in the location of stocks, the
availability of raw materials and the timing of production in these entities' systems.
Aluminum can be sold at the prevailing LME price at minimum, and sometimes at
a higher price, given its particular shape, grade and location.

For much of this decade, China has been the largest alumina consuming market, and its rapid growth in demand (at the rate of approximately 10% per annum
until recently) has fueled the growth of the worldwide alumina market. Alumina
is generally sold on a fixed price basis or as a percentage of the LME price for
aluminum. Percent of LME contracts have terms of up to 5 years, and generally

contain specified puts and calls. Under this arrangement, buyers typically have the right to call when prices reach a certain threshold, and sellers have the right to put if prices fall below a specified floor; when prices are within the put/call range, the transactions price is arrived at by mutual negotiation on an annual basis.

11.1.3 Core Assets and Skills

A good deal of trading in physicals is customer-based, although proprietary trading is also fairly common. Traders realize profits, in essence, by creating market efficiencies and exploiting short-lived price differentials over time and across markets. For example, on customer-based business, traders engage in time and location swaps, thereby eliminating the need to store and transport product. Through their comprehensive knowledge of infrastructure and their ability to manage risk, they are also able to move product more cost-effectively than large and less nimble producers and consumers when called upon to do so. By maintaining stocks of certain metals in particular shapes and qualities in various locations, traders are often able to meet specialized demand quickly, and sell metals at higher prices than the prevailing LME price. Proprietary trading generally entails making markets and earning a bid/ask spread, taking positions and taking advantage of arbitrage opportunities.

There are a number of key prerequisites to successful physicals commodities trading: (1) access to financing; (2) access to product; (3) a reputation for reliability; (4) a set of administrative controls that prevents enormously costly errors and facilitates the effective management of risk; (5) a sophisticated IT system that enables traders and risk managers to track activity in real time; and, (6) expertise in market fundamentals, trading strategies, risk management and market infrastructure and logistics. In some markets (e.g., natural gas and power), traders possess all of these forms of expertise. In other markets (e.g., copper concentrates, alumina and fuel oils), a separate group may have the necessary logistical expertise.

11.1.3.1 Access to Financing

Access to financial capital is a pivotal element of *all* trading companies' operations. The importance of financing varies to some degree, depending on the type of transaction and the commodity at issue. For example, significant financing is essential in structured finance, where producers are capital-constrained, and in alumina markets, where product is traded in very large volumes. In contrast, certain types of precious metals trades require substantially less financial capital by virtue of the way that they are structured. However, with very few exceptions, access to substantial lines of credit is a *sine qua non* of commodities trading. Commodities trading firms generally rely almost entirely on European bank lines. European banks have a much greater understanding and appreciation of the complexities of commodities trading than U.S. commercial banks, and have not exited the business, as U.S. lenders have.

Bank loans can be grouped into three categories: (a) structured finance; (b) working capital; and, (c) repurchase agreements. Structured finance is provided predominantly to the European (most often Swiss) offices of trading firms. This predilection for lending to European-based borrowers is explained by physical proximity, more effective means of legal recourse, and a generally higher comfort level with European entities.

Certain multinational groups or individual group members can only borrow on a transactions-specific basis. Loans are made to particular legal entities in many cases, although banks may also extend "swing lines" on which more than one group member may draw. Individual transactions are almost always financed entirely by one lending institution, despite the fact that they can be quite large, because this arrangement affords lenders greater legal protections in the event of default. In determining which lender to approach on an individual transaction, a trading firm generally considers the bank's flexibility on transactions financing in general, its proclivity to finance the specific type of transaction at issue, the complexity of the transaction, the need to keep unused capacity available at specific institutions and the need to provide each lender with a certain volume of business to preserve the relationship. Transactions-specific loans are administratively burdensome, in that trading firms are required to submit extensive information on the subject transaction to the lending institution.

Other trading groups or individual group members are able to negotiate more flexible borrowing arrangements, and can borrow against inventories and receivables. Such loans are generally secured by these assets. The borrower provides a *Letter of Pledge* to lenders on each borrowing, which stipulates the specific commodities and receivables that it is pledging as collateral, and provides the requisite supporting documentation.

11.1.3.2 Access to Product

In order to trade commodities, one obviously must have access to commodities. As suggested above, such access may take the form of long-term offtake arrangements and may be dependent on providing financing of various kinds to producers. Traders also source product in the spot market.

In the physicals markets, an extensive knowledge of individual suppliers, their current and projected output, future expansion plans, technologies and alternative distribution channels are key to ensuring reliable supplies of product. Relationships with suppliers (and customers) are often developed and maintained by marketers. Marketers (or "originators") may be part of trading firms' staff or independent agents. The latter are typically compensated by commission or on a fixed fee-per-ton basis.

While pre-financing was often necessary to ensure access to supplies of aluminum in the 1990s, investment in hard assets (ownership interests in mines and smelters) is increasingly viewed as the only truly effective strategy currently. Alumina and aluminum producers do not currently have the same financial constraints that they previously did (and addressed by means of pre-financing), for the reasons discussed below. Moreover, trading firms' customers themselves are reluctant to purchase essential raw materials from intermediaries with no direct sources of supply.

11.1.3.3 Trading, Risk Management and Logistical Expertise

Traders provide essential expertise in formulating and executing trading strategies, as clearly indicated by their very high compensation levels. An intimate knowledge of the fundamentals that drive individual markets is obviously part of this expertise, but it also often requires an equally extensive knowledge of infrastructural elements of the market, which may create trading opportunities or preclude certain trading strategies at different times. With respect to certain commodities (e.g., electricity, as well as natural gas), traders possess knowledge of both market fundamentals and infrastructural and logistical features.

However, when product is moved via ocean-going vessel, as is true of alumina and aluminum (as well as liquified natural gas), the chartering function is generally performed by a separate group within the trading firm. The chartering of vessels requires specialized knowledge regarding the optimal means of shipping different metals and bulk raw materials, how quickly one can load, how long the voyage will be, the identities of charter parties and ship owners seeking particular cargo sizes, the availability and locations of ships at specific points in time, which vessels have excess space on particular voyages, discharge rates and depths at individual ports, demurrage charges, etc. In general, local knowledge is extremely important in obtaining the requisite shipping capacity at reasonable cost.[3,4] When trading and logistics are handled by separate groups, traders are in frequent contact with individuals responsible for chartering vessels, requesting quotes multiple times daily. Shipping rates may determine whether a contemplated trade will be profitable.

While traders typically determine their individual transactions-specific hedging strategies, the trading group also performs a higher-level risk management function, which is often centralized. This activity entails establishing credit and position limits, continuously monitoring the group's exposure, and assessing the potential losses associated with adverse price movements and changes in spread (the differential in value from one month to the next).

11.1.3.4 Administrative Controls and IT Systems

Because of the large dollar value of individual contracts and the very high cost of potential errors, omissions or missed trades, an effective system of firm-wide controls is essential. Trading firms generally require that every contract for the purchase and/or sale of product be approved in writing from a credit standpoint as part of such

---

[3] Chartering teams generally work with brokers. Chartering brokers possess important market information that they develop and maintain through daily dialog with other market participants. It is also frequently advantageous to have a middleman in negotiations with vessel owners.

[4] The freight market is a commodity market, with many characteristics in common with other such markets. Freight rates move on a daily basis, and a futures market for freight (the Baltic Exchange) has developed to provide ship owners and firms leasing vessel space a means of hedging their exposure. However, only ships of certain sizes are covered on the Baltic Exchange; smaller vessels, constituting the "Handy Market," are not covered. Some trading firms have "gone long" on ships (i.e., purchased vessels) in recent years, as freight rates have increased dramatically.

internal controls. Every physical trade is also generally confirmed in writing with the counterparty, clearly specifying the terms that the parties intended. Moreover, all contracts are typically reviewed to ensure that they contain the correct legal clauses and are therefore enforceable, that the terms are correctly stated and accord with those originally agreed on verbally, etc. Such oversight is critically important to trading firms. Risk managers must also have effective systems and procedures in place to quantify and continuously monitor different types of risks (market risk, counterparty-related risk, operational risk and liquidity risk). Similarly, an IT system that permits risk managers to view transactions and hedges in "real time" is essential to effective risk management. While certain trading-specific applications software is available from third parties, generally by product or sector, it typically requires extensive customization.[5]

11.1.3.5 Reputation for Reliability

Broadly speaking, the counterparty-related risks referenced above entail non-payment (i.e., credit risk), delayed performance (i.e., the delayed delivery of product) or outright non-performance. If the first or third of these eventualities comes to pass, the financial downside will generally be enormous. Because such risks are so consequential, it is of the utmost importance that trading firms be viewed as reliable counterparties.

11.1.4 Recent Developments and Their Effect on the Relative Importance of Core Assets and Skills

The core trading elements identified above, including (a) access to financing and product, (b) trading, risk management and logistical expertise, (c) effective administrative controls, risk management procedures and IT systems, and (d) a reputation for reliability, taken as a whole, do not change overly much from year to year. However, their *relative* importance can shift substantially over a comparatively brief period. In the past 3–5 years, the commodities trading landscape has been dominated by four important developments:

1. Hedge funds have become a very significant factor in these markets.
2. China has diminished dramatically in importance, particularly in the alumina and aluminum markets.
3. Pre-payment prospects have dwindled because few producers now require financing.

---

[5] For example, energy trading software vendors include OpenLink and Triple Point Technology. Other vendors sell software for natural gas, alumina and aluminum, crude oil and most other traded commodities.

4. The supply sides of the alumina and aluminum markets (and certain other commodities markets) are more concentrated than previously, as a result of a number of large mergers.

11.1.4.1 Role of Hedge Funds

Hedge funds take speculative positions, and are sufficiently large to influence prices dramatically. As a result of hedge funds' comparatively recent movement into physicals, metals prices have increased by as much as 400% over the past several years. Prices are also *much* more volatile than previously, and are no longer driven by market fundamentals. Moreover, while hedge fund money has driven a wedge between market fundamentals and pricing to a significant degree, it has also influenced market fundamentals. High-cost mines that could not operate profitably in more stable markets, generally located in North America and Europe, are now able to produce metals profitably. The very high cost of certain metals (e.g., copper) has also motivated end-users to substitute other materials, such as plastics, where feasible (e.g., in plumbing applications).

11.1.4.2 Diminished Importance of China

As previously noted, China was the driving force behind the formerly buoyant alumina market for a number of years, and it exported significant volumes of aluminum as well. However, China has built up its alumina production capacity from 7 to 8 million tons several years ago to upwards of 20 million tons currently, and it imports commensurately smaller volumes. Moreover, because aluminum production is extremely energy-intensive, and China has been in the throes of a severe energy shortage for some time, it has also shifted from encouraging aluminum exports through tax rebates to imposing a tax on such exports. Hence, traders have been looking elsewhere for alumina customers and aluminum suppliers, and cultivating relationships with producers in Asian countries other than China.

11.1.4.3 Decline in Pre-payment Opportunities

As previously noted, in the latter part of the 1990s, metals trading firms were able to secure favorable offtake arrangements with Russian aluminum producers in exchange for pre-payment loans, because the latter were cash-strapped and required working capital. However, with metals and other commodities prices at record levels, producers no longer need such cash infusions.

11.1.4.4 Consolidation in Alumina and Aluminum Markets

As with many other industries, the alumina and aluminum markets have been consolidating over the past decade, with the rate of consolidation recently accelerating. Alcan previously acquired Alusuisse and Pechiney, and was in turn acquired by Rio Tinto in 2007. Alcoa acquired Alumax, Inespal, Almix and Reynolds. RUSAL and

SUAL were formed through the consolidation of Russian smelters and CIS refineries. In late 2006, Glencore agreed to merge certain of its alumina and aluminum assets with these entities in exchange for a 12% interest in the resulting combined company (United Company RUSAL). Chinese smelters and refiners combined to form Chalco.

11.1.5 Effects of Developments on Trading Activities

The developments described above have had a profound effect on (a) the risks associated with merchant trading, (b) trading firms' capital requirements; and, (c) the range of viable trading strategies. Each of these points is discussed in turn below.

11.1.5.1 Enhanced Risk

High and volatile commodities prices magnify price and credit risk, necessitating even greater due diligence and more "bullet-proof" risk management. Moreover, because a customer may enter into a contract to purchase materials at one price on a given day for delivery a month hence, and be able to purchase the materials at a much lower price later in the month, there is a real risk that the customer will not take delivery under the original contract. Given the increased risk of non-performance, a reputation for reliability is even more important than previously, and firms are reluctant to transact with counterparties with which they have limited experience. Moreover, large counterparties that require regular supplies of a given commodity are less apt to reneg on a deal than smaller counterparties, and pose a lower credit risk. Hence, smaller counterparties are at a significant competitive disadvantage in these environs.

11.1.5.2 Increased Need for Financing

Because commodities prices are considerably higher than they have historically been, traders need more money to finance a given transaction, and because prices are more volatile, they must also earn a higher return to compensate them for the increased risk. There is also the potential for very large margin calls on hedging transactions, which banks will not finance. Hence, trading firms must have sufficient cash available to meet potential margin calls.

11.1.5.3 Diminished Range of Viable Trading Strategies

Certain trading strategies are not feasible in the current trading environment. As previously noted, because suppliers do not need pre-financing, it is much more difficult to negotiate long-term offtake arrangements. As a result, trading firms are increasingly acquiring ownership interests in mines and smelters as an alternative means of securing reliable sources of supply. Traders are also much more reluctant to take positions of any length, and to carry inventories (particularly in the copper market, which has been in steep backwardation for an extended period of time). Instead, they have focussed to a much greater extent than previously on short-term trading.

11.1.6 Division of Labor and Risks Among Group Members

The firm that is the subject of this case study engages in a wide range of customer-based and proprietary trading activities. It is contending with all of the challenges posed by hedge fund participation, China's marked decline as an importer and exporter of key metals, dwindling pre-payment opportunities and ongoing consolidation in the aluminum markets. Each Group member that concludes trades has credit lines on which it can individually draw, and the group as a whole has a number of swing lines as well. Similarly, each entity that concludes trades has the requisite logistical and administrative support staff to verify contract terms with counterparties, review all contracts to ensure their enforceability, provide lending institutions with the necessary documentation, etc. FP performs risk management activities on a group-wide basis, evaluates customers' creditworthiness, and has developed and maintains the group's IT infrastructure. Firm-wide credit and position limits are established by a committee composed of representatives from all trading entities.

Natural gas, alumina and aluminum are traded by multiple group members, although the degree of interaction among traders in different offices varies considerably by commodity. UKS trades natural gas in the United Kingdom and on the Continent. USS and CAS trade natural gas in North America. Because of the lack of physical infrastructure (i.e., pipelines) spanning the Atlantic, and the fact that, to date, cross-Atlantic trades in LNG are the exception rather than the rule, natural gas traders in the United Kingdom have virtually no interaction with their opposite numbers in the United States and Canada.

USS and CAS engage in some, albeit a very limited volume of, intercompany transactions in natural gas. These transactions take place at index prices. USS' natural gas traders deal primarily with customers based in the United States and Western Canada, while CAS deals primarily with Eastern Canadian customers. However, originators and schedulers employed by CAS assist USS in developing and maintaining relationships with certain Western Canadian counterparties, and in nominating pipelines. (When a trader intends to move gas via pipeline, he or she notifies a scheduler on staff, who contacts the scheduling personnel employed by the pipeline operator, "nominates" (or designates) a particular pipeline, and makes the necessary contractual arrangements.)

FP, USS and UKS all employ alumina and aluminum traders; CHS employs marketers who act on behalf of these traders. As with natural gas, there are comparatively few intercompany transactions in alumina and aluminum. However, traders based in Switzerland, the United States and the United Kingdom routinely share market intelligence, jointly formulate trading strategies, identify sources of supply and outlets in their respective markets, and maintain a single book of business.

Moreover, one individual functions as the head trader of alumina and aluminum, with oversight responsibility vis-a-vis the other traders in all locations. Traders' discretionary bonuses are based on the Group-wide P&L for alumina and aluminum.

11.2 Transfer Pricing Issues

With regard to natural gas, intercompany transactions are largely limited to services (origination, scheduling and key support functions). As previously noted, the limited intercompany transactions in natural gas between USS and CAS take place at index prices, which constitute CUPs. With respect to alumina and aluminum, the group is a "functionally fully integrated" trading operation.

11.3 Analysis Under Existing Regime

The analysis of natural gas services under the current transfer pricing regime is comparatively straightforward. As noted, most trading houses utilize independent marketers in certain geographic markets, to supplement the efforts of employees who perform the same origination function internally. Compensation paid to third party marketers constitutes arm's length consideration for the origination functions performed by one Group member on behalf of another. Most trading firms perform logistics functions solely internally. However, Non-Vessel Operating Common Carriers (NVOCCs), which arrange for the transport of product but do not own transportation assets themselves, are reasonably good comparables.

The support services that FP renders to other Group members are also amenable to comparables-based analyses. For this purpose, we distinguish between lower and higher value-added services. To some degree, these distinctions are necessarily guided by the particular mix of services that standalone services providers render. Thus, for example, if standalone companies combine IT customization and credit risk assessment services under one roof, the corresponding intercompany services can be combined for analytical purposes as well. (As discussed below, we utilize a formulary apportionment methodology to allocate the Group's alumina and aluminum trading profits, and include a measure of administrative support in the formula. As such, services fees should *not* be charged on these product lines.)

The more challenging part of this transfer pricing analysis pertains to the trading of alumina and aluminum. As a functionally fully integrated trading operation, the Group has only *Notice 94–40* and the proposed Global dealing regulations[6] to rely on in determining the arm's length allocation of its income among taxing jurisdictions. As discussed in Chapter 3, *Notice 94–40* details the formulary apportionment methodologies that have formed the basis of global trading firms' APAs with the IRS, and the proposed global dealing regulations expand upon and generalize these methodologies. To reiterate, allocation formulas generally consist of three factors:

---

[6] As previously noted, these regulations do not even technically apply to commodities traders.

1. The "relative value" of individual trading locations;
2. The "risk" associated with each trading location; and,
3. The extent of "activity" at each trading location.

Measures of these individual factors vary across cases, and are weighted to reflect their perceived relative importance. The formula as a whole is "intended to measure the economic activity of each trading location and its contribution to the overall profitability of the worldwide business."[7] The income to be allocated is defined as "worldwide profits and losses from trading the class of commodities or derivative financial instruments and related hedges ... [included] within the APA, less expenses that are directly related to the production of trading income or loss, such as compensation of certain personnel, computer trading systems, and broker commissions (the 'worldwide net income or loss')."[8]

Consistent with the approach outlined in *Notice 94–40*, our analysis of the Group's alumina and aluminum trading activities is based on a formulary methodology. We measure the "relative value" of each trading location by total compensation paid to alumina and aluminum traders by location. In recognition of the fact that non-performance risk is currently the most dominant form of risk, we measure "relative risk" by average physicals transactions volumes by office. Lastly, we measure "activity" by compensation paid to key support personnel in each location.

It remains to weight each factor. Trader compensation (our measure of the "relative value" of individual trading locations, as noted) is typically ascribed the greatest weight. However, the current trading environment has greatly circumscribed traders' ability to exercise their skills. At the same time, the extreme volatility of commodities prices has heightened both risk and the importance of certain key support functions (primarily those related to credit and risk management). In view of these considerations, we assign the greatest weight (0.50) to physicals transactions volumes (our measure of "relative risk"), and weight value and activity factors equally (0.25 and 0.25, respectively). As noted, the resulting ratios are used to allocate the Group's trading profits, as defined above, on alumina and aluminum transactions.

11.4 Analysis Under Alternative Regime

Next, we analyze this case by application of the proposed simplified profit split method. Using this methodology, one allocates combined after-tax free cash flows based on the fair market value of assets employed by each Group member in its alumina and aluminum trading activities (or a reliable proxy therefor). Hence, the first order of business is to identify all assets employed by the Group in its trading

---

[7] See *Notice 94–40, Global Trading Advance Pricing Agreements*, 1994-1 C.B. 351; 1994 I.R.B. LEXIS 213; 1994-17 I.R.B. 22, April 25, 2004.

[8] Ibid.

of alumina and aluminum, and, where feasible, to assign ownership of each such asset to individual Group members. However, as discussed at greater length below, functionally fully integrated trading groups generally develop important intangible assets *jointly*, in the normal course of their business. As a result, ownership (and the associated income) cannot be ascribed to an individual Group member.

Consider first the intangible assets employed in alumina and aluminum trading. As discussed at Section 11.1, the key prerequisites to commodities trading include:

- Access to financing;
- Access to product;
- A reputation for reliability;
- A set of administrative controls that prevents enormously costly errors and facilitates the effective management of risk;
- A sophisticated IT system that enables traders and risk managers to track activity in real time; and,
- Expertise in market fundamentals, trading strategies, risk management and logistics.

Access to financing in and of itself does not constitute an intangible asset in competitive financial markets. Expertise in market fundamentals and the like does not exist separate and apart from the traders that possess this expertise; as such, it too does not constitute an intangible asset.[9] Administrative procedures, systems and controls, while critical, are not proprietary, and, as such, should be considered "routine" intangible assets (in the parlance of the U.S. regulations).

A reputation for reliability is also centrally important, in that it is a precondition of access to product, financing and, ultimately, counterparties. Moreover, it constitutes an intangible asset. However, a reputation for reliability is a natural outgrowth of conducting a successful global dealing operation over a period of years.[10] In this instance (and in virtually all cases involving functionally fully integrated global trading operations), individual Group members have contributed equally to the development of the Group's reputation. As such, the "reputational" intangible asset cannot be used to allocate income among Group members.

Access to product constitutes an intangible asset under some circumstances. For example, if pre-payment arrangements, coupled with long-term offtake agreements, ensure access to alumina or aluminum in tight markets or on favorable terms, such contracts should be considered valuable intangible assets. However, as discussed at length above, long-term offtake arrangements are largely a thing of the past, replaced by direct investment in upstream hard assets. Established relationships that

---

[9] The Section 482 regulations define intangible assets as patents, inventions, designs, processes, copyrights, trademarks, franchises, methods, programs, etc., that have "substantial value independent of the services of any individual." See Treas. Reg. Section 1.482-4(b).

[10] For this reason, the capitalization–amortization approach often used to value intellectual property for residual profit split purposes cannot be used to value this intangible asset (leaving aside the fact that a cost-based valuation method often yields results that bear no relationship to fair market value).

ensure access to product are also potentially important intangible assets in a trading context. However, as with its reputation, the Group has historically developed such relationships jointly, not through investment per se, but in the ordinary course of business. (Moreover, in the alumina and aluminum markets in particular, established relationships with customers and suppliers have greatly diminished in value recently as a result of China's substantially reduced role in these markets.)

Most trading firms utilize off-the-shelf software developed specifically for trading applications, and this Group is no exception. However, the software generally has to be extensively customized. Hence, the customization component constitutes an intangible asset of some significance, owned by FP in this case.

In sum, FP has created an intangible asset through the customization of software. Expenditures on customization activities are a reasonable approximation of the asset's value: One would not pay more than this amount to purchase the customization features, because the software engineering work can readily be replicated.[11] The Group's offtake arrangements have largely expired; if this were not the case, they would also be valuable intangible assets, and ownership should be ascribed to the Group member that is the legal counterparty.[12] A reputation for reliability, while a highly valuable intangible asset, has been developed jointly by all members of the Group, and, as such, cannot be used to allocate trading profits among members. Established relationships likewise have been developed jointly, and now have *de minimis* value in any event. More broadly, in circumstances where one is justified in applying the formulary apportionment method, joint ownership of intangible assets that are developed in the normal course of business is the rule rather than the exception.

Where most intangible assets are jointly developed and owned by all members of a controlled trading group (as in this case), the allocation of after-tax free cash flows by entity should be based primarily on each entity's contribution (or utilization) of capital over the course of the year, and the degree of risk assumed thereby. As described in the summary of key facts above, in many instances (including this case), individual group members have their own designated lines of credit, extended by third party lenders, and bear the associated interest costs. Under these circumstances, the borrower should retain the after-tax free cash flows earned on all trades financed by drawdowns on its credit lines (out of which it will repay principal and interest). For swing lines, loans extended to the Group as a whole, or equity capital, the same basic logic applies: The entity that draws on such capital to finance trades incurs the associated cost of capital, and should retain the associated after-tax free cash flows, out of which it compensates lenders and investors.[13]

---

[11] The Constructive Cost Model (COCOMO) is a widely used means of estimating software development costs.

[12] Under the U.S. Temporary Regulations issued in 2006, "[t]he legal owner of an intangible pursuant to the intellectual property law of the relevant jurisdiction ... will be considered the sole owner of the respective intangible ..." See Temp. Treas. Reg. Section 1.482-4T(f)(3)(i)(A).

[13] To illustrate, consider an extreme case where a single group member provides all of the capital necessary to finance transactions, while other group members employ only as much working

A more readily available proxy for capital employed (and certain types of risks assumed thereby) may serve the same purpose. Commodities trading firms measure and monitor their market risk continuously.[14] They also invest significant resources in the development and refinement of risk models and stress testing.[15] Value at risk (VaR) is one common means of measuring market risk. It entails quantifying potential losses resulting from adverse price movements of a given percentage over a specified time horizon. Trading firms generally calculate VaR on a position-by-position basis and aggregate these individual measures into an overall risk position. VaR measures jointly capture the amount of capital invested in a given position and the degree of price risk associated with the position: The larger the investment and/or the greater the risk (as calibrated by the assumed percentage price change), the higher the VaR, all other things equal. As such, individual group members with larger VaRs will have a higher cost of capital.

VaRs could serve as a proxy for the *relative* amount of, and risk to, capital employed by individual group members, for purposes of allocating after-tax free cash flows among them. Ideally, one would average VaRs over days, rather than weeks or months, given the fluidity of trading firms' positions. Such an analysis presupposes that individual group members own limited intangible assets. However, even where this is not the case (e.g., where one group member is the counterparty to an offtake arrangement with discounted pricing), allocations of intangible income are more readily handled separately, prior to a VaR-based allocation of the remaining trading income. (Stated differently, the income allocated to individual group members as a result of their ownership of intangible assets should be removed from the pool of after-tax free cash flows to be allocated based on average VaRs.) For this purpose, intangible assets do not need to be valued explicitly. Instead, one need only estimate the amount of income generated by each such asset during the period at issue, a much more manageable task. Given the one- or two-step allocation of combined after-tax free cash flows based on (a) income generated by intangible assets and/or (b) average VaRs, it remains to convert such flows into before-tax net income (see Chapters 4 and 9 for discussions of this issue).

It should be noted that VaRs measure market risk, not credit or counterparty risk. However, as the latter risks become more pronounced, trading firms' measures of risk will be refined accordingly. As such, the more general point to be made is that

---

capital as is necessary to maintain a staff and premises. The latter members are effectively services providers and should retain only enough free cash flows to compensate the providers of working capital in limited quantities. All other free cash flows should accrue to the group member that finances transactions, inasmuch as it must pay its shareholders and lenders for the use of their funds on a much larger scale.

[14] For the results of a survey of 17 commodities trading firms' risk management procedures and practices, see Commodity Firms Regulatory Capital Working Group, "An Alternative Approach to the Application of the full CRD to Commodity Firms Active in the EU," 2006, Appendix 3.

[15] Stress testing entails assuming dire financial market conditions and determining whether the firm could withstand these conditions.

trading firms' own measures of risk will be both more comprehensive and more readily available than ad hoc measures of risk designed expressly for tax purposes.

11.5 Comparison

The formulary apportionment methodology presupposes that there is a predictable (and possibly causal) relationship between (a) the measure of profits defined in *Notice 94–40*, and (b) the "factors" used to allocate such profits among group companies.

However, the market-determined compensation paid to traders, originators, logistics personnel, risk managers and others *already reflects* the value of their contributions to the generation of gross profits. Segmenting compensation paid to different groupings (e.g., traders and key support personnel, respectively) and superimposing weights onto the resulting "value" and "activity" factors, simply substitutes subjective judgment for an existing, and much more reliable, measure of each groupings' economic value.

The "risk" factor, as the IRS has applied it, is also problematic. Here, the distinction between accounting profits and free cash flows becomes paramount. As stated in *Notice 94–40*, the risk factor is intended to "measure the potential risk to which a particular trading location exposes the worldwide capital of the organization." As illustrated by our proposed simplified profit split method, risk, appropriately measured, can in fact serve this purpose. However, reducing risk to a single, point-in-time measure, as described in *Notice 94–40* (e.g., open positions at year end), cannot possibly capture all the dimensions of risk to which a functionally fully integrated trading firm is subject over the course of a year. Given trading firms' fully justified preoccupation with risk, and their dedication of resources to the measurement thereof, it makes far more sense to rely on such internal measures. Additionally, as noted, the formulary method applies to "worldwide net income," rather than after-tax free cash flows. The latter, rather than the former, should be allocated based on capital employed and risks assumed thereby.

In summary, the formulary apportionment method's attribution of worldwide net income to value, activity and risk factors in itself is unfounded. The measures and weighting of value, activity and risk are also flawed, and the resulting allocation is therefore wholly arbitrary. One can significantly improve on the IRS' formulary apportionment methodology vis-a-vis global dealing operations by substituting assets for factors, fair market values for weights and after-tax free cash flows for the accounting-based measure of profits defined in *Notice 94–40*. With these modifications, which the proposed simplified profit split method incorporates, the approach has a far more solid economic footing.

Chapter 12
Decentralized Ownership of Intellectual Property

This case study involves an Internet-based multinational firm with operations in numerous countries. Its intangible assets consist largely of discrete user communities, which have been developed by separate legal entities operating in various taxing jurisdictions, and secondarily of an IT platform used in all locations. Hence, ownership of intangible assets is not concentrated in a single Group member.

Diffuse ownership of intangible assets other than trademarks is comparatively unusual (and trademarks can generally be addressed in a transfer pricing context through methods other than profit splits). This fact pattern arises primarily when one established company acquires another, and has not yet integrated the separate research and marketing groups within each organization. A multinational firm that has been built up in part through acquisitions may also decide *not* to integrate the separate research and/or marketing groups. For example, this may be the case if (a) the research groups have complementary, but clearly distinct, areas of expertise, (b) consumers in individual countries have markedly different preferences (as is often the case vis-a-vis the United States and Europe), or (c) the firm manufactures electronics products and must therefore deal with different voltage requirements and standard-setting and certification bodies.

In short, contrary to several examples in the Section 482 regulations (e.g., the example under Treas. Reg. Section 1.482-6 and Example 8 under Treas. Reg. Section 1.482-8), it is relatively uncommon for individual members of a multinational group that has developed organically to maintain separate research facilities, or otherwise independently develop intangible assets other than trademarks. (The large fixed costs associated with many types of research facilities create a compelling incentive to centralize the research function. Additionally, in many instances, research activities are, by their nature, cooperative, and face-to-face interaction among researchers can be extremely important.) Some notable exceptions to this general observation, ironically, are e-commerce companies. Despite the fact that such firms often have a limited physical presence, and national boundaries do not exist in cyberspace, there are numerous impediments to the formation of genuinely border-free e-commerce websites. Such obstacles include:

E. King, *Transfer Pricing and Corporate Taxation*,
DOI 10.1007/978-0-387-78183-9_12, © Springer Science+Business Media, LLC 2009

- Language;
- Local customs, tastes and preferences, not only for particular types of goods and services but also for the "look and feel" of websites and user interface features;
- Differing legal protections regarding the transfer of personal information over the Internet, and consumers' comfort level in doing so;
- Differing legal restrictions on the types of products that can be sold over the Internet;
- Currency;
- Payment mechanisms;
- Customs duties; and,
- Shipping.

In view of the above impediments to border-free e-commerce websites, individual members of multinational e-commerce groups generally customize their sites and develop their own user networks (although the development and maintenance of an IT platform is often centralized). Such is the case with individual members of the multinational Group featured in this case study. We analyze this case under the residual profit split method, the proposed joint venture method and the (officially) proposed cost-sharing regulations.

12.1 Summary of Key Facts

As noted above, the multinational firm in this case is a large Internet-based company with operations in numerous countries. Its tangible assets consist predominantly of servers (along with headquarters and local offices), and its intangible assets consist of a number of discrete user communities, a trademark and an IT platform (consisting of server-side and client-side software). The firm as a whole is in the business of providing web-based information services and a forum in which users can interact directly. Its income consists primarily of advertising revenues.

The Group's sites in different countries, while generally extremely successful, have remained discrete; users in one country rarely interact with users in another country (even within the EU), and user interfaces have been extensively customized. Such customization goes far beyond translation and spelling to include virtually all aspects of the "look and feel" of the sites and the specific functionality that users in different countries demand. The U.S. site is operated by the parent company (USP), and it was the first site to be established. It developed the business model used by all Group members (which is not proprietary, and has been extensively replicated by third parties), and the IT platform, also used by all Group members. All of the Group's non-U.S. sites are operated by its wholly-owned subsidiary in Europe (FS), each through a separate legal entity (themselves subsidiaries of FS). Network effects have been an extremely important factor in the Group's success.

The telephone industry in its early stages is an often-cited example of network effects. At the outset, the industry consisted of very small local networks, or local exchanges, that could not communicate with one another. AT&T provided the infrastructure (an interconnector) that enabled subscribers of one local exchange to connect to subscribers of other local exchanges. The more such cross-connections individual subscribers could make (equivalently, the larger the network), the more valuable the service. Hence the birth of a monopoly: Because individual local exchanges were worth far more as part of AT&T's growing network, it could pay more than their value on a standalone basis to acquire them.

The analogy to the Internet is so straightforward that it is barely an analogy at all: The Internet has rapidly become an integral part of the world economy, and of the way in which individuals communicate and socialize, because it is a massive network of networks that facilitates billions of cross-connections at minimal cost. If it were only half as large, it would be much less than half as valuable and influential. The same observation applies to user networks on the Internet: eBay, Flickr, YouTube and Face Book are extremely valuable companies primarily because they have very large user communities. It is very difficult for new entrants in the same product space to attract users, because the size of a user network generally determines the desirability of joining in the first instance. (Hence Microsoft's aggressive pursuit of Yahoo.) Large begets larger, and smaller firms fall by the wayside. This dynamic, while applicable to certain companies and industries without a presence on the Internet, is amplified in cyberspace, as has long been recognized. Thus, for example, Morgan Stanley Dean Witter equity researchers made the following observation in June 1999:

> Even as Internet companies grow at torrid speed, many have yet to generate positive earnings because they are spending heavily now to build market leadership for the future. The lesson is clear to us: first-mover advantage and the law of increasing returns are more pronounced on the Net than anywhere else in the economy.[1]

While USP was the first mover in its product space in the United States, other companies in non-U.S. markets were quick to duplicate its business model, as noted. Largely because of network effects and the resulting first-mover advantage, USP expanded into foreign markets where there was a clear market leader through acquisitions. It rebranded the acquired sites and migrated users to its own IT platform, to eliminate duplication in network assets and costs. USP also entered into several joint venture partnerships in key non-U.S. markets.

Shortly before USP's first major acquisition, FS was established, and USP contributed the shares of the acquired company thereto on a cost-free basis. USP and FS also entered into a joint venture (JV) agreement, which set out the following division of labor:

- USP contributes its existing IT platform.
- USP has sole responsibility for maintaining and upgrading the IT platform at its own cost and risk. Servers are located solely in the United States, for use worldwide.
- USP agrees to customize individual foreign sites based on specifications provided by FS.

---

[1] Morgan Stanley Dean Witter, *The European Internet Report*, June 1999, p. 181.

- FS has sole responsibility for developing international markets (with the exceptions of Germany and Japan) at its own cost and risk.
- FS is contractually obligated to develop and promote USP's brand identity in international markets (heretofore unknown outside of the United States), and indemnifies USP against all losses, damages, expenses and other costs incurred as a result of alleged claims of improper use of USP's brand name.

Under the terms of its JV agreement with FS, USP is entitled to 20% of FS' operating profits. Since USP and FS entered into this agreement, FS has established a number of greenfield sites in various countries. USP also purchased two other firms providing similar or complementary information services and forums, and again contributed the acquired companies' shares to FS on a cost-free basis. USP has joint venture agreements with third parties in Germany and Japan; hence their exclusion from FS' territory in the intercompany JV agreement. (These third party JV agreements pre-dated FS' JV agreement with USP.)

Due to the sheer size of the U.S. population, the fact that Silicon Valley was the launching pad for vast numbers of Internet start-ups and, relatedly, because U.S. consumers were among the first to fully embrace the Internet, the U.S. website has remained the largest of the Group's individual sites. Because it was the Group's first site, it has also traveled further along the trajectory of development and maturation. Primarily in response to flagging interest among U.S. users, USP recently acquired two domestic companies with complementary e-commerce businesses. Both acquisitions were stock transactions, and the acquired companies do not have overseas operations. FS' sites now collectively rival the size of the U.S. site (and generate comparable revenues and free cash flows), although they are individually much smaller and the markets less mature.

USP has invested considerable sums in its IT platform over the past several years, primarily for purposes of refining the U.S. user interface and building scalability into its system. The latter is an important issue in the United States, but much less so in foreign markets, because the user networks are much smaller in these markets. Investments in IT are only one-quarter of those in marketing on a Group-wide basis. Such marketing is primarily Internet-based, and is designed to maximize traffic to the Group's sites.

12.2 Transfer Pricing Issues

This case raises the following transfer pricing issues:

1. Should FS compensate USP for its contribution of the three acquired foreign companies' assets, and should USP compensate FS for its partial financing of USP's two domestic acquisitions (both of which were much larger than the foreign target companies at the time of their acquisitions)?
2. How much should FS pay USP for:

- Rights to use USP's IT platform and its upgrades to server-side and client-side software on an ongoing basis;
- USP's customization of its platform undertaken on FS' behalf; and,
- USP's performance of site operations functions on FS' behalf.

3. Should FS compensate USP for its rights to use the latter's brand identity in international markets, and if so, what constitutes arm's length consideration?

12.3 Analysis Under Existing Regime

The range of potential approaches to the transfer pricing issues listed above depend in part on whether one treats FS and USP as joint venture partners or purely standalone companies.

12.3.1 Assuming USP and FS Act to Maximize Their Individual Profits

If we assume that FS and USP each act to maximize their *individual* profits rather than their *combined* profits, certain of the transfer pricing issues can be addressed fairly simply.

FS and USP should compensate one another for their respective contributions of assets and acquisition financing. The fair market value of assets contributed by USP to FS is straightforward, inasmuch as these contributions took place shortly after the acquisitions (all of which were cash transactions), and a market price therefore existed.

FS' contributions to the financing of USP's domestic acquisitions are more complex. As noted, these transactions were stock acquisitions. When the first such acquisition took place, FS' cash flows accounted for approximately 30% of Group-wide cash flows. When the second such acquisition took place, FS' cash flows accounted for close to 40% of Group-wide cash flows. At both points in time, the Group's international sites were growing substantially more rapidly than USP's domestic site.

An implication of these facts is that a substantial part of the future cash flow stream represented by the Group's stock, used to acquire the domestic target companies, will be generated in international markets. Therefore, in effect, USP and FS *jointly* acquired the domestic companies, jointly own their assets, and should divide the cash flow attributable thereto in proportion to their respective ownership interests. (Alternatively, USP could purchase FS' interests outright.) One might argue instead that an implicit back-to-back securitization transaction has taken place: First, FS issued USP notes entitling the latter to a portion of its future cash flows, in exchange for the face amount of the notes up front; second, USP transferred these notes to the sellers of the domestic target companies as partial consideration. Under this scenario, USP owes FS the face amount of the notes (and foregone interest).

Under most circumstances, FS' use of USP's IT platform and brand identity, and USP's performance of customization and site operations services, could be analyzed by reference to arm's length licensing and services arrangements. However, in this instance, FS would presumably pay USP a nominal amount, if anything, for the use of its IT platform and its customization services on an arm's length basis. Each of the foreign companies that USP acquired had IT platforms sufficient to meet FS' functionality and scalability requirements in these markets. Further, the user interfaces were already customized by country. USP contributed these platforms, along with the remaining acquired assets, to FS, and, as analyzed above, it should have been compensated at arm's length therefor. Hence, USP's IT platform was entirely duplicative. The decision to use a single platform was motivated solely by the fact that, over the longer term, having a single platform would conserve IT expenses on a consolidated basis.

12.3.2 Assuming FS and USP Act as Joint Venture Partners

Because FS does, in fact, utilize USP's IT platform and has, in fact, relied on USP to perform certain customization activities, the line of reasoning outlined above, which follows directly from treating FS as a standalone company, would almost certainly be unacceptable to U.S. taxing authorities.

While the U.S. and OECD transfer pricing regulations and Guidelines clearly require that FS and USP be treated as independent companies, this does not preclude characterizing them as joint venture partners, inasmuch as third parties often enter into such arrangements. Moreover, the division of labor between USP and FS, as set forth in the intercompany JV Agreement summarized above, clearly indicates that this is how the Companies actually structured their affairs. As such, for purposes of further analyzing the transfer pricing issues in this case, we assume that FS and USP are independent companies acting as joint venture partners.

In view of this conclusion, it is clear, in principle, that we should look first to USP's third party joint venture arrangements with companies in Germany and Japan to determine the arm's length division of income between USP and FS. However, as a practical matter, the IRS tends to reject out of hand the use of joint venture arrangements as comparable uncontrolled transactions. Therefore, while continuing with our assumption that USP and FS are joint venture partners, we apply the residual profit split method under the current transfer pricing regime, in lieu of the CUP method.

As described in detail in Chapter 3, one applies the residual profit split method by (a) imputing arm's length "returns" to the routine contributions made by each member of the controlled group; (b) determining the relative value of each member's intangible assets; (c) adjusting combined reported operating profits in two steps: increasing such income by intangibles-creating expenditures, and decreasing the resulting magnitude by amortization deductions; (d) quantifying combined "residual income" by reducing combined adjusted operating profits by each member's returns to routine contributions; and, (e) allocating residual income based on each group member's relative intangible asset values. (In contrast to standard applications of the residual profit split method, in which one allocates the combined income of all group members participating in the subject transactions, our application in this case entails apportioning only FS' income.)

Transfer pricing practitioners generally value the intangible assets contributed by each group member by capitalizing and amortizing their "intangibles-creating expenditures," rather than by application of standard valuation methodologies, such as the Discounted Cash Flow (DCF) method.[2] Hence, in applying the residual profit split method, the first several implementation steps entail:

- Determining which expenditures give rise to intangible assets;
- Estimating the "gestation lag" associated with each such category of expenditure (that is, the lag between investment and the realization of benefits in the form of improved products or processes); and,
- Establishing the economically useful life of each type of intangible asset.

Each of these steps is highly subjective, and consequential in determining the allocation of consolidated income. In this instance, we *temporarily* sidestep these issues by making certain simplifying assumptions, most of which we then sequentially relax. (This is done for expository purposes, and to illustrate the qualitative and quantitative significance of individual assumptions.) Our simplifying assumptions are listed below:

1. All of FS' marketing expenditures give rise to intangible assets;
2. All of USP's software development expenditures give rise to intangible assets;
3. No other expenditures give rise to intangible assets;
4. USP's IT platform and FS' marketing-related intangible assets have *identical* gestation lags and useful lives;
5. The scalability of USP's IT platform benefits FS, despite the fact that FS' sites are individually much smaller than the U.S. site;
6. FS performs no routine functions; and,
7. USP performs no routine functions vis-a-vis international markets.

Given these simplifying assumptions, approximately 25% of FS' adjusted operating profits (all of which are residual profits, in view of assumptions #6 and #7 above) should accrue to USP.[3] Given our assumption that FS performs no routine functions, we also reduce its operating expenses (and thereby increase its operating profits) by the costs of such functions.

---

[2] It is unclear why these more standard valuation methods are not discussed in any detail in the transfer pricing regulations.

[3] For purposes of this analysis, FS' adjusted operating profits are computed as (a) its reported operating profits, plus (b) its marketing expenditures in the current year, less (c) the estimated amortization of its marketing intangible assets in the current year. These adjustments to FS' reported operating income conform the treatment of investment in intangible assets to investment in tangible assets for accounting purposes. (As discussed at Chapter 3, one should, in principle, utilize after-tax free cash flows in lieu of adjusted operating profits, but the regulations are framed in terms of operating profits.)

While the calculation of asset values is arithmetically simple, it is tedious and time-consuming in direct proportion to the length of assumed gestation lags and economically useful lives. Hence, for the sake of illustration only, we assume that FS' marketing intangible assets have a gestation lag of one month and an economically useful life of 2 years. Moreover, we assume that FS expends a uniform amount per month on marketing over the course of a year, determined by dividing its annual marketing expenses by 12. As noted, benefits from these monthly outlays are realized over the subsequent 24 months. (The gestation lag is very brief because most marketing efforts are geared toward directing Internet traffic to FS' sites. Individuals respond quickly or not at all to these efforts.) Lastly, we assume that FS invests \$19,440,000, \$43,524,000 and \$112,800,000, respectively, on marketing during its first 3 years of operations. This set of assumptions generates the amortization deductions per annum (in thousands of U.S. dollars) shown in Table 12.1 during years 1–3.

We determine the division of FS' adjusted operating profits between FS and USP under the residual profit split method, given the simplifying assumptions noted above, in the following steps:

1. USP's software development outlays, expressed as a percentage of consolidated intangibles-creating expenditures, are consistently in the range of 23.0%–27.0%.
2. With identical gestation lags and useful lives, relative intangible asset values will equal relative intangibles-creating expenditures.
3. Therefore, under this set of assumptions, USP's IT platform has a value of between 23.0% and 27.0% of the Group's combined IT- and marketing-related intangible assets.
4. The relative values of (a) USP's IT platform in international markets, and (b) FS' marketing intangible assets, should be approximately equal to the relative values of these assets on a consolidated basis if platform scalability benefits FS (as we assume for the time being).

Next, we sequentially eliminate certain of our simplifying assumptions. First, USP and FS *do* perform routine functions. More particularly, in addition to its sales and marketing role, FS performs customer support, payment processing and general and administrative support functions. USP performs site operations services vis-a-vis FS' international operations. Utilizing several sets of standalone services providers that (a) perform a subset of the same support functions on a fee-for-service basis, and (b) do not own intangible assets, we conclude that FS should earn a weighted average markup of 8% over the costs of performing its routine functions. We conclude that USP should earn a markup of 10.0% over the costs of performing site operations services on behalf of FS. Hence, we reduce FS' adjusted operating profits by (i) the costs that USP bears in rendering site operations services to FS, (ii) the 10.0% return that USP should earn on these routine services, and (iii) the 8.0% weighted average markup that FS should earn in performing its routine

Table 12.1 Amortization of FS' Marketing Intangibles, Years 1–3

YEAR 1

1	2	3	4	5	6	7	8	9	10	11	12
1620	1620	1620	1620	1620	1620	1620	1620	1620	1620	1620	1620
	−68	−68	−68	−68	−68	−68	−68	−68	−68	−68	−68
		−68	−68	−68	−68	−68	−68	−68	−68	−68	−68
			−68	−68	−68	−68	−68	−68	−68	−68	−68
				−68	−68	−68	−68	−68	−68	−68	−68
					−68	−68	−68	−68	−68	−68	−68
						−68	−68	−68	−68	−68	−68
							−68	−68	−68	−68	−68
								−68	−68	−68	−68
									−68	−68	−68
										−68	−68
											−68
	68	136	204	272	340	408	476	544	612	680	748

Year 1 Amortization: 4,488 Euros

YEAR 2

1	2	3	4	5	6	7	8	9	10	11	12
3627	3627	3627	3627	3627	3627	3627	3627	3627	3627	3627	3627
−68	−68	−68	−68	−68	−68	−68	−68	−68	−68	−68	−68
−68	−68	−68	−68	−68	−68	−68	−68	−68	−68	−68	−68
−68	−68	−68	−68	−68	−68	−68	−68	−68	−68	−68	−68
−68	−68	−68	−68	−68	−68	−68	−68	−68	−68	−68	−68
−68	−68	−68	−68	−68	−68	−68	−68	−68	−68	−68	−68
−68	−68	−68	−68	−68	−68	−68	−68	−68	−68	−68	−68
−68	−68	−68	−68	−68	−68	−68	−68	−68	−68	−68	−68
−68	−68	−68	−68	−68	−68	−68	−68	−68	−68	−68	−68
−68	−68	−68	−68	−68	−68	−68	−68	−68	−68	−68	−68
−68	−68	−68	−68	−68	−68	−68	−68	−68	−68	−68	−68
−68	−68	−68	−68	−68	−68	−68	−68	−68	−68	−68	−68
−68	−68	−68	−68	−68	−68	−68	−68	−68	−68	−68	−68
	−151	−151	−151	−151	−151	−151	−151	−151	−151	−151	−151
		−151	−151	−151	−151	−151	−151	−151	−151	−151	−151
			−151	−151	−151	−151	−151	−151	−151	−151	−151
				−151	−151	−151	−151	−151	−151	−151	−151
					−151	−151	−151	−151	−151	−151	−151
						−151	−151	−151	−151	−151	−151
							−151	−151	−151	−151	−151
								−151	−151	−151	−151
									−151	−151	−151
										−151	−151
											−151
816	967	1118	1269	1420	1571	1722	1873	2024	2175	2326	2477

Year 2 Amortization: 19,758 Euros

YEAR 3

1	2	3	4	5	6	7	8	9	10	11	12
9400	9400	9400	9400	9400	9400	9400	9400	9400	9400	9400	9400
−68											
−68	−68										
−68	−68	−68									

Table 12.1 (continued)

−68	−68	−68	−68								
−68	−68	−68	−68	−68							
−68	−68	−68	−68	−68	−68						
−68	−68	−68	−68	−68	−68	−68					
−68	−68	−68	−68	−68	−68	−68	−68				
−68	−68	−68	−68	−68	−68	−68	−68	−68			
−68	−68	−68	−68	−68	−68	−68	−68	−68	−68		
−68	−68	−68	−68	−68	−68	−68	−68	−68	−68	−68	
−68	−68	−68	−68	−68	−68	−68	−68	−68	−68	−68	−68
−151	−151	−151	−151	−151	−151	−151	−151	−151	−151	−151	−151
−151	−151	−151	−151	−151	−151	−151	−151	−151	−151	−151	−151
−151	−151	−151	−151	−151	−151	−151	−151	−151	−151	−151	−151
−151	−151	−151	−151	−151	−151	−151	−151	−151	−151	−151	−151
−151	−151	−151	−151	−151	−151	−151	−151	−151	−151	−151	−151
−151	−151	−151	−151	−151	−151	−151	−151	−151	−151	−151	−151
−151	−151	−151	−151	−151	−151	−151	−151	−151	−151	−151	−151
−151	−151	−151	−151	−151	−151	−151	−151	−151	−151	−151	−151
−151	−151	−151	−151	−151	−151	−151	−151	−151	−151	−151	−151
−151	−151	−151	−151	−151	−151	−151	−151	−151	−151	−151	−151
−151	−151	−151	−151	−151	−151	−151	−151	−151	−151	−151	−151
−151	−151	−151	−151	−151	−151	−151	−151	−151	−151	−151	−151
−151	−151	−151	−151	−151	−151	−151	−151	−151	−151	−151	−151
	−392	−392	−392	−392	−392	−392	−392	−392	−392	−392	−392
		−392	−392	−392	−392	−392	−392	−392	−392	−392	−392
			−392	−392	−392	−392	−392	−392	−392	−392	−392
				−392	−392	−392	−392	−392	−392	−392	−392
					−392	−392	−392	−392	−392	−392	−392
						−392	−392	−392	−392	−392	−392
							−392	−392	−392	−392	−392
								−392	−392	−392	−392
									−392	−392	−392
										−392	−392
											−392
2628	2952	3276	3600	3924	4248	4572	4896	5220	5544	5868	6192

Year 3 Amortization: 52,920 Euros

functions.[4] These additional adjustments yield a revised (and reduced) estimate of FS' residual profits. Under this scenario, USP's share of residual profits remains the same 23.0%–27.0% (albeit applied to a smaller residual profit base). Moreover, it is entitled to services fees equal to the cost of site operations services rendered to FS, plus the aforementioned 10.0% markup.

In the third phase of our analysis, we incorporate the fact that FS does *not* benefit from USP's ongoing investments in scalability. The U.S. site is approximately three times the size of the single largest international site. As a result, international sites

---

[4] FS' adjusted operating profits would ordinarily be net of the costs of performing its routine functions. However, because we initially assumed that FS did not perform routine functions, we eliminated the associated deductions. As such, in relaxing this assumption, we also reduce FS' adjusted operating profits by these costs.

require only a fraction of the scalability built into USP's platform. This *substantially* diminishes the value of USP's IT platform in international markets. Consistent with the residual profit split method in general, we parse USP's IT platform value into its component parts (scalability and "all other") based on relative IT expenditures. This analysis suggests that approximately 60% of the value of USP's IT platform is attributable to scalability. Hence, whereas USP's contribution of intellectual property constituted 23%–27% of the value of all intangible assets used in international markets under our initial assumptions, it now constitutes only 9.2%–10.8%, after giving effect to the fact that scalability has *de minimis* value in international markets. (As noted above, in addition to this share of FS' residual profits, USP is also entitled to site operations services fees under the residual profit split method.)

Lastly, we eliminate our assumption that USP's IT platform and FS' active user base have uniform useful lives. The former has an estimated useful life of six years, and the latter, two years. Incorporating this element into our analysis *decreases* the relative value of FS' intangible assets and *increases* the percentage of FS' residual income that should accrue to USP. (USP's services fees for routine functions performed remain unchanged.)

12.4 Analysis Under Alternative Regime

As noted, taxing authorities generally do not consider joint venture arrangements between unaffiliated companies to be reliable comparable uncontrolled transactions. JV partners could conceivably collude to reduce their combined tax liability and compensate their opposite number through side transactions. More generally, JV partners' incentives are intrinsically more suspect than companies that have no mutual interests.[5]

This position is somewhat ironic, in that the relationships among members of a controlled group are more closely akin to a JV partnership than to two or more companies acting to maximize their individual profits. Moreover, in this instance, USP negotiated arm's length JV agreements with German and Japanese partners almost concurrently with its intercompany JV agreement with FS. The arm's length JV partnerships permit the separate JV companies to utilize USP's IT platform and brand identity, and USP performs ongoing software development, customization and site operations services on their behalf.

We use USP's (uniform) third party JV arrangements to establish arm's length consideration for (a) FS' use of USP's IT platform and brand identity, and (b) USP's

---

[5] Moreover, the U.S. proposed cost-sharing regulations (issued in 2005) and the Coordinated Issue Paper on cost sharing (released in 2007) reflect the drafters' belief that unaffiliated research joint venture partners routinely contribute pre-existing intellectual property of approximately equal value to their JV arrangement. As such, the drafters argue, intercompany cost-sharing arrangements, in which one party contributes only financing, are readily distinguishable from third party research joint venture partnerships.

performance of ongoing software development and site operations services. More particularly, we summarize and compare the key terms of USP's intercompany and third party JV agreements, respectively, and adjust the share of free cash flows that accrues to USP under the arm's length JV agreements to reflect differences in the intercompany JV agreement's key terms. The adjusted share of profits constitutes the proportion of free cash flows that should accrue to USP under its JV arrangement with FS.

12.4.1 Key Terms of JV Agreements

The key terms of USP's arm's length and intercompany JV agreements are summarized below.

12.4.1.1 Allocation of Costs and Risks

USP's JV agreement with FS provides that the latter has sole responsibility for developing international markets (with the exception of Germany and Japan) at its own cost and risk. More particularly, FS is obligated to establish, finance and manage the subsidiaries and call centers that USP and FS jointly agree to establish in the major international markets. In contrast, USP's arm's length JV agreements provide that a separate JV company will be established, and USP and its JV partner will each purchase and hold 50% of the JV company's shares. Moreover, each partner is responsible for contributing equal amounts of working capital to the JV company, up to a specified maximum. Hence, USP bears substantially higher costs and greater risks vis-a-vis its arm's length JV agreements, as compared with its intercompany JV agreement with FS.

12.4.1.2 Use of USP's IT Platform and Performance of Site Operations Services

Under the terms of USP's intercompany JV agreement, it contributes its existing IT platform and has sole responsibility for maintaining and upgrading the platform at its own cost and risk. USP also maintains FS' sites on its servers and allows FS to implement improvements in features and functions that USP develops, if desired. Under the terms of USP's arm's length JV agreements, it agrees to (a) design, develop, deploy, operate and maintain the JV company's site; (b) ensure that users of the JV company's site benefit from the same level of service that USP provides to its users; and, (c) allow the JV company to implement any feature or function made commercially available on USP's site. In sum, USP permits both its affiliated and independent JV partners to use its IT platform and provides the same range of ongoing software development and site operations support thereto.

12.4.1.3 Use and Promotion of USP's Marks

As noted above, FS is contractually obligated to develop and promote USP's brand identity in international markets and indemnify USP against all losses, damages, expenses and other costs incurred as a result of alleged claims of improper use of USP's brand name. In contrast, the companies owned jointly by USP and its unaffiliated JV partners have no obligation to develop and promote USP's brand name. Moreover, USP expressly indemnifies the JV companies against all losses, damages and expenses that arise due to claims of trademark infringement. Hence, FS bears significant costs and risks associated with the development of USP's marks in its territory, and is, for this reason, entitled to retain the associated intangible income. Neither USP's unaffiliated JV partners nor the separate JV companies bear any such costs or risks. Moreover, USP's arm's length JV agreements do not provide for the payment of trademark royalties. As such, there is no mechanism to transfer marketing intangible income from the JV companies to USP.

12.4.1.4 Marketing and Promotion of Websites

USP's JV agreement with FS does not stipulate minimum promotional expenditures or activities. As a practical matter, FS invests very heavily in the marketing and promotion of its international sites. USP's arm's length JV agreements describe its counterparties' obligations regarding marketing and promotion in detail, albeit in terms of specific numbers of editorial mentions, television spots, etc., rather than cost or a percentage of revenues. USP's JV partners' obligations in this regard decline over time. The JV partners have invested considerably less per annum, as a percentage of net revenues, than FS since the JV companies and FS commenced operations.

12.4.1.5 Allocation of JV Income

Inasmuch as USP owns 50% of the separate JV companies' shares, it has claims to 50% of their respective free cash flows (after payment of interest and repayment of principal on outstanding debt). Under the terms of its JV agreement with FS, USP has claims to 20% of the latter's free cash flows.

12.4.2 Summary of Qualitative Observations

In summary, USP bears substantially higher costs and risks under its arm's length JV agreements, as compared with its intercompany JV agreement. USP permits both its affiliated and independent JV partners to use its IT platform and brand identity, and provides the same range of IT and site operations support thereto. FS bears significant costs and risks associated with the development of USP's marks in its territory, and is therefore entitled to retain the associated intangible income. USP's third party JV partners do not bear costs or risks associated with the development of its brand identity in their respective territories, and, in principle, are therefore not entitled to retain any portion of associated intangible income. However, USP's arm's length JV agreements do not provide for the payment of trademark royalty fees; as such, there is no mechanism in place to channel marketing intangible income to USP. Lastly, the JV companies in which USP has a 50% stake have consistently invested substantially less in the marketing and promotion of their sites than FS.

In short, FS makes far greater contributions to the development and operation of sites in its territory, in the nature of working capital, risk-bearing, marketing, promotion and the development of USP's trademarks, than USP's third party JV partners. It is therefore entitled to retain substantially more than 50% of its free cash flows. Equivalently, USP makes substantially fewer contributions to FS than it makes to the JV companies in which it has a 50% stake: It bears virtually no risk vis-a-vis FS' international sites, contributes no working capital to FS to speak of, and assumes no responsibility for developing and defending its trademarks in FS' territory. It is therefore entitled to substantially less than 50% of FS' free cash flows.

12.4.3 Quantitative Analysis

As noted, USP contributes the same tangible and intangible assets (servers, an IT platform and its brand identity) to both affiliated and independent joint ventures, and provides the same ongoing IT support to both. However, USP does *not* bear risk vis-a-vis FS' operations, and *does* bear risk vis-a-vis the arm's length joint ventures. Therefore, among other things, we adjust USP's return on the latter investments to reflect this differential risk. Stated differently, we estimate the risk-free return that USP would have earned on its investment in the JV companies in which it owns a 50% interest, expressed as a percentage of their free cash flows. All other things equal, the same percentage of FS' free cash flows should accrue to USP. However, additional refinements, to account for FS' greater contributions of working capital, its development of USP's brand identity and its more intensive marketing and promotion activities, are necessary as well.

We assume that the risk-free rate of return during the relevant period is 4% (based on prevailing Treasury bill rates). The market risk premium is approximately 6.5%. On a consolidated basis, USP's and FS' beta is 1.35, and their cost of equity capital (equivalently, their required return on equity) is therefore 12.78%. We assume that the JV companies in which USP has a 50% ownership interest have the same required return on equity.[6] Therefore, the risk-free portion of the jointly-owned JV companies' required return on equity is equal to 31.0% (calculated by dividing 4% by 12.78%). Stated differently, if one breaks down USP's, FS' and the 50%-owned JV companies' required return on equity capital into its component parts, slightly less than one-third of the total required return would compensate investors for their commitment of capital per se, and the balance would compensate investors for the risks they assumed thereby.

---

[6] In view of the fact that these entities operate in the same industry and employ the same tangible and intangible assets, this is a plausible working assumption.

As noted, USP has claims to 50% of the separate JV companies' free cash flows, supplies 50% of their equity capital requirements, makes additional in-kind contributions to capital consisting of a portion of the JV companies' intellectual property, and bears the associated risks. The JV companies' free cash flows accruing to USP (net of any interest costs on funds that they borrow directly from third parties) constitute USP's total return on its equity investments therein. As such, these cash flows should yield the required return on investment of 12.78% on average. Applying 31.0% to USP's 50% share of the JV companies' free cash flows, we obtain USP's hypothetical risk-free return on investment in these entities, expressed as a percentage of their free cash flows. This adjusted return is equal to 16.0% of total free cash flows (net of interest costs) generated by the JV companies (and should yield the risk-free rate of return on investment of 4.0% on average). In sum, if 50% of the JV companies' free cash flows yields USP's total required return of 12.78%, 16.0% of the JV companies' free cash flows yields the return that USP would require if it bore *no* risks on its investment in these entities, all other things equal.
USP should earn approximately the same risk-free rate of return vis-a-vis FS, expressed as a percentage of the latter's free cash flows, all other things equal.

However, FS was self-funding, developed and promoted USP's marks in international markets at its own cost, and invested far more intensively in the marketing and promotion of its sites. As such, USP's arm's length return is *less than* 16.0% of FS' free cash flows (net of interest costs). The adjustments necessary to reflect these differences can be quantified using the same required return methodology. The aforementioned 16.0% of FS' free cash flows should be reduced by half of its equity capital, other than in-kind contributions, and multiplied by the risk-free rate of 4.0%.

12.5 Analysis Under 2005 Proposed Cost-Sharing Regulations

Consider lastly our analysis of this case under the 2005 proposed cost-sharing regulations. For purposes of this analysis, we assume that USP and FS entered into a cost-sharing agreement covering USP's IT platform, in lieu of their joint venture agreement. At this time, FS' intellectual property consisted of intangible assets that USP acquired from one competitor in Europe and contributed to FS, certain of which were immediately retired (among them an IT platform). The remaining assets would *not* have been contributed to the cost-sharing arrangement. USP had an established community of users, the IT platform and a brand identity (known only in North America).

As described in Part I, the proposed cost-sharing regulations proscribe five methods to select from in establishing the value of pre-existing intellectual property contributed to a cost-sharing arrangement: The CUT method, the acquisition price method, the income method, the market capitalization method, and the residual profit split method. We consider each of these methods in turn, other than the residual profit split and CUT methods (applied to these facts previously), and the acquisition price method (which does not apply given the assumed facts).

12.5.1 Income Method

Under the income method, one would first establish the equivalent of an arm's length royalty rate for FS' rights to use USP's existing IT platform (and rights to potential future improvements), either by application of the CUT method or an intertemporal variant of the CPM. This rate is referred to as the "Alternative Rate". Secondly, the Alternative Rate would be reduced by FS' "Cost Contribution Adjustment" (a means of reimbursing FS for its projected cost-sharing payments). The resulting percentage, effectively a discounted royalty rate, would then be applied to FS' actual revenues (on an ongoing basis) to determine its per-period buy-in payment. As discussed in Chapter 3, under the income method, FS would be treated as the licensee of both (a) USP's pre-existing IT platform, and (b) all future refinements and new versions thereof, developed under the aegis of the cost-sharing arrangement.

12.5.1.1 In Combination with the CUT Method

The income method is applied in conjunction with the CUT method in the following steps:

1. Establish an arm's length royalty rate for FS' rights to use USP's IT platform in its markets, expressed as a percentage of FS' sales, based on third party CUTs;
2. Separately calculate the discounted present value of (a) FS' projected cost-sharing payments (as determined by USP's IT research budget and FS' anticipated relative benefits therefrom), and (b) FS' projected sales; and,
3. Reduce the arm's length royalty rate by the ratio of (a) the present value of FS' projected cost-sharing payments to (b) the present value of FS' projected sales.

The percentage of sales calculated in Step 3 above constitutes FS' Applicable Rate, payable to USP. This Applicable Rate, applied to FS' actual sales, determines its per annum buy-in payment. Depending on the magnitude of R&D expenditures to be shared, it is easy to imagine a situation in which the Applicable Rate would be negative. For example, suppose a third party would pay 10.0% of net sales for rights to use USP's IT platform in non-U.S. markets. (The upper bound of this rate would be determined by the cost of reproducing the IT platform, divided by FS' revenues, but the market-determined rate might be significantly lower.) FS' projected cost-sharing payments, discounted to the start date of the cost-sharing arrangement, are $15 million. FS' projected sales, similarly discounted, are $120 million. Under these assumed facts, FS would pay an Applicable Rate (or, equivalently, an adjusted running royalty rate) equal to 10% less 12.5%, or –2.5%.

12.5.1.2 In Combination with the CPM

The income method is applied in conjunction with the comparable profits method in the following steps:

1. Determine arm's length returns to FS' routine functions;
2. Calculate the discounted present value of FS' projected operating profits, its projected returns to routine functions, its projected cost-sharing payments, and its projected sales;
3. Compute the Alternative Rate, equal to the ratio of (a) the present value of FS' projected operating profits, reduced by the present value of its projected routine returns, to (b) the present value of FS' projected sales; and,
4. Reduce the Alternative Rate by the cost contribution adjustment, equal to the ratio of (a) the present value of FS' projected cost-sharing contributions to (b) the present value of FS' projected sales.

The percentage of sales calculated in Step 4 above constitutes FS' Applicable Rate, payable to USP. (Under the *Commensurate with Income* Standard, the Alternative Rate should, by assumption, be approximately equal to an arm's length royalty rate *if FS owns no intangible assets in its own right*.)

As noted, under the CUT variant of the income method, FS is treated as a licensee of USP's IT platform (including future versions thereof) and is reimbursed for its projected cost-sharing contributions. As such, it has no incentive to participate in the cost-sharing arrangement (and no real opportunity to do so). However, FS *retains* intangible income attributable to its independent investments in marketing intangible assets. In contrast, under the CPM variant of the income method, FS' income is limited to projected routine returns on its tangible assets (or projected returns as measured by another profit level indicator). As such, it neither has an incentive to participate in the cost-sharing arrangement *nor* to invest independently in marketing intangible assets. As such, if USP and FS were to enter into a cost-sharing arrangement, USP would have to fund the development of marketing intangible assets in non-U.S. markets single-handedly, and FS would be consigned to the role of services provider.

12.5.1.3 On a Genuinely Arm's Length Basis

On a genuinely arm's length basis, USP would not enter into a cost-sharing arrangement if it could earn a higher return (as measured by the net present value of its projected after-tax free cash flows) by further developing its IT platform internally and (a) directly exploiting the platform in foreign markets, (b) licensing the platform at arm's length, or (c) entering into a JV arrangement. In computing the net present value associated with the first of these alternatives (the "self-develop and exploit internally" option), USP's projected after-tax free cash flows in international markets should incorporate the following components:

- FS' projected net revenues (which should be treated as USP's net revenues);

- FS' projected cash outlays (which should be treated as USP's expenses), including:

  - Projected intangibles-creating marketing and promotional expenses;
  - Projected investments in tangible assets and working capital; and,
  - Projected cash operating expenses.

- Projected investments in the further development of USP's IT platform that would otherwise be borne by FS;
- All site operations expenditures allocable to FS' territory; and,
- The estimated tax costs of operating in this manner (given the likelihood that USP would be deemed to have permanent establishments in FS' markets).

In computing the net present value associated with the "self-develop and license" option, USP's projected after-tax free cash flows should incorporate the following components:

- FS' projected net revenues, multiplied by an arm's length royalty rate for rights to use USP's successively refined platform in international markets (which would constitute USP's licensing income);
- Arm's length fees payable by FS to USP for site operations support;
- Projected investments in the further development of USP's IT platform that would otherwise be borne by FS; and,
- The estimated tax costs on licensing and services fee income earned by USP.

In computing the net present value associated with a JV arrangement, one would presumably assume that the (hypothetical) JV agreement would be identical to the actual JV agreements between USP and third parties. Projected free cash flows in total (half of which would accrue to USP) should reflect:

- The JV company's projected revenues and cash outlays (as defined above) in FS' territory;
- Projected investments in the further development of USP's IT platform that would otherwise be borne by FS;
- Site operations expenses allocable to FS;
- Projected interest costs; and,
- Projected tax costs.

Each option should be discounted at a different rate, reflective of the associated risks. The option that yields the highest net present value can be used to establish the minimum buy-in payment that FS should make to USP under the cost-sharing arrangement. USP should be indifferent between (a) the cost-sharing option, and (b) the "self-develop and exploit internally" option, the "self-develop and license" option or the JV option (depending on which has the highest net present value). The net present value of the cost-sharing option should incorporate FS' buy-in payment, its ongoing fees for site operations services rendered, USP's associated site operations expenses, FS' cost-sharing contributions and USP's associated tax costs. The discount rate applied to projected after-tax free cash flows under the cost-sharing option should be lower than the discount rate applied to projected results under the other three scenarios, to reflect USP's reduced market- and research-related risk. Denoting the buy-in payment as our unknown and equating the two net present values, one can solve for the minimum buy-in payable to USP. USP's results in its domestic market do not need to be incorporated into this analysis, inasmuch as they remain the same across all of our scenarios.

FS must also be willing to pay the derived buy-in fee on an arm's length basis, considering its feasible alternatives. Such alternatives include licensing another platform that satisfies its lesser functionality requirements and obtaining site operations support from a third party vendor, or relying on one of the IT platforms to which it obtained rights through the acquisition of competitors (and continuing to fund upgrades of this platform). If FS would earn a negative or zero net present value by paying the minimum buy-in fee computed above, it would not be willing to enter into the cost-sharing arrangement on a genuinely arm's length basis.

12.5.2 Market Capitalization Method

The market capitalization method could in principle be used in this instance as well. FS was established just prior to entering into the joint venture agreement with USP, which we have recharacterized as a cost-sharing agreement for analytical purposes. USP was a public company at this time. Therefore, USP's average market capitalization, increased by its liabilities and reduced by (a) the value of its tangible assets (primarily servers), (b) the value of its user community and brand identity, and (c) its goodwill and going concern value, constitutes the value of its IT platform. Under the market capitalization method, FS should pay a percentage of this residual value to USP, equal to its anticipated relative benefits from exploitation of the IT platform.

The difficulty here lies in determining reliable fair market values for USP's user community, brand identity and goodwill/going concern. Goodwill and going concern value are almost always determined as a residual. However, under the market capitalization method, the IT platform value is determined as a residual, necessitating that one explicitly value goodwill/going concern. It is unclear how one would do so in a reliable way.

12.6 Comparison

Our analysis of this case under the current transfer pricing regime is based on the residual profit split method. As discussed at length in Chapter 3, this methodology is fraught with weaknesses, chief among them being the assumption that expenditures on the development of intangible assets, on the one hand, and the value of such assets, on the other, bear any necessary relationship to one another. All of the conceptual and practical problems associated with the comparable profits method, detailed in Chapter 3, apply to the residual profit split method as well. As a result of these shortcomings, the allocation of income that we obtain in this case under the residual profit split method is essentially meaningless.

Moreover, the fact that USP entered into third party joint venture agreements at about the same time that it entered into its intercompany joint venture agreement with FS should be determinative. USP and FS clearly intended that they would function as JV partners, and in fact did so. Hence, taxing authorities' disinclination to use joint venture arrangements between third parties as comparable uncontrolled transactions is difficult to understand, and harder still to justify. In relying on USP's arm's length joint venture agreements, with adjustments for differences in key terms, we are able to establish arm's length results vis-a-vis the allocation of FS' income between itself and USP with a reasonable degree of confidence.

Under the 2005 proposed cost-sharing regulations, in combination with the Coordinated Issue Paper addressing buy-in payments released in 2007, the market capitalization method could theoretically be used to establish FS' arm's length buy-in payment. However, this would entail valuing goodwill and going concern explicitly, rather than as a residual.

The income method, applied in conjunction with the CUT method, is internally inconsistent: If USP retains all income attributable to improvements in its IT platform, FS would have no incentive to join the cost-sharing arrangement on an arm's length basis. More fundamentally, it would have no real opportunity to do so, because the income method, applied in combination with the CUT method, simply converts the cost-sharing arrangement into a licensing arrangement. The income method, applied in conjunction with the comparable profits method, also eliminates FS' incentives to develop and promote USP's brand identity and business model in non-U.S. markets. Hence, by modifying the way in which USP would be compensated for its external contributions, the relationship between USP and FS would be restructured in its entirety. A corrected version of the income method would substitute after-tax free cash flows for before-tax operating profits in all net present value calculations, and systematically analyze feasible alternatives available to *both* participants, not just USP. Both participants must be as well or better off under the cost-sharing arrangement than they would be under all feasible alternatives, and the net present value of participation must be positive for both FS and USP.

Part IV
Conclusions

Chapter 13
Concluding Observations

This final segment of the book culls certain general observations from the individual case studies reviewed in Chapters 5 through 12, and summarizes our conclusions.

In principle, a transfer pricing regime should achieve the following ends:

- Enable tax authorities in different jurisdictions to allocate income across the countries in which multinational firms operate both equitably and consistently, and thereby prevent double-taxation;
- Provide some certainty to firms regarding their tax liability; and,
- Minimize compliance, audit and dispute resolution costs.

These goals can be met under a variety of regimes, provided that all tax authorities uniformly apply consistent rules.

Ideally, tax laws and regulations should also be drafted so as to treat domestic and multinational firms uniformly. By doing so, one does not create incentives that may have unintended, and potentially undesirable, consequences.

The transfer pricing methodologies currently endorsed by the United States, OECD member countries and others do not achieve these objectives. In most cases, the sanctioned methods are based on assumptions about market structure and firm behavior that are neither theoretically nor empirically valid. Comparisons of profitability across firms at the gross or operating profit level have no real foundation and are highly sensitive to the particular firms one includes in samples of "comparable" companies. Moreover, the Internet has brought about fundamental economic changes that have given rise to entirely new methods of expansion internationally, and novel divisions of functions, risks and intangible assets among commonly controlled companies. These new fact patterns are inadequately addressed, or not addressed at all, under the existing transfer pricing regime.

The case studies presented herein contain analyses under both the existing transfer pricing regime and one or more proposed methods (where possible). The proposed methods seek to make use of all available arm's length data, inexact or otherwise, and are not founded on inaccurate assumptions about market structure and market participants' behavior. A common theme running throughout this book, and illustrated in several of the case studies, is that operating profits and other accounting measures of profits differ from free cash flows. To the extent that transfer pricing

E. King, *Transfer Pricing and Corporate Taxation*,
DOI 10.1007/978-0-387-78183-9_13, © Springer Science+Business Media, LLC 2009

methods are based on economic reasoning, economic measures of profits should be used in lieu of accounting profit measures.

Under certain of the proposed methods, much of the current compliance burden would be shifted from firms to taxing authorities. For example, the numerical standards approach would require taxing authorities to conduct comprehensive, industry-specific benchmarking studies annually, in lieu of the thousands of studies conducted by individual firms. However, with the exception of the required return method, the proposed methods would also greatly reduce the magnitude of this burden. They would, hopefully, also go much further than the current regime in reducing audit and dispute resolution costs, the likelihood of double-taxation and penalties, and uncertainty regarding individual firms' anticipated tax liabilities.

The case studies also highlight certain more specific observations. First, the numerical standards approach would remedy many of the shortcomings of the existing system in relatively straightforward transfer pricing cases. However, it should be applied on a skill- and/or an industry-specific basis. More particularly, in the case of services, taxing authorities should publish a range of safe harbors for services requiring different skill levels. As applied to distributors, safe harbors should also encompass advertising-to-sales ratios, inventory-to-sales ratios and other magnitudes that have proven to be controversial in a transfer pricing context, in addition to safe harbor resale margins by industry and geographic market. Inasmuch as numerical standards would be framed in terms of safe harbor resale margins and markups over cost, this approach would clearly not ameliorate the conceptual shortcomings of the resale price, cost plus and comparable profits methods. Rather, this approach is put forth in recognition of the fact that genuinely arm's length results are time-consuming and difficult to develop, and perhaps such efforts should be reserved for the more complex transfer pricing issues.

Moreover, even when numerical standards are applied, a careful analysis of market structure and the nature and extent of competition in the relevant markets is important. This type of analysis is the only means of ascertaining whether members of controlled groups have developed and utilize valuable intangible assets. While the OECD Guidelines strongly stress the importance of detailed analyses of market structure, competition, etc., the U.S. transfer pricing regulations, and, still more strikingly, the application of these regulations, are more formulaic than they ought to be.

The modified inexact CUP and CUT methods are intended to make use of information contained in product and intangible asset pricing to a greater extent than is currently permitted. A more flexible application of the CUP and CUT methods may yield the most reliable results in analyzing certain fact patterns. For example, the use of franchise agreements to analyze the intercompany pricing of bundled intangible assets is both empirically valid in some circumstances, and feasible from a practical standpoint, given the large number of such agreements and the fact that their terms are often publicly available. Moreover, existing methods do not satisfactorily address these types of transactions. Similarly, joint venture arrangements between unaffiliated companies should potentially be considered valid comparable uncontrolled transactions.

The required return methodology is an improvement over existing transfer pricing methods in a theoretical sense, but its applicability is somewhat limited from a practical standpoint. More particularly, the required return method should be applied only under one of the following circumstances:

Scenario A

- The tested party has recently been valued in the normal course of business for non-tax purposes, and the valuation is not potentially distorted by intercompany pricing; and,
- Tax authorities agree on the use of specific industry betas, interest rates on corporate debt of various kinds (or their safe harbor equivalents), risk-free rates and the market price of risk, and publish all such betas and rates on a monthly basis.

Scenario B

- Taxing authorities accept a baseline valuation done at multi-year intervals (e.g., every 3 years) absent significant changes in the business, with informed estimates of percentage increases or decreases in value in the interim; and
- Tax authorities agree on the use of, and publish, industry betas, interest rates on corporate debt, risk-free rates, and the market price of risk.

Scenario C

- A sufficient number of comparable companies can regularly be found to calculate valuation multiples (for which the denominator is independent of transfer prices), and these multiples fall within a reasonably narrow range; and,
- Tax authorities agree on both (a) industry-specific valuation multiples, and (b) the use of published industry betas, interest rates on corporate debt, risk-free rates, and the market price of risk.

The formulary apportionment method, as described in *Notice 94–40* (published in 1994) and the proposed global dealing regulations (published in 1998), incorrectly measures the pool of allocable income, and allocates such income on an arbitrary basis. One can significantly improve on the IRS' formulary apportionment methodology by substituting assets for "factors", fair market values for weights, and after-tax free cash flows for the accounting-based measure of profits put forth in *Notice 94–40*. With these modifications, which the proposed simplified profit split method incorporates, the approach has a far more solid economic footing.

Lastly, the 2005 proposed U.S. cost-sharing regulations, and the companion Coordinated Issue Paper on cost-sharing issued in 2007, are fundamentally flawed. The income method is strongly advocated in the latter document, although it is just one of a number of valuation methodologies put forth in the proposed cost-sharing regulations. The income method, as interpreted in the Coordinated Issue Paper, cannot be consistent with the arm's length standard, for the simple reason that participants (other than those making external contributions) would have no incentive to join under the conditions imposed, and no incentive to exploit the developed intangibles even if they did participate. Yet, third parties regularly enter into research joint ventures. A corrected version of the income method would substitute after-tax free cash flows for operating profits, and systematically analyze feasible alternatives available to *all* participants. All such participants must be as well or better off under the cost-sharing arrangement than they would be under all feasible alternatives, and the net present value of participation should be *positive* for all entities.

The other methods described in the proposed cost-sharing regulations are also problematic. Both the acquisition price method and the market capitalization method require valuing goodwill and going concern assets explicitly (unless, under the acquisition price method, a target company was acquired solely to obtain access to specific intellectual property, and ceased to be operated as a going concern). This simply cannot be done in a reliable way. In other valuation contexts, goodwill and going concern value are almost invariably determined as a residual. More broadly, where valuation issues arise, such as when firms are called upon to establish the value of pre-existing intellectual property for cost-sharing purposes, standard valuation principles and methods generally make a great deal more sense than the methods advocated in the proposed regulations and the Coordinated Issue Paper.

Finally, the U.S. tax authorities' unsubstantiated claim that third party research joint ventures are not comparable to intercompany cost-sharing arrangements needs to be revisited. In many respects, joint venture arrangements closely mimic the relationship between affiliated companies, albeit without the incentives for income-shifting that may arise in an intra-group context. Moreover, unaffiliated research joint venture partners can and do participate solely by providing financing in some instances, contrary to U.S. tax authorities' preconceptions. Venture capitalists routinely do so. As such, arm's length research joint ventures should in principle be extensively utilized in structuring and evaluating intra-group cost-sharing arrangements, barring regulatory prohibitions.

Index